CASH MANAGEMENT

Perspectives, Principles & Practices

R. N. JOSHI

NEW AGE INTERNATIONAL (P) LIMITED, PUBLISHERS
New Delhi • Bangalore • Calcutta • Chennai • Guwahati
Hyderabad • Lucknow • Mumbai

Reprint 2000

NEW AGE INTERNATIONAL (P) LIMITED, PUBLISHERS
4835/24, Ansari Road, Daryaganj,
New Delhi - 110 002

Offices at :
Bangalore, Calcutta, Chennai, Guwahati, Hyderabad,
Lucknow and Mumbai

ISBN : 81-224-1026-X

4 5 6 7 8 9 10

Published by K. K. Gupta for New Age International (P) Ltd.
4835/24, Ansari Road, Daryaganj, New Delhi - 110 002 and
printed in India at Taj Press, New Delhi - 110 064.

To My Father

Preface

Cash is an omnipresent phenomenon in a business. It is the 'life blood' of business. Like blood in a human body, it circulates to all the segments of a business activity. Every business activity has direct or indirect effect on finance, and anything done financially affects cash eventually. It is the most liquid asset, in fact liquidity of other assets is measured in terms of their convertibility into cash. It is also the most critical asset responsible for the successful running of a business. But if not managed skillfully, it is equally responsible in ruining the business. Even a profitable business becomes bankrupt when it runs out of cash. There is another dimension associated with cash, as well. Like any other asset, cash carries opportunity cost. No business can afford to have barren cash. It depreciates in terms of its real value. Prudent deployment of surplus cash is an important tenet of cash management. An alert Finance Manager can make cash management a 'profit centre' by investing the surplus cash in a most profitable manner. An effective and efficient cash management, thus, aims at ensuring ready cash available at all times to cater to the operating, investing and financing requirements of a business; not too much but never too little.

Cash is real and visible. It is free from any subjectivity, like the one we witness while calculating the 'profit'. Prof. David Tweedie, Chairman of the UK Accounting Standard Board, stressing the need to have cash based approach, observed that cash was a "very difficult figure to fiddle". The inherent feature of 'reality' ingrained in cash has given cash flow approach a definite edge over fund flow approach which embraces both cash and non cash elements. The comparison between two has been beautifully illustrated in the editorial of the official journal of the Institute of Chartered Accountants of India. *

> No single argument could have contributed to the primacy of the Cash Flow approach as did the demise of Polly Peck—an international trading group. This Group had recorded a healthy "funds" inflow of Pd. Stg. 172 million in 1989. Had the same information been presented on a "Cash Flow" approach, it would have showed

---

* *The Chartered Accountant,* March, 1995.

> an out-flow of Pd. Stg. 129 million. This no doubt was an extreme case and a well publicized one, which brought home the point that apparently solvent companies could collapse through lack of liquidity. It illustrated that a Funds Flow statement with its emphasis on working capital was capable of misinterpretation in that, a significant decrease in cash could be obscured by an increase in stocks or debtors. Obscuring movements relevant to liquidity and viability was not difficult.

The extract highlights the limitation of fund flow approach. It also eloquently establishes the imperativity of having astute cash control programme for a business. In fact, of late, the Accountants the world over are switching their emphasis from fund flow approach to cash flow approach. In the UK SAP-10 : 'Statements of Source and Application of Funds' with its emphasis on changes in working capital was superseeded by the Financial Reporting Standard-1 (FRS-1): Cash Flow Statement w.e.f. March 23, 1992. The International Accounting Standards Committee changed its earlier International Accounting Standard-7 (IAS-7): 'Statement of Changes in Financial Position by revised IAS-7 : 'Cash Flow Statement' effective from January 1, 1994. The Institute of Chartered Accountants of India, too, has circulated a Discussion Draft on the cash flow statements modelled on the revised IAS-7. The stock exchanges of India have also made it obligatory for all the companies listed with them to prepare the cash flow statements, and present it to the share holders alongwith the annual balance sheets effective from accounting period ending on or after March 31, 1996. Beside providing information regarding ability of a business to generate cash and the needs to utilise the cash flows, such cash flow statement will also mirror the efficiency of cash management programme followed in a business.

The book discusses the principles and practices of cash management in a lucid and simple manner with a non-mathematical approach, in general. The book consists of 15 chapters. Chapter 1 outlines role of cash in a business. Chapter 2 explains the intricacies of cash flow cycle. Next four chapters provide comprehensive coverage to cash budget, acclaimed as back bone of cash management by mandarins of financial management. The first in the series, Chapter 3, presents principles of forecasting in general and cash forecasting in particular. This is followed in Chapter 4 by detailed frame work on formating of a cash budget. The next Chapter 5 provides indepth study in respect of short term cash budget. The last chapter in the series, Chapter 6, concentrates on the long term cash budget. An exclusive Chapter 7 is devoted to cash management techniques aggressively deployed in the developed countries. Chapter 8 contains in simplified and logical manner the concept of liquidity and efficient usage of cash. The cash management would be viewed myopically, if the other prominent components of working capital are not considered for their impact on cash flow. In the light of this, Chapter 9 discusses the management of receivables and Chapter 10 deals with inventory management. Chapter 11 concentrates on the various means available for investment of short-term cash surplus. The next two chapters deal with the various sources of raising funds. Chapter 12 discusses the sources of short-term financing, and those of long-term financing are explained in Chapter 13. Chapter 14 describes various kinds of money market instruments and the assistance they provide to a business in maintaining desired level of liquidity. Finally, Chapter 15 details internal control mechanisms separately for cash and treasury instruments to ward off possibilities of misappropriations and defalcations.

The book is useful for postgraduate students doing MBAs and those pursuing professional courses like CA, ICWA, CFA and Company Secretary. Due to practical slant of the subject, the practising finance professionals and Treasury & Finance Managers shall also find the book a helpful guide for planning, executing and monitoring their cash-based assignments.

I acknowledge my indebtedness to late Mr. Asang Machwe, of New Age International (P) Limited, Publishers who persuaded me to write this book, but unfortunately left for his heavenly abode while the book was under print. But for his encouragement the book would not have seen the light of the day.

This being the first edition of the book, possibilities of some infirmities creeping in its presentation cannot be ruled out. I shall be grateful if the readers communicate the deficiencies and suggestions for its improvement.

R.N. Joshi

Contents

1

CASH IN BUSINESS

1.1 INTRODUCTION

Business is a matter of using money to make more money. Start-up capital is invested as seed money to earn incremental money generated by profit as its fruit which, in turn, becomes seed money to earn more money. Money thus becomes both basic input and ultimate output for a business. The obvious question then arises as to what is money which propels the business to voyage for its further acquisition. Economists world over have propounded a wide variety of definitions from time to time. It has been described by Walker as "money is that money does". Saligman defined it as "one thing that possesses general acceptability". D.H. Robertson put forward a more practical definition "anything which is widely accepted in payment for goods, or in discharge of other kinds of business obligations." These definitions reveal inherent features of money - an agent through which values are measured and goods are exchanged. Thus money can be defined as medium of exchange having general acceptability which provides value to a transaction and acts as a means for its settlement.

The money of present-day is Ready Money - a product of centuries of evolutionary process. It consists of currency notes and bank notes and is popularly known as Cash. We can appreciate cash and its role in business in a better way by studying evolution of money and its transformation into present-day form of Ready Money.

1.2 ORIGIN OF CASH

All business transactions involve give and take. Earlier this give and take was settled through commodities. One commodity was exchanged with another. This system of barter had three difficulties: presence of two persons who could satisfy each other's needs; determination of the rate of exchange and problem of exchange of large with smaller commodities. The clumsiness and inconvenience of barter has been very well illustrated by Lt. Cameron. When he wanted to buy a boat in Africa, he discovered, "Syde's agent wished to be paid in ivory of which I had none; but I found that Mohammad Ibn Sahib had ivory and wanted cloth. Since I had no cloth, this did not assist me greatly until I heard that Mohammad Ibn Gharib had cloth and wanted wire. This I fortunately possessed. So I gave Ibn Gharib requisite amount of wire; whereupon he handed over cloth to Ibn Sahib who in his turn gave Syde's agent the wished-for-Ivory. Then he allowed me to have a boat."*

1.2.1 Early Cash

It was to overcome the disadvantages of barter that a need for a medium of exchange was felt and commodity as medium entered the business arena. There was no special commodity which was picked up for this purpose; it all depended on factors like location, community, climate, economic development of the region, *etc*. Wheat, rice, cattle being the most commonly consumed commodities were the first to be chosen for this purpose. The areas with cold climate preferred fur & skins as money. Coastal areas developed cowrie shell as medium of exchange, and so on.

The commodity money did not serve the purpose well because it was devoid of basic features of good money, *i.e.*, durability, divisibility and portability. With the progress of civilisation and advancement in economic development metal became the medium of exchange. First, it was silver then gold. These metals were weighed every time a transaction was settled. Later on, to overcome the difficulties of weighment every time, the metal was cut into pieces of definite weightage and coinage got into circulation. It served well as a medium of exchange but it suffered with problems of debasement and tampering by dishonest persons. Also it was troublesome and risky to carry gold or silver coins.

1.2.2 Present Day Cash

With the increase in business and trade it became increasingly difficult to use commodity money as a medium of exchange due to the problems explained above. Consequently, search was made for an item which could serve as a medium of exchange sans negative features of commodity money. Thus, started the era of Paper Money. The initial use of paper money was in the form of receipts given by London goldsmiths for deposit of coins. In the first phase of paper money, these receipts were accepted as medium of exchange only if these were convertible into coins of same value. However with the expansion of business particularly in the twentieth century the inconvertible paper money became acceptable as an established medium of

*From All Across Africa, quoted in "Money" by Foster and Catchings.

exchange. It has now been made a legal tender since it consists of Currency Notes issued by central bank or the government of the country. In addition to currency notes, it is Bank Notes which are gaining credence in the business world of today. Bank notes refers to the deposits in the bank which can be converted into currency notes any time on demand. There has been multifarious growth of business and banking infra-structure too, has kept pace with its development. As a result, bank money though not legal tender, is as much in circulation as the paper money. The business of today has broken national barriers and has become cross-country. It is the bank money which facilitate cross-currency trade. As a matter of fact in the present era of jet age business it is not cash represented by paper currency but the cash represented by paperless bank currency which settles most of the business deals.Instead of physical movement of cash from one place to another the entries in "nostro" and "vostro" accounts kept by banks are highwayed through electronic media. Such entries or credit signified by such entries can be converted into cash whenever and wherever required.

1.2.3 Future Cash

Computer has entered every segment of commercial world. The advent of Internet has further intensified its penetration. Cash too, has not remained aloof from its impact. In fact, mass experiments are going on which could transform the way we could think about money. A new breed of cash, which is basically a software is being developed for circulation in future. It is a kind of electronic money known as "E-cash". Money under this system will move along multiple channels largely outside the network of banks and paper currency. There are many big and small computer companies as well as banks in the race for development of their own brands of E-money. These include corporate icons like Microsoft, Xerox, Visa, Citicorp, Digicash and Cybercash.

Under the system, one may have E-cash in the form of a credit card size piece of plastic with an embedded microchip that one can load with E-money purchased with traditional currency. Or one can have E-cash in his personal computer or electronic "wallet" down loaded over phone lines from the issuer of E-money. This digital money will enable shopping on line and zapping money to the sellers over the internet. Businesses can also keep stash of E-cash on hand for buying supplies and transmitting money without involving banks.

E-cash can be issued both by banks and non-banks. As on date, non-banking corporations are more aggressive in this process of cash replacement. This may pose a big problem for the banks which have big stakes in the present monetary system. Commercial banks are entrusted with the creation of money by central banks of the concerned countries by keeping a fraction of deposits as Reserve. If the same practice is followed by non-banking companies which are largely unregulated, they shall also create money as commercial banks now do. The banking industry may suffer a lot.

It is said that in many ways E-cash represents the biggest revolution in the currency since gold replaced cowrie shells. Some experts look at it as a revolution similar to Industrial Revolution. Many benefits are attributed to the new system. Firstly, E-cash is more convenient and feasible than traditional money. Secondly, banks that issue E-cash could find it much cheaper than handling cheques and papers that accompany traditional money. Thirdly, unlike credit cards which provide no privacy to its users, E-cash offers virtually complete anonymity. Fourthly, money can move with lightening speed. E-money has several potential dangers as well. Uncontrolled growth of E-cash systems could undermine bank and government controlled money systems. E-money being a stateless currency can be sent in and out of a country undetected facilitating money laundering on a grand scale. Tax evasion can become a matter of pushing a button. Counterfeiters can replicate the series of digits that constitutes E-money. E-money is less secured than bank money. Money stored on a personal computer can be lost for ever if the system crashes.

What exactly is going to be the currency scenario when various brands of E-money start floating, is not very clear. Many issues need to be solved. Who shall be the issuers and who will regulate issuers? How to insulate against tax evasion, money laundering and counterfeiting on private networks? How will taxes be imposed in cyberspace which transcends physical boundaries? How will consumers be protected? Whatever may be the solutions to these and many other such issues, it is certain that the day of electronic monetary system is not very far off. Looking at the accelerating pace of development in this field, one is constrained to comment that digital money is the ultimate - an inevitable medium of exchange for an increasingly wired world.

1.3 PROFIT AND CASH

There can be many reasons for one to go in for a business. It may be due to ancestral legacy making it an automatic choice or one finds himself temperamentally better fitted to its functionary independence or one may have acquired the right business acumen to plunge into it. But there is only one real purpose for doing a business and that is to earn profit. Profit is a return which one gets on his investment in the business. And profit so earned is the most important source for generating cash flow in a business.Erroneously, some people think that profit and cash are synonyms. In other words, there is a mistaken belief that cash-in-till should swell at the year end by the amount indicated as profit in the Profit and Loss account. This is not correct. Profit and cash are two different phenomena. Was it not so, how would one explain a profitable venture facing cash drought going into bankruptcy, whereas a losing concern having no difficulty in discharging its liabilities. It is necessary, therefore, to understand the distinction between the two so as to appreciate the role of cash in a business in its proper perspective.

Commercially, profit is a return on investment which from the accounting angle is calculated by deducting all expenses from the revenue. Cash, on the other hand, is the liquid asset of the business which keeps on flowing in and out of the business. As a matter of fact, distinction between profit and cash is distinction between something abstract and real. Profit as quantified by the accountant is determined taking into consideration accounting principles, conventions, customs and standards. Cash on the contrary is something real and visible. Profit is a concept, an opinion. Cash is a bare simple fact. The study of the following items will highlight the distinguishing features of the two.

1.3.1 Depreciation

Depreciation is an accounting convention of allocating the cost of a fixed asset over its useful life. There are many factors, commercial and statutory which determine the useful life of a fixed asset and therefore the depreciation charge is at best a reasonable estimate only. Profit is arrived at after charging this reasonable estimate year after year during the tenure of the useful life of the asset. Cash, on the other hand, is affected only once, in the year in which the asset is acquired and payment made.

1.3.2 Sale and Purchase on Credit

The system of commercial accounting permits non-cash sales or purchases to be recorded in the accounts as soon as the transaction is complete. Movement of cash is of no relevance. Profit is thus determined on the basis of income and expenditure considering bill/invoice prices of sales and purchases irrespective of receipt or payment of cash or delivery of goods. Cashflow, however, is affected only when payment is received or made to debtors and creditors, respectively. Occurence of sale or purchase transaction in that year is of no relevance to the cash flow.

1.3.3 Prepaid Expenses

Profit of a business pertains to a pre-defined period of time normally an year better known as 'accounting year'. The expenses charged against the profit are relevant for the said period only. However,there are certain expenses which are incurred in a particular accounting year while benefits accruing therefrom extend beyond that period.

Profit in such cases is subject to charge of the expenses pertaining to the relevant period only. It is not burdened with that portion of expense which is attributable to future years. Cash flow, on the other hand, is immune to such adjustments. Cash outflow is affected in the period in which payment is made irrespective of the fact whether the payment belongs to one or more years.

1.3.4 Inventories

Inventory plays an important role in the determination of profit. At the year end, inventory with the business is valued and due credit is accorded while quantifying profit of the year. There are many methods in vogue for valuation of inventory, *e.g.*, LIFO, FIFO, average, weighted average methods. Each method is likely to reveal different figure of inventory valuation, resulting in different figures of profits. Cash does not accord any such special treatment to inventories. It is in no way affected by the existence or non-existence of inventory at the year end or its valuation. Cash outflow takes place when the payment is actually made for the inventory.

1.3.5 Accounting Amortisation

Due to statutory requirements or conventionally, certain costs are charged to profit over a period of time. An example is preliminary expenses. Profit is reduced by a regular amount till the whole cost stands amortised. However, so far as cash flow is concerned there is an immediate outflow of cash as soon as total amount is paid.

1.3.6 Interest Bearing Obligations

Most of the short-term and long-term interest bearing loans and advances require periodical payments of principal and interest till the whole of the amount is paid or retrieved. Some times loan amount is programmed into equated instalments merging both principal and interest. Only the interest portion of such instalment is reflected in profit. While cash flow is affected by both the principal as well as interset. Likewise, investment of surplus funds in short or long term investments shall involve cash outflow as and when investment is made, but profit will be affected to the extent of interests on such investments only.

1.3.7 Capital and Revenue

Profit is affected by revenue items only. Cost of capital items are not charged to profit. The discriminating characteristic is whether the item is "used up" or "used in" the business. Profit is affected by used-up items only whereas cash is affected by both used-up and used-in items. Goods are purchased to be 'used up' in the day to day doing of the business. Hence, these constitute an important part of profit calculation. Cash, on the other hand, is affected both by capital and revenue items. Not only purchase of goods but also purchase of assets acquired to be used in the business shall result in cash outflow. Acquisition of land may create a big dent in the cash outflow in view of the magnitude of the amount. As for profit, since land is never depreciated, profit is never affected. Similarly, additional capital introduced into the business will not affect the profit figure. Cash, however,will substantially increase.

It can be seen from the above that profit is an abstract figure which is computed from income and expenditure of a business whereas cash is a matter of fact which is free from problems of computation. It is an visible asset which is immune to niceties of accounting conventions for its valuation. Its valuation is what it is.

1.4 MOTIVES FOR HOLDING CASH

We have seen that for a business cash is an important and crucial asset. But it is also a fact that cash by itself is a zero earning asset. Cash-in-till or even a cash in current account of a bank does not earn any revenue. It rather depreciates with inflation in the economy. Nonetheless, every business holds cash. We discuss below the motives which prompt a business to keep ready cash in its hands.

1.4.1 Transaction Motive

Transaction is a media through which a business activity is conducted. Transaction motive refers to requirement of cash for the conduct of day to day business activity. A business enters into a wide variety of transactions and cash being legal tender, these are settled through cash. The transactions occasion both inflows and outflows of cash. Outflows of cash are on account of purchases, wages, other cash expenses and inflows are through cash sales and collection from the customers. Inflows and outflows of cash never synchronise. At times, the receipts are more than payments and at other times payments exceed receipts. A business has to maintain enough cash to meet its requirements. The cardinal principle is to keep just the right amount, not too much but never too little. The transaction balance can be held in cash or short term marketable securities. Whenever a cash is invested in such securities the idea is to earn some interest so that surplus cash does not remain infertile. An important consideration for such short term securities is that their maturity should coincide with the needs, because the primary motive is not to earn profit but to keep them liquid. The quantum of cash to be held for transaction purpose will depend on a number of factors, prominent being size of cash inflow and outflow, the nature of transactions, the time gap between receipt of cash and its exit on account of payments.

The transaction motive covers cash requirement for normal routine functions. The requirement for this purpose is substantially certain and can be predicted with good degree of accuracy.

1.4.2 Precautionary Motive

Transaction motive takes care of normal routine functions but the business during its currency is engrossed with various contingencies and emergencies. It has to protect itself for such contingencies by holding additional cash in hand. This is known as precautionary motive. Such cash balance provides a cushion or buffer to meet unexpected cash demands. Some of the events warranting additional cash can arise owing to cancellation of an order, lock out, strikes, levy of duty or cess on raw materials *etc*. The volume of cash required for this purpose depends upon a number of factors, *e.g.*, the nature of the business, the accuracy with which cash needs of the business can be predicted - greater the accuracy lesser the 'cash balance' required for this purpose. Another important factor in this regard is accessability to the Credit Market. In case a business can raise required funds from the market at short notice it needs only to retain a moderate balance for precautionary purpose.

Precautionary cash balance provides cushion generally to meet non-routine demands.The requirement remains uncertain making its predictability somewhat difficult.

Both in the case of transaction motive and precautionary motive, the cash is held to meet transaction needs. In the case of former, cash is held for normal and ordinary transactions whereas in the case of latter it is retained for meeting unexpected and unforeseen transactions.

1.4.3 Speculative Motive

As the name suggests, in this case motive is to encash the opportunities which may unexpectedly surface in future. Cash, therefore, is retained in addition to transactions and precautionary motives for speculative purposes also. The speculative motive for holding cash can well be explained by an example. A common item for speculation is security prices. Suppose the present rate of long term interest is 10%. A Rs. 100 bond which carries 12% rate of interest is then worth Rs. 120. If it is expected that rate of interest is likely to fall (increasing the price of bond), the business will like to buy such securities out of the funds earmarked for speculative purposes. Similarly, a business may speculate in material prices also. It may delay the purchase of the raw materials if it expects that raw material prices are likely to fall and make purchases in future when prices actually fall. Keyens has aptly defined the speculative motive as "the desire of earning profit by knowing better than the market what the future will bring forth."

The speculative motive covers events which are most uncertain, unforeseen and unpredictable to forecast.

1.4.4 Other Motives

In addition to these three basic motives there are some other motives for holding cash. One such motive is compensating motive. Business of today is predominently dependent on the commercial banks for the financial support. For some of services the bank charges a commission or service charges but for some others it insists that a predetermined minimum balance be kept with the bank which should not be withdrawn in the ordinary course of business. For instance, if a bank guarantee is issued by the bank, guarantee charges based on the period and amount are debited by the bank. In addition, it may ask for retention of some minimum balance too. Such balance is known as Compensating Balance.

Yet another motive for holding cash is attributable to business expansion. It refers to the motive of accumulating cash to meet the requirements of expansion envisaged by the business. Despite the existence of various financial institutions to fund such expansions, a business has to provide part of the funds from its own resources necessitating needed cash accumulation. Besides, in the present era of mergers and acquisitions ready availability of cash helps in implementing such schemes smoothly. Also many "corporate raiders" can use such handy cash for seizure of ownership shares of a sought-after-unit in a secret move. Holding of cash for such purposes have been described as business expansion motive.

1.5 FACTORS INFLUENCING CASH AVAILABILITY IN A BUSINESS

The cash flow in a business is influenced by a number of factors. These can be classified into two categories—internal and external.Internal factors are those factors which are internal to the business, and by and large arise as a result of management decisions. These are under the direct control of management. External factors, on the other hand, are such environmental factors which are not under the direct control of the management. Such factors affect the economy as a whole and their ramifications are felt by an individual business as well. It is a case of macro affecting micro. Another kind of external factors are the factors which affect the concerned industry as a whole and not the whole economy. These too, exercise influence on the availability of cash in a business. We shall study these factors in detail.

1.5.1 Internal Factors

Internal factors are products of management policies followed either consciously and positively, or unconsciously by default, or combination of both. These are unique to the concerned business concern and are under its direct control. Following are some of the avenues from where these factors emanate and affect the cash in a business.

(a) *Operating Policies:* These refer to all types of decisions which make the business operative. Every business desires to operate at its optimum level. For this it has to gear up all of its segments to the utmost efficiency. On the production front decisions are taken to determine utilisable level of capacity based on the break-even analysis, make or buy decisions considering its own production line, pricing policy, *etc.* which have direct bearing on cash flow. Also, a business has to decide about salary structure which constitute a substantial part of administrative expenses. For selling of the products an important decision is whether to have its own dedicated outlets or selling should be done by giving franchise to other parties. Both the alternatives shall require cash but the magnitude in the case of former will be substantially more than the latter. Another important decision is regarding fund allocation for research and development. All these decisions have a direct bearing on cash in business.

(b) *Fixed Assets:* Fixed assets are the long lived properties of a business which it owns and uses as an aid to generate profits. These are not bought and sold in the normal course of business. So far as cash is concerned investment in fixed assets embodies two important features. First, it requires cash outlay of high order and secondly, the cash is 'sunk' for a longer period whenever these are purchased. Business policies towards automation, expansion, technological development, competition in the market *etc.* are some of the important factors which influence its policy towards investments in the fixed assets which, in turn, affect the requirements of cash in the business.

(c) *Management of Receivables:* In the modern competitive business environment there is no escape from selling goods on credit. Such a course entitles the customer to use immediately the goods sold against deferred payments. In a way, a customer's business is financed through the cash resources of the seller. The credit policy followed by the business has a direct bearing on the cash in business. The cash remains 'blocked' to the extent and period of credit allowed. Also terms of credit like cash discount will affect the flow of cash from debtors. Weak credit control increases the possibilities of bad debts which result in depletion of cash.

(d) *Inventory:* Inventory refers to stocks held by a business. Funds are normally tied up in three kinds of inventory - raw materials, work in process (semi-finished goods) and finished goods. Investment in inventory has great impact on business cash. In addition to cost of goods lying in stock, cash is required to meet carrying cost of inventory, *e.g.* interest, godown rent, insurance, *etc.* A business endeavours to strike a balance between two conflicting aims - one of minimising inventory and second ensuring that enough quantity is always available to meet the demand as and when it arises. This is done by efficiently organising the production and sales operations. Business is also guided by basic parameters of material management like minimum and maximum level of stock, re-ordering level of quantity, stock-velocity ratio *etc.* At times management ignores all these parameters and buys heavy inventory when it expects substantial price rise in the near future. Obviously, it affects business cash adversely.

(e) *Payment Policies:* It refers to policies concerning the payments to be released to creditors and suppliers. A business's efficiency to exploit this element of OPM (Other Peoples Money) has an important affect on business cash. 'Pay only when due' is the guiding rule. Extracting maximum credit from suppliers, utilising cash discount offered by them are some of the ingredients of prudent purchase management policies resulting in decelerating of cash outflow.

(f) *Miscellaneous:* Other factors which affect the cashflow may arise due to commercial and statutory requirements. Some of the examples are periodic deposit of advance tax instalment, contribution of provident fund, payment for electricity, telephone bills *etc.* In their own ways these also have an impact on the cash in business.

1.5.2 External Factors

External factors cover all determinants relevant to the overall economy and/or a particular industry. First, we will discuss the factors which influence the economy in general.

(a) *Monetary and Fiscal Factors:* These factors relate to the money supply in the economy. During periods of inflation, the economy is flushed with money, price rise has a cascading effect on the output and the business has cash in abundance. On the other hand, during recessionary conditions demand for goods contracts and economy faces cash drought. The result is an epidemic of bankruptcy of the cash starved businesses.

The fiscal factors too, have a direct bearing on the cash availability in a business. Tax is an important fiscal factor which determines the size of disposable cash in the hands of business. For instance, corporate tax is a charge against profit and has direct influence in reducing the amount of cash in a business to that extent. Higher the tax rate lower the cash volume. Indirect tax also has its toll. An increase in excise or custom duty on the raw materials consumed by a business shall increase the cash outflow of the business.

(b) *Special Factors Relevant to an Industry:* In addition to monetary and fiscal factors, there may be some special factors unique to a particular industry as well. These also influence the cash flow of a business. Some examples are given below:

(i) Some retailers have the advantage of having favourable cash-flow position because sale proceeds are collected in cash over the counter whereas payments to the suppliers on account of cost of the products sold is made much later. Contrary to it, in some retail businesses cash is collected from innumerable small customers over a period of time for the sale of merchandise which have been purchased by depositing money in advance.

(ii) Some industries warrant blocking of funds for a considerable period of time in the inventories before it could mature in sale, for instance tea, tobacco, wine distilling *etc.*

(iii) The peaks and valleys of cash movement are glaringly visible in the case of building and construction industry. The industry is fed, at a given point of time, with a relatively small number of large discrete contracts. The initial cash inflow under such contracts is normally restricted to limited percentage of payment as mobilisation advance whereas substantial cash outflow has to be arranged for principal cost components—material, machines and manpower. The regular inflow, however, starts when the construction activity picks up: This is in the form of progress payments against running account bills but that too is invariably subject to deduction on account of retention money, and unamortised amount of advance paid earlier. The endeavour in such contracts is to execute the contract as a 'self financing project' failing which the firm has to dwelve upon 'bridging finance'—finance for the period of deficit when the payment is made to supplier/sub contractor and amount is received from client. Any prolongation in the completion schedule of the project has a multiplier effect in the escalation of cost and cash outflow. This probably, is the reason that this industry produces bumper crop of bankruptcies and unhappily will continue to do so because of the unique constraints which it have to encounter.

(iv) Some firms deal in highly volatile products like pop records, newspapers, and there is little time to regulate the cash movement if the things begin to move adversely.

(v) Consultancy and professional firms because of their relatively low overhead cost and receipt of good part of funds before the initiation of activity normally do not face cash crunch.

Thus we see that cash supply to a business is dependent on a plethora of factors both internal and external. The supreme art of handling these factors is to control internal factors and manage external factors. The only way this can be done is by implementing an efficient and effective cash management programme in the business.

1.6 MANAGEMENT OF CASH

In a business anything done financially affects cash eventually. Cash is to business what blood is to a living body. A business cannot operate without its life-blood cash, and without cash management, there may remain no cash to operate. Cash movement in a business is a two-way traffic. It keeps on moving in and out of business. The inflow and outflow of cash never coincides. We have studied above the factors influencing demand of cash, *i.e.*, the motives for holding cash and also the factors influencing availability of cash in the business. Effective control of these constitute two important aspects of management of cash. Another important aspect which is unique to cash management is time dimension associated with the movement of cash. Due to non-synchronicity of cash inflow and outflow, the inflow may be more than the outflow or the outflow may be more than the inflow at a particular point of time. This needs regulation. Left to itself cash flow is apt to follow monsoonic pattern, and showers of cash may be heavy, scanty or just normal. Hence there is a dire need to control its movement through skillful cash management. The primary aim of cash management is to ensure that there should be enough cash available when the need arises, not too much, but never too little.

An astute cash management programme is concerned with past, present and future business activities:

— Past is relevant for analysing cash movements historically, so as to figure out the trends of such movements. Such an analysis can provide vital information regarding cash needs during season or off-season; actual receipt of cash (inflow) from the customers vis-a-vis projections made, quantum and periodicity of various cash expenses *etc.* Equipped with such historical data, a business develops its cash flow programme for the present and future operations.

— Present is relevant for monitoring current cash movement so that it is effectively regulated and controlled. Many business avenues warrant constant watch. A business has to be lean and mean to be successful and close monitoring of cash movement provides great assistance in this regard. It helps in identifying areas which require immediate attention. Further, an efficient cash management programme is capable of making itself a "profit centre" by judicious deployment of surplus short term funds.

— Future is relevant for forecasting the anticipated cash movements of the ensuing budget period. Cash forecasting is the most effective instrument of cash control and cash control is the most important tool of financial management. Cash forecasting reveals the time and extent of probable cash deficits and surpluses in the future period. A business can take action in advance for replenishing the cash during the deficit period, and arrange for its profitable investment when it is expected to be in surplus. On the longer time frame, cash forecasting helps the management to appreciate cash implications of long term policies it has envisaged in its corporate plan.

Cash management programme aims at evolving strategies for dealing with various facets of cash management. These facets include the following:

1.6.1 Optimum Utilisation of Operating Cash Flow

Implementation of a sound cash management programme is based on rapid generation, efficient utilisation and effective conservation of its cash resources. Cash flows in a circle. The quantum and speed of the flow can be regulated through prudent financial planning facilitating the running of business with the minimum cash balance. This can be achieved by making a proper analysis of operative cash flow cycle alongwith efficient management of working capital. Chapters 2, 9 and 10 deal with these issues in detail. Chapter 15 spells out various internal control measures to insulate cash and other liquid assets against any kind of pilferage.

1.6.2 Cash Forecasting

Cash forecasting is backbone of cash planning. It forewarns a business regarding expected cash problems which it may encounter, thus assisting it to regulate future cash flow movements. Lack of cash planning results in spasmodic cash flows. The subject has been extensively dealt in Chapters 3, 4, 5 and 6.

1.6.3 Cash Management Techniques

Every business is interested in accelerating its cash collections and decelerating cash payments so as to exploit its scarce cash resources to the maximum. There are techniques in the cash management which help a business to achieve this objective. These techniques are elaborated in Chapter 7.

1.6.4 Liquidity Analysis

The importance of liquidity in a business cannot be overemphasised. If one does the autopsies of the businesses that failed, he would find that the major reason for the failure was their unability to remain liquid. Liquidity has an intimate relationship with efficient utilisation of cash. It helps in the attainment of optimum level of liquidity. There are many ways to measure the liquidity and efficient use of cash in a business. These are explained in detail in Chapter 8.

1.6.5 Profitable Deployment of Surplus Funds

Due to non-synchronisation of cash inflows and cash outflows the surplus cash may arise at certain points of time. If this cash surplus is deployed judiciously cash management will itself become a profit centre. However, much depends on the quantum of cash surplus and acceptability of market for its short term investments. Details regarding chalking out a short term investment programme and avenues for such investments are dealt in Chapters 11 and 14.

1.6.6 Economical Borrowings

Another product of non-synchronisation of cash inflows and outflows is emergence of deficits at various points of time. A business has to raise funds to the extent and for the period of deficits. Raising of funds at minimum cost is one of the important facets of cash management. Raising of funds from various short and medium term sources as well as long term sources have been explained in Chapters 12 and 13.

Cash is the most liquid and critical asset of a business. The skilful management of cash is vital for the efficient functioning of a business. Despite this generally, cash management programme does not receive the attention it deserves. At times this nonchalant attitude can become suicidal for a business. A business which ignores the basic tenets of cash management is bound to be trapped in the mire of usurary, and ultimately falls into bankruptcy.

QUESTIONS

1. What are the principal motives for holding cash in a business?
2. "It is wrong to believe that cash at the year end should increase by an amount equal to the profit earned during the year". Explain the statement by highlighting the distinguishing features of profit and cash.
3. What are the internal and external factors responsible for the cash availability in a business?
4. Explain the objectives of cash management.
5. Explain barter and the problem encountered in the barter trade.
6. What are the basic features of money as a good medium of exchange and to what extent present day cash possesses these features?
7. Explain electronic cash(E-cash) and its role in the future business.
8. What do you understand by cash management and what are its basic tenets?

2

CASH FLOW CYCLE

2.1 INTRODUCTION

Cash is life blood of a business. No business can exist without cash just as no human can live without blood. Stretching this analogy a bit further, in a going concern cash is apt to take a circulatory route like that of blood in the body. Blood affects each and every part of the human body, cash affects each and every segment of business activity. A man can live better if he keeps his blood pressure under proper control; a business can do better if it keeps its cash flow cycle duly regulated.

Cash is required to meet short term and long term requirements of a business. Accordingly, there are short term and long term cash flow cycles in operation. Short term cash requirement covers acquisition of current assets like stock and involves a constant process of generation and consumption of cash. Cash is consumed in procurement of materials, and processing them for production. It is generated through sale of such production to customers who pay cash, which again is utilised for procurement and processing of material to be sold resulting in generation of cash, and so the cycle goes on. Long term cash requirements are relatively for a longer duration. Cash is utilised for purchase of fixed assets which are used in a business for much longer period. The operational features of long term cash flow cycle are, therefore, different from those of short term cash flow cycle.

2.2 FEATURES OF SHORT TERM CASH FLOW CYCLE

The basic features of short term cash flow cycle are:

— Cash flow is cyclical in its nature.

— The movement of cash is influenced by a number of events and there is a time lag between one event and an other.

— Cash inflows and outflows remain non-synchronised resulting in surpluses and deficits during its movement.

2.2.1 Cyclical Flow of Cash

The first trait of business cash flow is its movement which is cyclical in character. Continuous circulatory flow of cash is the vital force of a going business concern. The initial cash put in the business is used for acquiring goods, *i.e.*, conversion of cash into stock. The goods so acquired when sold result in receipt of cash, *i.e.*, re-conversion into cash through sale of stock. The cycle is complete to be followed by another tranche of purchase and sale and in this way the merry-go-round goes on. This simple cash flow cycle is shown in Exhibit 2.1.

Exhibit 2.1
CASH FLOW CYCLE (TRADING)

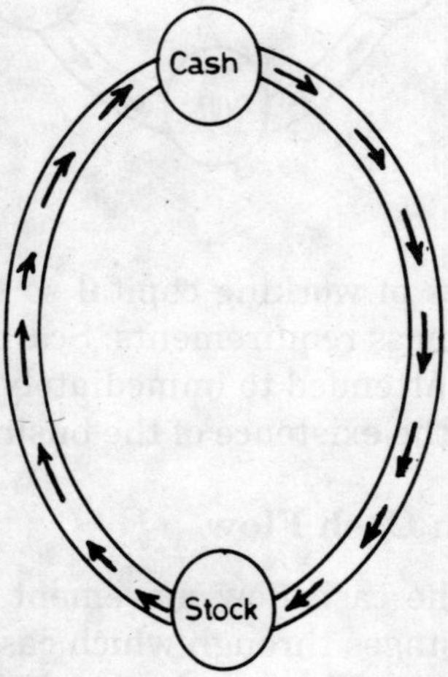

In the instant case, purchases and sales are on cash basis and the business is engaged in trading activity. Obviously, no business worth its name can function without affording credit for its sales. Also, there exists a complete process of production line, converting "raw materials" into "work in process" and finally into "finished products". Finished products are then sold to buyers on credit and cash is received from them at a later date. The cash flow cycle then will be as displayed in Exhibit 2.2.

This cyclical movement of cash flow is a process involving constant conversion of cash into other elements of working capital, *i.e.* creditors, stock, debtors and vice versa. It is working capital which is involved in the day-to-day working of the business. It covers all the routine operations generating a momentum which is appropriately reflected in the cash flow. Sound cash management aims at ensuring proper proportion

Exhibit 2.2
CASH FLOW CYCLE (MANUFACTURING)

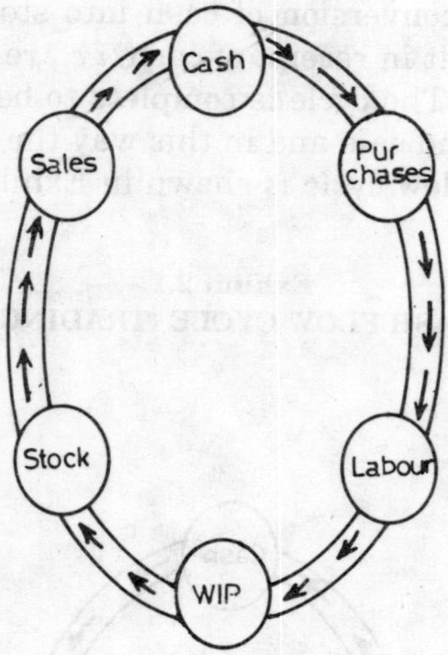

among these elements of working capital so that flow remains co-ordinated with the business requirements. Scarcity or surfeit in the flow at any stage must be attended to immediately otherwise it will have a devastating effect on the existence of the business.

2.2.2 Time Factor in Cash Flow

The orbital time of the cash flow movement can be analysed by examining the various stages through which cash moves and measuring the stage-wise time gaps. This can further be supplemented by determining the rate of cash turnover in terms of total operating annual outlay. These are explained below.

(a) *Events Affecting Cash Flow Movement:* The cash flow passes through various stages along its circulatory track. These stages are marked by events forming a chain in a sequential order. Three points merit consideration in this regard. First, events affect both cash and non-cash activities. Secondly, events affecting cash either concern generation of cash or consumption of cash resulting in the increase or decrease in the cash flow, respectively. Thirdly, there is a gap between one event and the other. This gap is the travel time of cash between the two events. The management policies play a vital role in shortening or lengthening of this time gap. The exact impact of this gap on the optimisation of cash flow movement shall be examined later on in this chapter.

A typical cash flow cycle has been tabulated in the Exhibit 2.3.

The cash flow cycle has been reduced to various activities influencing the movement of cash. Broadly, the activities can be categorised into four phases.In the first phase, materials are procured resulting in creditors for payment. The second phase starts with conversion of procured materials into work-in-progress followed by manufacture of finished products. In the third phase, finished products are kept in the stock waiting for sale. The final phase consists of sale of products and receipt of cash from customers. The full cycle is complete to be repeated again.

In terms of activities, the first activity starts with the placement of order. This activity is a non-cash centre (column 5) because there is no involvement of cash in this event. The second activity (also a non cash centre) starts on the receipt of materials and with this the count down for cash payment starts which becomes due after the expiry of 10 days credit period. The payment released on the 10th day is the first activity involving cash movement. It is to be noted that 10 days have been added to the processing days(column 3) but the cumulative effect reflected on the cash flow cycle (column 4) has been indicated as negative number of days since it involves outflow of cash. The time gap between receipt of materials and manufacture of final finished products is 30 days involving various processes of production. Inventory of product remains with the business for 15 days after which sale is effected generating debtors who have been offered a credit of 40 days. This activity, too, has no impact on cash movement till the expiry of 40 days when the cash is received from the sundry debtors. This way the cash flow cycle is complete in a period of 85 days as detailed below:

1. Procurement time	10 days
2. Processing time	30 days
3. Inventory storage time	15 days
4. Credit allowed	40 days
	95 days
Less Credit availed	10 days
Complete Cash flow cycle	85 days

(b) *Cash Turn Over Ratio*: Once orbital time of the cash flow cycle is determined, one can calculate the cash turnover ratio of the business. This ratio indicates the velocity of cash flow cycle in a year. It can be calculated by the following formula:

$$\text{CTR} = \frac{\text{D}}{\text{CD}}$$

Where,

CTR = Cash turnover ratio,

Exhibit 2.3 : Events Affecting Cash Flow Movement

Date	Activity	No. of Days		Non Cash Centres Impact	Cash Centres Impact	
		Processing	Cumulative		Cash Enter	Exit
(1)	(2)	(3)	(4)	(5)	(6)	(7)
April 5	Material ordered	—	—	Commitment made	—	—
April 15	Material received	0	0	Creditors created	—	—
April 25	Payment released	10	(–)10	—	—	(–)
May 15	Material processed	30	30#	Inventory generated	—	—
May 30	Sales effected	15	45	Debtors created	—	—
Jul 9	Payment received	40	85	—	(+)	—

#Days = 10 + 30 – 10 = 30

D = Number Of Days. (Normally, a year is considered as having 360 days)

CD = Cash flow cycle days.

In the present case, the cash turn over ratio $= \frac{360}{85} = 4.24$

2.3 SURPLUSES AND DEFICITS IN THE CASH FLOWS

The third trait of cash flow cycle emerges due to non-synchronisation of cash inflow and cash outflow resulting in deficits and surpluses en-route the flow movement. In the non-static business environment of today it is difficult to have a perfect coincidence of in-flows and out-flows of cash.During certain periods, business may encounter instances of negative cash flow, *i.e.*, cash out-flow is more than cash in-flow or positive cash flow, *i.e.*, cash in-flow is more than cash out-flow. Such periodical deficits should not be considered as indicative of weak financial position nor the surpluses as an index of strong financial strength. However, constant deficits or surpluses should be matters of concern. The former flashes a red signal for liquidity crisis whereas the latter is a sign of inefficient deployment of funds.

Like any other item cash also has a cost. It can be subdivided into three groups: cost of holding surplus cash, cost of holding less cash and procurement cost. The cost manifestation can be in the form of direct expenditure or indirect expenditure. It can be on revenue account or capital account.

2.3.1 Cost of Cash Surplus

The obvious question can be that if excess cash results in cost then why business allows the cash to be piled up? The excessive surplus cash may arise due to a number of factors which may be a fallout of occasional, seasonal or cyclical occurrences.

First of all, let us consider occasional cash surplus which can be routine or exceptional. Internal factors are responsible for such a surplus. Normal mismatching of receipts and disbursements of cash may result in excessive cash at particular times. Also, in certain cases which are exceptional in nature, business may find itself flushed with surplus cash for a short period of time, *e.g.*, after the issue of shares/debentures for a particular project and till the actual utilisation in the project, huge funds may become available to the business for parking in short term marketable securities.

External factors influenced by seasonal and cyclical forces are also instrumental in creating cash surpluses in the business. A business engaged in seasonal business activity will find excessive cash during the season, *e.g.*, a woollen garment manufacturer may find excess cash during winter season. Similarly, idle cash may become available due to cyclical pattern in the economy too. During recession there may be idle cash waiting for consumption in business operations.

Surplus cash if deployed judiciously can bring extra revenue to the business. Non-deployment of such cash will result in missed opportunity cost known as "cost of surplus". Such surplus cash results in loss of revenue in the form of interests which would have been earned through its investment. Hence, the missed opportunity costs. This is a direct cost of holding fallow cash, and the quantum of cost is dependent on the prevalent rate of interest in the market. Higher the interest rate more the cost. Surplus cash entails indirect cost as well. This is on capital account. Cash depreciates by losing its purchasing power in the present era of inflation. Barren cash remaining idle loses its own value as time passes.

2.3.2 Cost of Cash Deficit

Non-synchronisation of cash receipts and cash payments result in cash deficits at particular points of time. Some of these points would have been pin-pointed by cash budget. The costs associated with the cash deficit may be direct or indirect.

The business may have to borrow funds to meet the deficit. All costs associated with the arrangement of such loans are attributable to cost of deficits which would include interest on loans, negotiation charges, stamp duty and other costs involved in borrowing cash for the business. Another example of cost of cash deficit is the conversion cost. Even if the firm is not required to borrow funds and intends to use the funds temporarily parked by it in marketable securities, it may incur some expenditure by way of brokerage while converting these securities into cash. Also, non-availability of funds at times may force a business to forego a trade discount which it otherwise might have availed of. To that extent the business suffers and bears the cost of cash deficit.

The indirect cost associated with cost of cash deficit is in the form of deterioration in the credit rating of a business. Though it looks subjective, it is very important from the point of view of practical aspect of the business operations. Frequent or persistent cash deficits may lead to loss of creditability. Once it happens, the bank may offer loan on less favourable terms, supplier may withdraw credit facilities and insist on cash payments as a result of which the business may have to incur additional costs.

2.3.3 Procurement Cost

In addition to the above referred cost of deficit and cost of surplus, there is one more cost known as "procurement cost". This is the cost associated with operating the cash management programme. According to Bolten: "there are clerks and book keepers who run the daily routine. There is the overhead of an office. All these costs must also be considered."* These are fixed costs and remain constant whether there is surplus or deficit cash in the business.

2.4 MINIMUM OPERATING CASH BALANCE

Cash flow cycle is very critical to the running of a successful business and its constituent factors "Amount" and "Rate" are very critical for the effective running of a cash flow cycle. The Amount refers to the volume of cash flowing in the cycle and Rate connotes speed with which it flows in its circulatory route. Both affect each other and jointly they influence determination of minimum cash required in a business.

2.4.1 Amount of Cash

The volume of cash depends on the level of transactional activity of a business and on the buffer the business wants to create as a measure of precaution. Though general factors such as inflation and the like also play their role in the availability of cash in a business, the management policies have more vital and direct impact on the cash quantum in the business.

For the determination of minimal cash balance, all the three costs associated with the cash, viz., cost of deficit, cost of surplus and procurement cost have to be considered. As the cash supply increases, cost of deficit decreases whereas cost of surplus increases. Conversely, reduction in cash quantum increases cost of deficit and decreases cost of surplus. Procurement cost remains more or less immune to the variations in cash quantum. The 'total cost' represents cost of deficit, cost of surplus and cost of procurement. Optimal cash balance is the point wherein total cost is minimum. This is explained in the Exhibits 2.4 and 2.5.

Exhibit 2.4
OPTIMAL CASH BALANCE

Rupees

Cash Balance	Cost of Deficit	Cost of Surplus	Procurement Cost	Total Cost
1	2	3	4	5
10,00,000	1,80,000	1,00,000	1,00,000	3,80,000
15,00,000	1,08,000	1,40,000	1,00,000	3,48,000
20,00,000	10,000	2,00,000	1,00,000	3,10,000
25,00,000	5,000	2,60,000	1,00,000	3,65,000
30,00,000	—	3,00,000	1,00,000	4,00,000

It can be observed from Exhibit 2.4 that cost of deficit decreases as the cash balance increases while cost of surplus increases as the cash balance increases. Procurement cost being fixed in nature remains unchanged. Total cost representing all the three costs is reflected in

*Managerial Finance Principles and Practices—Bolten

column 5. The lowest point in the total cost, *i.e.*, Rs. 3,10,000 indicates optimal cash balance, of Rs. 20,00,000 under column 1. This is the ideal cash balance for the business. This is graphically presented in Exhibit 2.5.

In the Exhibit 2.5 Cash Balance is plotted along X-axis and Cost of Holding Cash along Y-axis. The Cost of Deficit curve declines as cash balance increases. Conversely, Cost of Surplus curve moves upward with increase in the cash balance. The Procurement Cost curve

Exhibit 2.5
OPTIMAL CASH BALANCE (GRAPHICAL PRESENTATION)

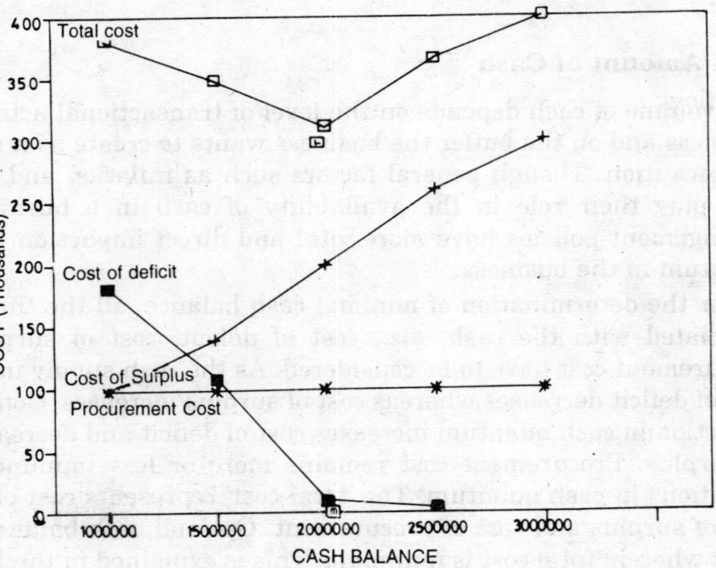

remains constantly straight indicating immunity to any change in the cash balance. It is the Total Cost curve which indicates the ideal cash balance for the business. The lowest point in this curve is at L where the total cost is minimal. The corresponding cash balance to this point is M at Rs 20 lakhs. This is the optimal cash balance for the business.

2.4.2 Rate of Cash Flow

The second important factor in the cash flow is the speed with which it flows in the circulatory track. It is a continuous process of generation and consumption of cash through conversion of stock, creditors and debtors into cash followed by conversion of cash into these assets again. The time factor involved in this conversion and reconversion is the index of efficiency with which the business is making use of these basic components of working capital. This has a direct bearing on minimising operating cash requirements. By adopting astute cash management policies the rate of cash flow can be increased culminating in the reduction in the cost of holding cash.

As may be observed in Exhibit 2.3, the cash flow cycle passes through four phases. The first phase starts with the receipt of materials, creation of creditors and release of payments. The second phase involves processing of materials into finished products. In the third phase, finished products lie in the inventory, waiting for sale. The fourth phase consists of sale of finished products and receipt of cash from debtors. All these four phases contribute to the speed of cash flow.

(a) *Payment to Creditors (Phase I):* The more a business delays its payment to creditors, the shorter it makes its cash flow cycle. However, in deciding on delaying the payment to the creditor the economics of discount offered by the creditors should be given due consideration. In the Exhibits 2.3 and 2.4, we see that the cash turnover ratio is 4.24 (360/85) and the optimum cash balance is Rs 20 lakhs. This makes the total operating annual outlay as Rs. 84.80 lakhs (Rs 20 lakhs x 4.24). In the cash turnover ratio we considered a credit period of 10 days as offered by the supplier. In case the business is in a position to successfully avail a credit period of 20 days then the cash turnover ratio will increase to 4.8 (360/75). This will have effect on minimum cash requirement which will now come down from Rs.20 lakhs to Rs 17.67 lakhs (Rs 84.80 lakhs / 4.8), a reduction of Rs 2.33 lakhs. If the opportunity cost is assumed @ 10%, there is net saving of Rs. 23,300 in the present example.

(b) *Conversion of Raw Materials into Finished Products (Phase II):* A business can shorten this time factor by following better policies of material management and production techniques. In the Exhibit 2.3, if processing time of 30 days is reduced to 23 days, the time of cash flow cycle will be shortened from 85 to 78 days. The cash turnover ratio will increase from 4.24 to 4.62 (360 / 78). The minimum cash requirement will come down to Rs. 18.35 lakh (Rs. 84.80 / 4.62). The saving in cash of Rs 1.65 lakhs can earn interest of Rs 16,500 at the assumed rate of 10%

(c) *Inventory Wait-in-Time (Phase III):* The time factor in this phase can be reduced by proper coordination of demand and production, and aggressive marketing. In the instant case, if the time gap of 15 days is reduced to 10 days it will have the effect of shortening cash flow cycle by 5 days, thus improving cash turn over ratio from 4.24 to 4.5 (360 /

80). The effect on minimum cash will be a reduction from Rs. 20.00 lakhs to Rs 18.84 lakhs (Rs. 84.80 lakh / 4.5). The saving of cash by Rs. 1,16,000 can earn a interest of Rs 11,600, assuming an interest rate of 10%.

(d) *Receipt of Cash from Debtors (Phase IV):* The importance of early realisation of debtors in the cash flow cycle cannot be overemphasised. Management policies in respect of credit terms offered to debtors, collection policies adopted *etc.* play important role in this. The cash flow cycle if improved by 15 days through early collections from debtors (from 40 days to 25 days) will increase the cash turn over ratio from 4.24 to 5.14 (360 / 70). The requirement of minimum cash balance will get reduced to Rs 16.50 lakh(Rs 84.80 lakh/5.14). The effect will be a substantial reduction of Rs 3.50 lakhs. This will lead to interest earnings of Rs 35000 at the assumed rate of 10%.

While taking decisions in respect of reduction in the time factors in all the four phases, the business must give due respect to the 'limits' relevant to each phase. In the first phase it should be seen that the delay in payment must not lead to evaporation of credit-worthiness of the business. In the second phase cutting inventory level should not lead to stoppage of production at shop floor. In the third phase,the business must ensure that enough stock is available to meet the market demand. The fourth phase which is sensitive of all, stringent credit terms and credit policies should not lead to reduction in sales.

2.5 LONG TERM CASH FLOW CYCLE

Short term cash flow confines its operations to working capital and for that matter some times is described as operating working capital. In addition to cash required in working capital (for day-to-day needs, technically known as floating capital requirements) cash is extensively used in the permanent avenues of business operations known as fixed capital requirements. Common instances are cash sunk in fixed assets and non-short-term securities. Working capital cash cannot be disturbed for this lest the business may starve and becomes incapable of meeting its day-to-day requirements. The present business requires heavy investments and the owners normally have to arrange loans to supplement their own contributions in the business. These become the sources for the inflows of long term cash flow.

The long term cash flow may not have a regulated and defined route like that of a short term cash flow. On the contrary, each item of long term cash flow may have its own orbit for movement. The features of long term cash flow cycle are:

- The quantum of cash flow involved is much bigger than that of short term cash flow cycle.
- It covers normally fixed assets and long term liabilities.

— The orbital time is much longer than that of short term cash flow.
— It is less volatile.

The movements of long term cash flow vis-a-vis short term cash flow have been exhibited in the Exhibit 2.6. The start up capital introduced by the owners is first instance of long term cash inflow. The outflows in this are in the form of dividends declared periodically by the business. Similarly, the loan capital is provided by the agencies which have been roped in to provide cash for longer duration. The outflows of cash in this instance are in the form of payment of interest and repayment of the loans in piecemeal instalments or at one go. On the assets side, the business invests some of the funds in long term investments. The inflow from the investment is in the form of interests/dividends, and also encashment of investments periodically for consumption in the business or for investment in some other

Exhibit 2.6
SHORT-TERM AND LONG-TERM CASH FLOW CYCLES

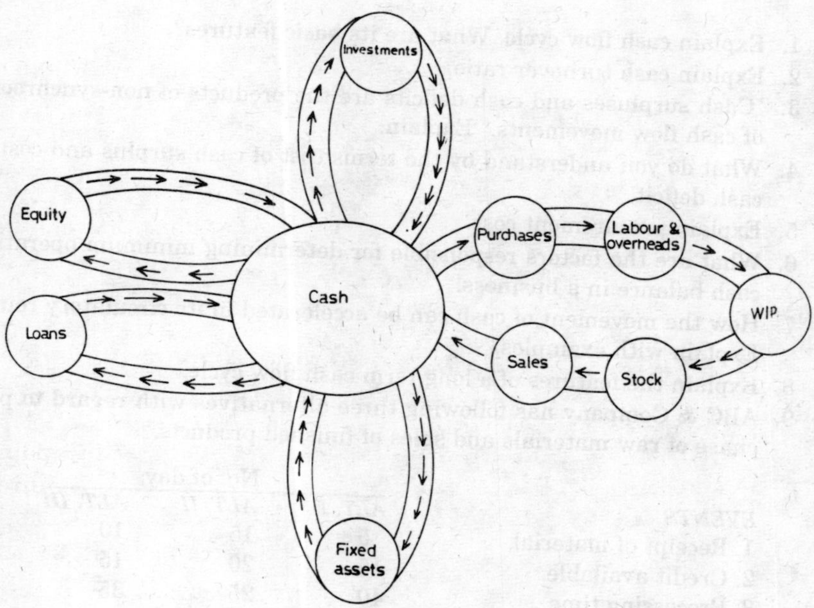

securities. A significant item which consumes cash for long term is fixed assets. According to one school of thought cash outflow in fixed assets is consumed permanently and that is the end of it. However, another school of thought holds that even the cash invested in fixed assets has got the effect on the inflow cash movement. This effect is direct in the form of realisation of the salvage value of a fixed asset which eventually is disposed of after its use. Of course, inflow of cash in such case will be very moderate as compared to outflow made a few years earlier. The indirect effect pointed out is concerning the depreciation and its impact on the tax liability. Depreciation as an item of expenditure is admissible in the determination of profit of a business but it does not make any dent on the cash outflow. Rather cash stands to increase to this extent. The profit determined for the taxation admits depreciation as an expenditure, and as such results in reduced amount to be paid as taxes. To that extent the fixed assets manage to reduce the cash outflow and contribute towards cash conservation in the business.

QUESTIONS

1. Explain cash flow cycle. What are its basic features?
2. Explain cash turnover ratio.
3. "Cash surpluses and cash deficits are the products of non-synchrocity of cash flow movements." Explain.
4. What do you understand by the terms cost of cash surplus and cost of cash deficit.
5. Explain procurement cost.
6. What are the factors responsible for determining minimum operating cash balance in a business.
7. How the movement of cash can be accelerated in its circulatory route? Explain with examples.
8. Explain the features of a long-term cash flow cycle.
9. ABC & Company has following three alternatives with regard to purchase of raw materials and sales of finished products.

	No. of days		
EVENTS	*ALT. I*	*ALT. II*	*ALT. III*
1. Receipt of material	5	15	10
2. Credit available	15	20	15
3. Processing time	40	25	35
4. Inventory storage time	15	35	25
5. Credit allowed	30	25	15

Which alternative is the best from the point of view of cash flow cycle?

10. ABC and Company is successful in getting the minimum time frame in respect of events No. 1, 3, 4 and 5 and maximum for event No. 2 among the three alternatives mentioned in the question No. 9 above. Further, its annual operating outlay is Rs. 27,00,000.

Determine the following :

a) Period in terms of number of days of cash flow cycle.
b) Cash turnover ratio
c) Minimum operating cash balance

11. XYZ & Company provides the following information:

a) Cash turnover ratio	5
b) Optimum cash balance	Rs.15 lakhs
c) Credit period allowed to customers	80 days
d) Rate of interest	10%

The Company decides to reduce credit to customers to 70 days. Calculate the savings effected by the Company due to shortening of credit period.

3

CASH BUDGET— GENESIS OF FORECASTING

3.1 INTRODUCTION

A cash budget is a summary statement presented in an orderly format containing forecasted figures of receipts and disbursements of cash over a given period of time. Cash budget like any other budget is concerned with future events, events which can be approximated or "best guessed" taking into consideration past results, present strengths and future trends. It is the technique of forecasting which generates raw material for budgeting and provides the best approximation.

The three basic features of business forecasting are:

— Forecasts relate to projections for an identified activity at a specific point of time, in future.

— Despite advancement in the scientific methods and concepts like market survey, statistical techniques *etc.*, forecasting has to grapple with uncertainty. The uncertainty may crop up due to a definite cycle or trend in a business or because of various unpredictable occurrences.

— The "best guess" under forecasting is made based on the past (historical data), present (existing facts) and future (expected trends).

Forecasting has acquired an enviable position in the concept of strategic management necessary to run a modern business. Gone are the days when first the demand in the market emerged and then the production was oriented to meet the demand. In the present day a successful business has to forecast demand of the product and gear up its production to meet the anticipated demand. Anticipation is the key to forecasting.

A business cannot remain content with a position of status quo. It has to opt for an aggressive attitude towards its development, otherwise its competitors are likely to outmarket it. For its growth and development; it has to look into the future. A dynamic business has to be farsighted. The blueprint for this foresight is provided by a 'Plan'.

3.2 PLANNING AND FORECASTING

A few words about Plan before we look into plan-forecasting relationship.

"The business which fails to plan, plans to fail"—goes an old saying. Business Plan has been described as an investment and like any good investment returns income in the form of increase in flow of profit and capital appreciation in the form of growth of the business. The spirit behind a business plan is to know where a business is at present and where it intends to go. Steps of business planning are:

— establishing where a business is at present;
— deciding where it intends to reach;
— chalking out a strategy for reaching there.

A business plan encompasses all actions for measuring benefits from the existing opportunities, mobilising resources for enhancing capabilities and ensuring adequacy of finance so that business achieves its objective of maximising return from the investment.

The relationship of a business plan and forecasting is confronted with a chicken-egg conundrum—which comes first: plans or forecasts. Some feel that a business first formulates a plan as to what it intends to achieve. Financial forecasts are then prepared to support the plan. Some others opine that forecasts are the first stage of planning process and play a key role in determining the contours of a plan.

The relationship of these two can well be appreciated if we study the equation under which these two phenomena, work in a business. Business plans relate to future events. Events are expressed in terms of objectives. Objectives are quantified through forecasting. So forecasting provides financial expressions to goals which a business plan aspires to achieve. These goals are in fact 'best guess' estimates in the 'scenario' blueprinted by a plan.

3.3 CASH FORECASTING

Forecasting thus is a planning tool. It is used for projecting future operational results of all the activities of a business - marketing, production, personnel, finance *etc.* All these activities have a chain-link-effect. A successful business has to anticipate the demand of the product by making a sales forecast. As a second step, production forecasts are made by estimating the requirements of material, men and machinery. And finally, the requirements for finance are assessed to execute all these activities which lead us to make cash forecasting because in a business anything done or to be done financially affects the cash eventually. However, there is one major difference between business forecasting covering other functional activities and cash forecasting. All other forecasts are on accrual basis whereas cash forecasts are on cash basis.

Cash forecasting is very important in the realm of overall business forecasting. It is concerned with every segment of business environment, be it permanent or temporary, capital or revenue, income or expense.

3.4 TIME HORIZON

The variables are forecasted for a predetermined period of time. This in business parlance is known as "time horizon". It refers to the time span for which the forecasting is made. There cannot be rigid rules to determine length of a time horizon. Conventionally, accounts of a business are prepared for a period of twelve months; forecasts are also made for twelve months so as to have an equitable ground for comparison of the forecasts with the accounting results. We have seen that cash forecasts act as a hub of all other forecasts like sales forecasts, purchase forecasts, production forecasts, *etc.* It, therefore, is prepared for identical period of twelve months too, to synchronise with the period of other forecasts. However, cash being very important and volatile warrants close scrutiny of its movement. The time horizon of twelve months of cash forecasting, therefore, is subdivided into months or weeks. This enables better forecast and control of cash flow in a business. Forecasts having time horizon of twelve months or less are known as short-term forecasts. But a business needs forecasts for longer time frame as well.

The time horizon of long-term forecasts largely depends upon the corporate plan constructed by the business. Some important factors which are taken into consideration for determining the forecasts period of long-term forecasts are as follows.

— Nature of business of some enterprises requires longer time frame to develop a meaningful plan. For instance, a construction company having big construction projects like hydro dam projects, need a bigger time horizon because of the long life span of the individual projects.

— The business which is dealing in items sensitive to quick obsolescence will have a shorter time horizon. Conversely, if a product has a longer life, forecasting shall have to be done for a longer period. Accordingly, time horizon shall be fixed for a longer duration.

— Products involving extensive research and development shall be having a longer time horizon.

— Capital intensive units will have a time horizon of longer duration.

3.5 FORECASTING AND UNCERTAINTY

"Those who foretell the future lie, even if they tell the truth", says an old Arab proverb. Future is pregnant with uncertainty and uncertainty is inherent in forecasting. Then why forecasting be attempted at all, argue some experts. According to them even if in some cases future has been forecasted accurately, the accuracy is for some other reasons and not because of any contribution of forecasting.

Uncertainty is a fact of modern business life. One has to live with it. The only way through which influence of the uncertainty can be diminished is by trying to predict the future. And the prediction can best be done by forecasting the 'best guess' of the future events. The business which plans and forecasts has at least some light to follow. One who is shy of it will have to grapple in the dark. Keynes has rightly put—"It is better to be vaguely right than precisely wrong."

Uncertainty and forecasting are inseparable. Uncertainty may arise due to a number of factors—seasonal, cyclical or random events. Seasonal factors have more or less a regular pattern that recur year after year. Such a regularity reduces the element of uncertainty and increases the accuracy of prediction. Cyclical factors caused by booms and recessions are difficult to be anticipated with accuracy and hence are more unpredictable. Random events may affect a particular business or industry as a whole. Some examples are sudden obsolescence of the product, strike, imposition of levy by the state or spurt in demand due to failure of a competitor. Such events are most unpredictable.

Uncertainty does dilute the accuracy of a forecast. But this should not prompt one to declare the forecasting a futile exercise. In order to appreciate forecasting in proper perspective we must not lose sight of the spirit behind forecasting. The basic objective of forecasting is to provide necessary guidance to a business enabling it to take timely action before the future unfolds itself. For this a good forecast need not be wholly 'correct'; it need only be 'fair' in its estimation.

3.6 IMPORTANCE OF CASH FORECASTING

"Forecasting is forewarning and forewarned is forearmed". Despite the uncertainty of future and number of other factors which affect accuracy of forecasted figures, the fact remains that if the business is successful in drawing reasonably dependable forecasts it can get sufficiently reliable signposts to indicate where, when and what type of actions should be taken to salvage the situation.

In brief, the following are the benefits of cash forecasting:

3.6.1 Cash Flow Requirements

Cash forecasting helps the management to gauge cash requirements of a business. This assists the business to firm up its policies towards working capital management — its policies towards management of stock, production, credit to customers, *etc.* Cash forecasting provides an insight to the cash flow cycle ultimately inducing the business to improve its cash-turn over ratio.

3.6.2 Cash Deficits

Cash flow forecasting reveals the quantum and period when the business is likely to face cash deficits so that appropriate action is taken for arranging additional funds before the actual deficit manifests itself. In short-term period, normally, a business depends upon bank finance for meeting the deficit. If action for arranging such finance is taken well in advance, better terms can be negotiated with the bank. A business rushing to bank just at the nick of the time falls at the mercy of the bank who scorn such business for lack of prudent financial management.

3.6.3 Cash Surpluses

Cash flow forecasting points out period of cash surpluses too, so that the same can be utilised by proper investment in the short term securities. Idle cash incurs opportunity costs. With cash forecasting a business acquires advance intimation and is in a position to chalk out its strategy for short term investments well in advance. Securities with desirable maturities and expected returns can be selected. Even alternative arrangements can be thought of to reduce the risk and increase the return avoiding wastage of time, and loss due to opportunity costs.

3.6.4 Pooling of Cash

Cash forecasting is of special importance for a business engaged in construction activity having numerous scattered projects or a business having multi divisional units. Cash forecasting of individual projects or units and its consolidation into overall forecasting for a business reveal the deficits/surpluses of cash of various projects and the business as a whole. It is possible that at a certain point of time there is surplus in one project and deficit in another. With such forecasting in hand, advance action can be taken for the inter project transfer of funds, so as to optimise the use of cash resources of the business.

3.6.5 Long-Term Cash Requirements

For its growth, a business designs strategic plan. Long-term cash forecasting provide necessary input with regard to working capital and fixed capital requirements for the implementaion of such plan. In the event of various plans being considered for a business, financial impact of each one is considered in the light of projections, made by long-term cash forecasts.

3.6.6 Avoidance of Bankruptcy

Cash forecasting may not insulate any business from bankruptcy. But it can flash red signals of impending future financial crisis giving ample time and opportunity to take remedial actions.

3.7 SHORT-TERM CASH FORECASTS

Short-term cash forecasting is for a shorter period. Minimum period may be as near as next day but the maximum period is not stretched beyond twelve months. Normally, the period of twelve months is favoured since it synchronises with other functional budgets which too are prepared for an year. Because of shorter time horizon, forecasts are more realistic and dependable. In forecasting for short term, entire thrust is on day to day cash. Forecasts help in ensuring that the cash flow of a business does not get dried up and it is in a position to meet its financial commitments even if necessary lubrication has to be done by injecting additional cash on temporary basis. Focus remains constantly on how cash enters and exits the business. It provides tactical control by revealing the points of time of deficits in the immediate near future and also the surpluses so that they can be better utilised. The underlying idea is to ensure that the business is in a position to meet its financial commitments and continues to operate successfully. Because of the shorter time horizon, short-time forecasts bank upon short-time financing like bank overdraft as a means of additional funds.

3.8 LONG-TERM CASH FORECASTS

Long-term forecasts have a longer time horizon. Long-term cash forecasts are not much concerned with display of detailed cash receipts and payments. The forecasts concentrate on issues like cash resource requirements for fixed assets, changes in working capital funds *etc.* thereby educating management regarding financial consequences of the strategic plans which a business intends to pursue. The underlying idea in this case is to determine which of the future alternative courses of action are best for adoption and the cash resources required to implement the preferred alternative. Unlike short-term forecasts, long-term forecasts are not much concerned with present situation but focus on the future development and growth of the business. For its financing as well, long-term cash forecasts explore and evaluate various patterns of long-term financing within the framework of debt equity parity. Long-term cash forecasts, because of the involvement of longer period are exposed to innumerable unpredictabilities in business environment and are, therefore likely to lack precision of short-term cash forecasts.

3.9 METHODS OF CASH FORECASTING

Primarily, there are two methods for making cash forecasts:

— Receipts and Disbursements method;
— Net Adjusted Income method.

Though both the methods can be used for estimating short-term and long-term cash requirements of a business but normally due to basic difference in the approach followed under each method, the Receipts and Disbursements method is used for short term cash forecasts, and Net Adjustment Income method is deployed for drawing long term cash forecasts.

3.9.1 Receipt and Disbursements Method

The method aims at cash forecasting as an abbreviated version of Cash Book of a future period. Under this method the individual items which involve movement of cash during the forecast period are estimated. Since such a forecast is for a shorter period, normally upto one year, estimates are made for all items of receipts and payments having some significant value. Such forecasts are fairly accurate.

3.9.2 Net Adjusted Income Method

Net Adjusted Income method is deployed where estimates for a longer period are required. Obviously, it may not be easy to estimate each and every item of income and expenditure for a longer period say five years, as meticulously as in the case of short-term forecasting. This method involves culling out of information pertinent to movement of cash from the already prepared accounting statements like forecasted profit and loss account and balance sheet to make future projections of cash requirements. Then, true to its name the method makes necessary adjustments in the accounting figures appearing in such forecasted profit and loss account and balance sheet which have been prepared on accrual basis. The 'adjustment' is effected to convert accrual based figures to cash based figures. The statement so prepared is known as Forecasted Cash Flow Statement.

The two methods are explained in detail in the following chapters.

QUESTIONS

1. Define a cash budget.
2. What are the basic features of business forecasting?
3. What is a plan? Explain the mutual relationship of planning and forecasting.
4. What do you understand by cash forecasting and how does it differ from forecasting of other functional activities of a business?
5. Describe time horizon and the factors responsible for determining the length of a time horizon.
6. Explain the influence of uncertainty in the forecasting.
7. "Forecasting is forewarning and forewarned is forearmed". In the light of this statement explain the benefits of cash forecasting.
8. Compare the short-term cash forecasting with long-term cash forecasting.
9. What are the different methods of cash forecasting?

4

CASH BUDGET — FORMATING

4.1 INTRODUCTION

Cash forecasting estimates the receipts and payments of cash from various accounts for a future period. It anticipates figures which are likely to be there during and at the end of the forecasted period. But a business is not content with this. It is interested to know what these figures should be so that business operates smoothly. Certain adjustments are required to make what the estimates are "likely to be" to what the estimates "should be". Thus, cash forecasting by itself may not achieve the desired objective. In order to make it an effective instrument of control in the mechanics of cash management, it has to be converted into a Cash Budget.

4.2 CONVERSION: CASH FORECAST TO CASH BUDGET

As stated above, forecasting helps in determining the anticipated cash receipts and payments of a future period. Of its own it does not indicate as to what is to be done with these estimates. It, however, provides the input for initiating appropriate action. We have also observed that cash receipts and cash payments of a business are seldom synchronised because of the unstatic business environment. This non-synchronising leads to positive or negative cash balances at given points of time during the budgeted period. Once these balances are known, business initiates steps for remedial actions. Such actions include arrangement of funds to tide over deficits or utilise the cash surplus in short term investments. The document prepared after effecting these adjustments is known as Cash budget. "A forecast is merely passive, while a budget should reflect the results of positive actions that management plans to take in order to influence, adapt to, future events."* In a way cash budget forecasts figures duly doctored

---

**Fundamentals of Management Accounting*—Anthony & Welsch.

by the management. These figures then become part of the overall budgetary control system.

4.3 CONSTRUCTION OF CASH BUDGET

Cash budget has been defined in the previous chapter as a statement presented in an orderly format containing forecasted figures of receipts and disbursements of cash over a given period of time. The following characteristics emerge from the definition.

— Statement contains forecasted figures.

— Forecasts are made for a predetermined period known as budget period.

— It is designed and presented in an orderly format.

The first two features, *i.e.*, forecasting and budget period have already been examined in the previous chapter. We will now study the formating and its importance.

4.4 FORMATING OF CASH BUDGET

Proper formating of the cash budget is very important. It ensures prompt, regular and accurate assimilation and comprehensive display of data year after year in case a standard format is followed. Another benefit of following a standard format is its admissibility for sensitivity analysis, *i.e.,* preparation of cash budget at different levels of activity. Also, it enhances comparability of the budgeted figures with the actuals.

Formating of cash budget involves study of two inter-related aspects:

— Layout.

— Presentation of Data.

4.4.1 Layout of Format

From the layout point of view cash budget can be divided into following two sections:

(a) **Caption Section:** Caption section discloses the identity and depicts name of the business, division, unit for which cash budget is prepared. In addition to it, other facts like period of the cash budget, *i.e.*, weekly/monthly/quarterly/yearly *etc.,* and date of preparation are also mentioned.

(b) **Contents Section:** Contents section contains the basic data of the budget. It can further be subdivided into four subsections.

(i) *Receipt Section:* Receipt Section takes into consideration anticipated cash receipts from various sources during the budget period. Receipts can be on capital or revenue account. A few examples of such receipts are sales of merchandise, sale of plant and equipment, cash receipts from repayment of advances, issuing of shares, *etc.*

(ii) *Payment Section:* This section records expected cash payments which have been projected to be released during the budget period. A few examples are payments to creditors, payments on account of wages and salaries, operational, administrative and selling expenses, payments on account of income tax, capital equipment purchases, dividend, *etc.*

(iii) *Deficit or Surplus Section:* This section represents arithmetical difference of cash receipts minus cash payments or *vice versa*. As explained earlier, cash inflows and cash outflows are generally non-synchronised. This results in deficits or surpluses at fixed intervals during the budget period. For determining the amount of cash surplus or deficit, balance in the beginning of the fixed interval period is also taken into consideration so as to arrive at an exact figure of cash for which remedial actions become necessary.

(iv) *Adjustment Section:* Adjustment section projects detailed account of the arrangements to be made for dealing with deficit or surplus. The business first decides the amount of desired cash balance which it would like to maintain to meet its requirements. In case the forecasted figures reveal a deficit, action is to be taken to make arrangements for borrowing funds from banks or other institutions and conversely if the cash surplus has been shown, to invest the funds in the short-term deposits known as Cash Equivalents in the realm of cash management.

Sample format of cash budget is shown in Exhibit 4.1.

4.4.2 Presentation of Data

Basic data spawned in the cash budget vary from business to business. However, one need not be over-concerned with unnecessary details while incorporating the data since indulgence in minute details shall make the whole process very cumbersome prompting the finance manager to avoid the whole exercise which might prove fatal for the business.

"International Accounting Standard" has issued an accounting standard for Cash Flow Statements—International Accounting Standard (7) Revised (IAS 7). Following the issue of the Standard, the Institute of Chartered Accountants of India too, has circulated a draft of proposed accounting standard on Cash Flow Statement. The objective of a Cash Flow Statement as explained in the proposed standard is to provide information about the 'historical' changes in cash and cash equivalents of an enterprise by means of a cash flow statement. In other words, how cash flowed inward and outward during a given period for which financial statements like profit and loss account and balance sheet fail to give any detail. Though the cash flow statement so recommended reveals the cash movement of the past period, its format can be borrowed to design the cash budget which portrays cash movement of the future period. Cash budget constructed in such a format will ensure identical paradigm making comparison of budgeted figures with actual figures easier, comprehensible and meaningful.

Exhibit 4.1
CASH BUDGET

Date: 25th March, 1995

Period : April to September, 1995

Basis : Monthly

Particulars	April	May	June	July	August	September
1. Cash Receipt						
2. Cash Payment						
3. Deficit/Surplus						
4. Adjustments						

Prepared by ....

Under the proposed standard, cash generating activity of an enterprise have been categorised into three classes:

— Operating

— Investing
— Financing

It would be advisable if the contents of the cash budget are also grouped into these classes so as to enable the business to critically examine the impact of individual activity on the financial position of the company. It would also help to evaluate the relationship *inter se* these activities. Justifying the presentation in a classified manner, the proposed standard comments: "Classification by activity provides information that allows users to assess the impact of those activities on the financial position of the enterprise and the amount of its cash and cash equivalent. This information may also be used to evaluate the relationships among those activities."

(a) *Operating Activities:* Proposed standard has defined these as, "Operating activities are the principal revenue- producing activities of an enterprise; and other activities that are not investing or financing activities."

Operating activities are the key activities of a business. Every business 'operates', be it a manufacturing, trading, contracting, or mining unit. While determining classification of operating activities both the nature of transactions and nature of business of the enterprise should be taken into consideration. Sale and purchase of securities may be investing activities for a manufacturing concern but is operating activity for a financial institution dealing in such securities. Quoting from the proposed standard, "Cash flows from operating activities are primarily derived from the principal revenue-producing activities of the enterprise, therefore, they generally result from the transactions and other events that enter into the determination of net profit or loss. Examples of cash flows operating activities are:

(a) cash receipts from the sale of goods and the rendering of services;
(b) cash receipts from royalties, fees, commissions and other revenue;
(c) cash payments to suppliers for goods and services;
(d) cash payments to and on behalf of employees;
(e) cash receipts and cash payments of an insurance enterprise for premiums and claims, annuities and other policy benefits.
(f) cash payments or refunds of income taxes unless they can be specifically identified with financing and investing activities; and
(g) cash receipts and payments from contracts held for dealing or trading purposes."

(b) *Investing Activities:* Proposed standard has defined these as: "Investing activities are the acquisition and disposal of long-term assets and other investments not included in cash equivalents". (Cash equivalents are short term highly liquid investments that are readily convertible to known amounts of cash and which are subject to an insignificant risk of changes in values.) Primarily, these relate to deployment of funds for the acquisition of assets required to facilitate operational activities. Investing activities reflect the extent to which expenditures have been made for resources intended to generate future income and cash flows. The exact magnitude of funds required for this purpose and its comparability *inter se* operating activities shall depend upon industry to industry. Some industries like large scale steel plants, road building, are capital intensive and may require investment of huge cash in long-term assets as compared to some other businesses like retail trade where operational activities may warrant deployment of more funds. Examples of investing activities as mentioned in the proposed standard are:

"(a) cash payments to acquire fixed assets (including intangibles). These payments include those relating to capitalised research and development costs and self constructed fixed assets;

(b) cash receipts from disposal of fixed assets (including intangibles);

(c) cash payments to acquire shares, warrants or debt instruments of other enterprises and interests in joint ventures (other than payments for those instruments considered to be cash equivalents or those held for dealing or trading purposes);

(d) cash receipts from disposal of shares, warrants or debt instruments of other enterprises and interests in joint ventures (other than receipts for those instruments considered to be cash equivalents and those held for dealing or trading purposes);

(e) cash advances and loans made to other parties (other than advances and loans made by a financial enterprise);

(f) cash receipts from the repayment of advances and loans made to other parties (other than advances and loans of a financial enterprise);

(g) cash payments for future contracts, forward contracts, option contracts and swap contracts except when the contracts are held for dealing or trading purposes, or the payments are classified as financing activities; and

(h) cash receipts from future contracts, forward contracts, option contracts and swap contracts, except when the contracts are held for dealing or trading purposes, or the receipts are classified as financing activities."

(c) *Financing Activity:* Proposed standard has defined these as: "Financing activities are activities that result in changes in the size and composition of the owners' capital (including preference share capital in the case of a company) and borrowings of the enterprise." As the name suggests, financing activities include the activities concerning raising of funds and repayment of loans. Such activities have got a direct bearing on the total capital employed in an enterprise. The separate projection of financing activities is useful in predicting claims on future cash flows by the providers of equity and loan capital to the enterprise. Examples as mentioned in the proposed standard are:

"(a) cash proceeds from issuing shares or other similar instruments;
(b) cash payments to owners to acquire or redeem the enterprise's shares;
(c) cash proceeds from issuing debentures, loans, notes, bonds, and other short or long term borrowings; and
(d) cash repayments of amounts borrowed."

4.5 WORK SHEETS

Forecasting of figures and documenting them into cash budget may involve detailed exercises, records of which are maintained in Work Sheets. Items which appear in cash budget normally do not have readymade values for filling therein. These require some calculations and estimation both in terms of quantum of amount of cash involved as well as timing of cash movement. Work sheets contain all such calculations and arithmetical derivations necessary for arriving at the figures to be put in the cash budget. There is no standard format for such work sheets. Every business is to tailor them as per their own requirements. However, it should be ensured that the work sheets provide enough root material for getting an insight of the budgeted figures, whenever unearthed. The work sheets need contain the information with regard to the following:

4.5.1 List of Items

List of items having significant values and generating cash movements. These include both routine items, *e.g.,* receipt from debtors and non-routine items, *e.g.,* receipt from disposal of fixed assets. Whenever some items have been grouped, break-up of the group should be detailed in work sheets.

4.5.2 Arithmetical Calculations

All arithmetical calculations necessary to arrive at budgeted figures concerning both revenue and expenditure should find place in the work sheets. If it is estimated that 20% will be cash sales and 80% on credit, the calculations of both the sales figures as derived from the total sales projected in sales budget should be detailed in the work sheets.

4.5.3 Timing of Cash Movement

Time being one of the most important factors in the preparation of cash budget, work sheets should contain sufficient information as to on what basis a particular figure of cash movement has been projected at a particular point of time. In the case of above instance of credit sales of 80% it is possible that receipts from debtors may mature in the following fashion:

— 50% after one month
— 20% after two months
— 10% after three months.

The working of cash receipts in different months should be detailed in work sheets.

4.5.4 Assumptions

Preparation of cash budget rests upon certain assumptions like growth rate, inflation rate, *etc.* All the calculations concerning these assumptions are mentioned in the work sheets for future reference. Well maintained work sheets, surprisingly prove extremely beneficial whenever these are referred to. Following are some of the benefits of keeping work sheets in a proper way.

— It helps in the preparation of cash budget by assimilation of information of all cash generating items, in an orderly manner. This way it is ensured that all items involved in the preparation of cash budget have been taken care of, attended to and projected accurately.

— These assist in variance analysis of budgeted versus actual figures, whenever referred to, during the currency of budget period. Whether the receipts from the sundry debtors are maturing as per the phased-out period considered in the cash budget and if not its impact on the cash receipts and cash in hand. Issues like these can be conveniently examined by referring to the work sheets.

— Assumptions for framing the cash budget are spelt out in the work sheets. Reference of these assumptions provide useful guidance, while doing sensitivity analysis of the cash budget for different levels of operations.

QUESTIONS

1. Explain the difference between cash forecast and cash budget.
2. What are the advantages of following a standard format for the preparation of a cash budget?
3. Describe the layout of a cash budget. Design a sample format of a cash budget.
4. What are operating activities? Give three examples.
5. Describe investing activities. Give three examples.
6. Describe financing activities. Give three examples.
7. Explain the role of worksheets in the exercise of budget preparation. What are the benefits of preserving these worksheets?

5

CASH BUDGET — SHORT-TERM

5.1 INTRODUCTION

Short-term cash budget limits its vision to a shorter time horizon, not beyond a period of 12 months. The thrust of short-term budget is to pinpoint periods and magnitudes of the cash deficits and surpluses during a budget period. Equipped with this information,the business gears itself to take advance action for borrowing the funds or investing them in short-term deposits as the case may be. It is easier to forecast for a short period. Short-term cash budget, therefore, projects fairly accurate and reliable figures. Receipts and disbursements method is most suited for making short-term forecasting. Under this method cash inflows and cash outflows concerning major items of receipts and payments for a future period are forecasted; and a summary statement is prepared. Such statement is in standard format known as short-term cash budget. However, there are certain factors which merit consideration before initiating the exercise of short-term forecast. These are explained below.

5.1.1 Annual Growth Rate

For its survival and future expansion, a business formulates its corporate plan and fixes its goals for the achievement of which annual growth rate is targeted. The management may decide that the business should have 25 per cent increase in its turnover and/or profit during a budget period. Once such a goal is established, estimation of individual items of revenue and expenses are tuned to the growth rate.

5.1.2 Inflation

Inflation is order of the day. In addition to general inflation witnessed in the economy, there may be some items of expense being dealt by a business, which bear a different rate of inflation. Projection of such expenses shall involve due consideration of both the inflation rates.

For calculating the combined impact of growth rate and inflation rate, it is imperative that at the first instance effect of growth rate should be applied, which then should be jacked up by inflation rate, otherwise the figures calculated may yield inaccurate results.

5.1.3 Timing

Most of the items of cost or expense have two dimensions — quantity multiplied by rate. But when such an expense involves movement of cash, then a third dimension of 'time' is also added. This dimension is of immense importance in the mechanics of cash forecasting. Even if, the expenses have been forecasted accurately, the timing is incorrect; the enterprise will land into financial problems. For instance, the expenses on account of cash purchases of a business were estimated correctly but it transpired that the business had to part with the requisite cash in the month of October instead of December as projected in the budget. The result was sudden deficiency of cash necessitating raising of short-term loan for two months.

We shall now study the mechanics of forecasting for all the three classes of activities—operating, investing and financing.

5.2 FORECASTING OF OPERATING ACTIVITIES

Operating activities are activities concerning main operation of the business. Among the three activities of the business, operating activities are most important. And in the whole gamut of operating activities, sales and purchases play decisive roles. Cash flow on account of these shall include cash generated by cash sales, payments to be received from the customers, cash purchases and payments to be released to suppliers. For the purpose of cash budget, sales and purchases are two sides of a coin.

5.2.1 Sales

"Nothing moves unless you sell something" goes an old saying. Also, sales provide an index to the magnitude of company's operations. Higher the sales, bigger the company. Understandably, some conglomerates in the business world continue some not very remunerative operations to retain their berths in the list of 'Big Companies', normally arrayed on the basis of sales. Sales to be achieved during a particular period is forecasted in the sales budget. However, from the point of view of cash budget, the following facets of sales deserve examination.

(a) *Cash Sales and Credit Sales:* Broadly, the sales fall into two categories—Cash and Credit. Cash sales generate instantaneous inflow of cash and are accordingly reflected in the cash budget. However, in almost all the disciplines of trade and industry, credit is allowed to attract more customers and increase turnover. Cash receipts on account of credit sales are phased out for a period based on terms of credit. Quite obviously, projection of cash receipts from cash sales is comparatively easier whereas that of cash receipts from credit sales is dependent on a number of factors like terms of credit, trade conventions, creditworthiness of the debtors, *etc.* Another important factor from the point of view of cash budget is proper determination of *inter se* proportion of cash sales and credit sales so that correct timings of cash inflows in a business are determined. To illustrate this we consider the following example.

Example: ABC Ltd. started a new business and for the next six months period the sales forecast are as follows:

(Rupees in lakhs)

	Months					
	April	May	June	July	August	September
Total Sales:	50	60	70	70	80	90

It is expected that 20% of the sales will be cash sales and the balance 80% shall be on credit. The receipts from debtors on account of credit sales shall be in the following manner.

50%	during the month of sale
20%	during next month after sale
10%	during second month after sale

Based on the above, determine the cash inflow of ABC Ltd. for the next six months.

Solution of example is shown in Exhibit 5.1

(b) *Payment Terms:* Payment terms play a significant role in projecting receipts from the debtors. In some industries, manufacturing tailor made equipment, it is customary that substantial amounts, some times even upto 100%, are received as advance. In some other industries, like construction industry, payment terms consist of mobilisation advance and on account progress payments subject to deduction of retention money. It is imperative that in such cases projection of cash receipts is made after taking into consideration such payment terms.

(c) *Discount:* Quantification of potential discount is an important factor since cash budget warrants display of realistic cash flow figures. Discount has two-fold impact.

Exhibit 5.1

EXPECTED CASH RECEIPTS FROM SALES

Rs. in lakh

Cash Receipts		Amount	April	May	June	July	August	Sept.	Oct.	Nov
(A)	Cash Sales		10	12	14	14	16	18		
(B)	Receipts from Debtors for credit sales:									
	Months	Amount								
	April	40	25	10	5					
	May	48		30	12	6				
	June	56			35	14	7			
	July	56				35	14	7		
	August	64					40	16	8	
	Sept.	72						45	18	9
			25	40	52	55	61	68		
	Total Cash Receipts A+B		35	52	66	69	77	86		

— The inflow from debtors is reduced by the discount amount. Quantum effected.

— The receipt of inflow is accelerated by the period for which discount is offered by the seller. Timing effected.

Both these factors influence the cash flow projections. Discount is of two types:

(i) *Trade Discount:* Trade discount may take the form of a rebate on the prices displayed in a price list. The business engaged in selling various items may not offer identical discount on all the items. Discount may be offered more in the case of slow moving items and less where the items have ready acceptability in the market. In such cases anticipated receipts from the debtors may require detailed calculations. First by identifying sales forecast of each item and then calculating the discounted price for it. The exercise involved may require minute and cumbersome processes. For the sake of simplicity, average discount price may be considered for the total number of product items expected to be sold during budget period. This would obviate the necessity of multiplying each quantity with its dedicated rate, thereby reducing arithmetic calculations to the minimum. For the purpose of projection in cash budget, receipt from debtors is shown at net price; *i.e.,* after reducing discount amount from the forecasted sales figures.

(ii) *Cash Discount:* Cash discount is a deduction from a price if payment is made before a certain date — an incentive to pay quickly. Unlike trade discount, cash discount is offered after trade debt has been registered so as to attract early settlement of dues. Normally, it is quoted as 2/10, net/60 terms. This means that the buyer is entitled to a discount of 2% if he settles his dues within 10 days as against the permitted credit period of 60 days.

The economics of cash discount can be studied in comparison with cost of capital in the market at a given point of time. When a business offers the terms of 2/10, net/60, it implies that sale price consists of two elements — 98% cash sale price and 2% as financing cost. The business would like to compare the 2% financing cost with the interest rate for borrowing funds in the market to know whether it will be economical to offer the incentive of discount or not. A discount of 2% will work out to be 0.04% rate per day, *i.e.*, 2 ÷ 50 days (60 – 10 days) and an annualised rate of 14.4%, *i.e.,* 0.04% × 360. If the market rate of interest is more than 14.4%; the business will do well to offer discount to the customer.

(d) *Sales Returns and bad debts:* Sales returns which influence cash budget are those which are returned by the customer after the sale has been effected. Sales returns has become a normal activity due to severity of competition among the sellers making the customer a privileged mortal. The returns of sales can affect both cash sales and credit sales. Past trend can provide a suitable guide for making a provision on this account.

Bad debts are those debts which are impossible to be retrieved from the customers. Despite all efforts made by the company with regard to ensuring creditworthiness of the buyers and also closely monitoring the receipts of the sundry debtors, some debts are bound to become bad. In the case of bad debts also, one gets influenced by the past experience for the creation of provision. Normally in the case of both sales returns and bad debts, a fixed percentage is reduced from forecasted sales figures lowering the cash inflow to that extent. This is explained in the Exhibit 5.2 which projects the figures of cash inflow from sales after discounting 1% each for credit sales returns and bad debts. The sales data is as per Exhibit 5.1.

5.3 FORECASTING OF EXPENSES

Business expenses are heterogenous elements of cost required to be incurred to earn revenue. There cannot be a single method which can be blanketly applied for estimation of all the expenses of a business. Each expense item is required to be assessed independently taking into consideration its past quantum and future requirements. However, there are certain general factors which need to be taken into consideration before starting the exercise of estimation of expenses.

5.3.1 Nature of Expenses

Expenses are of three kinds—fixed, variable and semi-variable. Such a categorisation necessitates proper appreciation of the nature of expenditure which in turn enhances accuracy of the estimates.

(a) *Fixed Expenses:* Fixed expenses are those expenses which remain same irrespective of the level of business activity. If fixed expenses are Rs 20,000 and volume of production 4000 units, they would remain at Rs 20,000 even if volume of production is increased to 6000 units. These are the obligations which a business has to honour whether the business is making profit or incurring loss. Whenever increased, they register a quantum jump, *e.g.,* rent of the office shall continue to be same irrespective of the turnover or profit/loss of the business. However, in case the business decides to hire another accommodation the expense under this head will shoot up. A successful enterprise always tries to get maximum out of the fixed expenses by stretching their benefits to the larger operational base. A few instances of fixed expenses are rents, rates, property taxes, supervisors' costs .

(b) *Variable Expenses:* Variable expenses move in total sympathy with the business activity. They register change in identical proportion to the change in the level of business activity. If the variable ex-

Exhibit 5.2

EXPECTED CASH RECEIPTS FROM SALES

(Rs. in lakhs)

Cash Receipts			Months							
			April	May	June	July	August	Sept.	Oct.	Nov
(A) Cash Sales			10	12	14	14	16	18		
(B) Receipts from Debtors for credit sales:	Months	Amount								
	April	39.20	24.50	9.80	4.90					
	May	47.04		29.40	11.76	5.88				
	June	54.88			34.30	13.72	6.86			
	July	54.88				34.30	13.72	6.86		
	August	62.72					39.20	15.68	7.84	
	Sept	70.56						44.10	17.64	8.82
			24.50	39.20	50.96	53.90	59.78	66.64		
Total Cash Receipts A+B			34.50	51.20	64.96	67.90	75.78	84.64		

penses are Rs 20,000 and volume of production is 4000 units, they would change to Rs 30,000 if volume of production is increased to 6000 units. The variable expenses per unit is fixed at Rs.5 whereas in the case of fixed expenses, total expenses are fixed and the cost per unit varies. Changes in variable expenses do not take place over time nor due to seasons of the year. The singular reason responsible in the changes of variable expenses are changes in the volume of business activity. A few examples are direct material, direct labour, electricity and power used in production.

(c) *Semi Variable Expenses:* According to Batty, "Semi-variable costs are hybrid costs; each is made up of a fixed element and a fully variable element". These expenses move in the same direction in which the business activity moves but not in the same proportion. The variation in their case is irregular. If semi-variable expenses are Rs 20,000 and volume of production 4000 units, they would be higher than Rs 20,000 if volume of production is increased by say 50 per cent to 6000 units. But increase in semi-variable expenses shall be less than 50 per cent because fixed element of semi-variable cost may not increase. A few examples are telephone, stationery, advertising *etc*.

5.3.2 List of Expenses

A business has a wide variety of expenses. For the preparation of a meaningful cash budget, it is necessary that no expenditure having significant value remains unbudgeted. This can be done if itemised list of expenses is prepared before embarking upon the activity of expense forecasting. A few sources from where such type of list can be modelled are as follows:

(a) *Independent List:* Attempt can be made for preparing an independent list of all the expenses of a business. In the case of small organisation, it may be possible first to divide the activities in each division and then jot down division-wise expenses. The finance manager responsible for cash budget can himself do this exercise. In a big business house all the concerned divisions, *e.g.*, production, marketing, administration, finance, *etc.* can be advised to prepare a list of expenses of their divisions independently. All such lists of expenses are then scrutinised and a final list for the business is compiled by the finance manager. While doing so, care should be taken that common expenses, *e.g.*, salary appearing in various divisional lists, are not duplicated. Also, expenses of smaller magnitude are clubbed with the similar items having major values.

(b) *Financial Statements:* The annual accounts, *i.e.*, profit & loss account, balance sheet alongwith schedules offer a very good source for preparation of such a list. One added advantage of borrowing items from such statements is the presentation of items in key heads of accounts obviating the possibility of being bogged down in the avoidable jumble of expense heads.

(c) *Accounting Code:* Accounting code can also offer inventory for preparation of such a list but problem in the case of following accounting code is that there can be so many items of expense which are not backed by cash movement, *e.g.,* depreciation. Further, normal long detailed accounting code list requires pruning to make it acceptable for cash budget.

(d) *Uniform Costing:* In some industries, uniform costing system is in vogue which adopts standard list of expenses unique to the industry. It provides a good source for preparation of list of expenses required to be forecasted.

(e) *Government controlled items:* In some other industries cost fixation of the proudct is done at the intervention of government agencies. This is more prevalent in developing countries where prices of necessities are controlled by the governments. The list acceptable to the government can also give an indication of expenses which need to be budgeted.

5.4 TYPICAL EXPENSES

Fleet of expenses arrayed in a business shall differ from enterprise to enterprise. A few instances which shall be relevant in almost all the cases are explained below:

5.4.1 Salary and Wages

Normally, salary is a combination of fixed and variable elements. Fixed element is popularly known as 'basic' and the variable element as 'allowance'. Further, every year salary cost may register some increase. The increase can be because of the following factors:

(a) *Basic Increase:* The employee's appointment agreement provides for annual increment. Even otherwise too, the employee is justified in expecting some additional pay to compensate for the continuation of his dedicated service to the organisation and enhancement in his service experience.

(b) *Inflationery Increase:* One of the variable elements of pay packet, 'dearness allowance' is normally linked with cost of living index prevalent in the economy. In the event of increase in latter, former is enhanced based on a predetermined formula.

(c) *Growth Rate Increase:* The increase in salary may have to be affected to meet the expansion envisaged as per the growth rate of the enterprise.

Similarly, in the case of wages there may be increase due to above referred factors. In some companies there exists an agreement between management and labour under which a review of wage structure is made periodically and necessary enhancement is made in the wages. In case a cash budget is prepared for that particular period under which such wage increase is due, provision for enhancement should be made while estimating the expenditure on wages.

In additon to remuneration, there are certain 'employee-related expenses' estimation of which is clubbed with forecasts of amounts for salaries and wages. These consist of perquisites like house rent allowance (HRA), leave travel concession (LTC), medical expenses, leave encashment, provident fund, gratuity, *etc.* Perquisites which are covered under statute are to be estimated in accordance with provisions of respective Acts. For others like HRA, LTC, medical expenses and the likes, employees' entitlements provide requisite guidance. Another approach followed in this regard is not to indulge in so minute details but to estimate these perquisites as a fixed percentage of salary and wages.

An important factor influencing the estimation of salary and wages is requirement of statutory deductions before the release of amounts to employees. A few instances are deduction on account of employee's contribution to provident fund, income tax and professional tax. Deduction on these accounts are effected from the salaries of individuals and deposited with the government agencies or trusts within the time period codified in the respective Acts. Cash budget, however, considers gross salary without giving effect to such deductions and their deposits with the statutory bodies. This is because there is very little time gap between the deduction and deposit of the money as a result of which timings of both the cash flows — entry and exit is not materially affected. One caution is to be exercised at this stage. The deduction on account of employee's own contribution to provident fund should not be mixed up with the employer's contribution to provident fund which is an additional liability of the business.

Timing: From the point of view of timing salaries are normally paid on monthly basis.

5.4.2 Freight and Cartage

Freight and cartage is incurred on account of purchase of materials and selling of finished goods. In addition to general factors like growth rate and inflation, the future expenses on this account are estimated taking into consideration load of raw materials and finished goods expected to be handled during the budget period. In case a new area is to be tapped for sale or raw materials are to be procured from far away places, additional provision of funds may be required and projections made accordingly.

Timing: If transport of goods is effected through one or more dedicated transporters, payments may be made on fortnightly/monthly basis. On the other hand, if despatch is affected through non-accredited transporters, payments shall have to be made in advance or at the time of delivery of goods at destination.

5.4.3 Rent

Rent falls under the category of fixed expenses, payment of which is determined as per the contract with the landlord. Whenever new accommodation is hired, some advance may be paid which is required to be provided for in estimation of this item in the cash budget.

Timing: Payment of rent is normally made in advance at the beginning of each month.

5.4.4 Travel

Travel may occasion on account of operational activities; *e.g.*, meeting buyers or suppliers, finance and accounts activities, *e.g.*, contacting financial institutions, banks, auditors *etc.*, selling and distributing activities, *e.g.*, dealing with advertising and distribution agencies, liaison with government or other influential agencies. In fact with the improvement in the means of transport this item has acquired great significance in domestic and international trade. Past amount incurred and future expansion programmes can provide guide for the estimation of this expenditure. Sufficient additional amount should be provided if the business intends to enter new territories.

Timing: Regarding timing of expense, if the travel arrangement are made through established travel agent, credit may be available for a fortnight or a month. However, if tickets are purchased directly from railway and airlines, payments shall have to be made in advance.

5.4.5 Advertising and Selling

In the present day of competitive environment and in view of cascading role of publicity, estimation of this expense has gathered immense importance. The forecasted amount under this head shall depend on the competitive strength of the business in the market and the strategies followed by competitors. If a new product is to be launched, business may have to provide for substantial amount under this head.

Timing: Advertising agencies extend credit in certain cases whereas some sources like television insist on advance payment.

5.4.6 Running and Maintenance

The estimate of cash expenditure shall depend upon the total strength of plant and machinery at the shop floor, construction equipment at the projects and the fleet of vehicles with the business. Normally, the past trend gives sufficient guidance to anticipate future expenditure. However, in case present machinery is becoming obsolete, more funds shall be required to cater for its increased wear and tear. Running and maintenance of vehicles normally has a set range which can be extracted from the past data. The office and township maintenance too, has a normal range of cash expenditure unless some exceptionally heavy repair is on the anvil.

Timing: The expenditure has to be incurred throughout the year as and when the need arises.

5.4.7 Electricity and Water

Electricity and water expenses have direct linkage with level of production activity in the case of manufacturing units. Obviously, the past trend is very important. However, any likely statutory hike by the government authorities should also be provided for. The licensed capacity, the installed capacity, utilised capacity and expected capacity must be taken into account while estimating the expenditure on electricity and water.

Timing: Normally, the expenditure in such cases is on monthly basis.

5.4.8 Insurance

Estimation of insurance expenditure is comparatively easier because of predetermined value of insurable assets and also the applicable rates of premium. The business must ensure that whatever is required to be insured has been taken care of. The insurance can be of the assets like buildings, machinery, vehicles, *etc.* New additions should also be covered. Forecasting of transit insurance can be made based on the average value of goods expected to be in transit during the year. If the business is engaged in international trade, marine insurance premium should be provided for on the basis of expected value of goods to be on high sea. Provision should also be made for cash insurance based on the average quantum of cash handled in the business at a particular point of time. In the specialised field of project exports institutions like Export Guarantee and Credit Corporation (ECGC) provides insurance covering political and commercial risks. Estimation of expenditure on this account can be conveniently made on the basis of insured value and the pre notified premium by the ECGC.

Timing: The dates for the due payment of premiums are mentioned in the insurance policies. For ECGC premium generally, the amount can be paid in instalment prefixed for particular dates.

5.4.9 Interest

Quite often, interest constitutes an important item in the total expense list of a business. Interest can be payable on account of bank overdrafts, loans taken from financial institutions, bonds issued by the business, fixed deposits accepted from the public and other such borrowings. Provisions for these can be made based on the terms of agreements with the respective agencies. The future cash deficits as revealed by the cash budget can also guide the business in this matter.

Timing: Terms of agreements with the agencies shall indicate exact dates on which the interest amounts become payable. Also the period of deficits can indicate the cash outflows for interest payments.

5.4.10 Bank Charges

Bank charges warrant a proper analysis. The general bank charges accruing in the normal course of business can be estimated based on the past actuals. However, if new letters of credits are to be opened or some additional bank guarantees are to be obtained sufficient provision should be created for all these in the estimation.

Timing: General bank charges like bank draft charges, cheque clearance charges are payable throughout the year. Timing of bulky bank expenses, *e.g.*, charges of letter of credit opening, bank guarantee charges can be judged based on the dates when these facilities are required to be availed of.

5.4.11 Auditors Remuneration

The remuneration to be paid to the auditors is dependent upon volume of work and time to be spent by auditors. Past can provide guidance. However, scope of the auditors assignment may increase if they are required to provide professional consultancy including advice on tax matters. Provision should be suitably increased.

Timing: Statutory audit fee is paid annually. For the professional services, payments can be released as mutually agreed.

5.5 FORECASTING OF INVESTING ACTIVITIES

Cash deployed in the investing activities reflect the extent to which expenditure has been made for resources intended to generate future income and cash flows. Obviously, amount spent on investing activities like operating activities is aimed at maximising profit and increasing cash inflow of the busines. The purpose of materials procured or other operating cost incurred is identical to procurement of assets; to increase cash flow generated by profit. However, in operating activities orbital time of incurring of expenditure (cash outflow) and receipts of revenue (cash inflow) is much shorter. But in the case of investing activities, funds are committed for a longer time frame and cash inflow stretches for a longer period upto the life span of the asset. Another unique feature of investing activity is that normally it involves locking of huge funds as compared to funds used for operating activities. Such revenue-producing assets warrant big capital outlay. This leads us to study reasons as to why long term assets are procured in a business. A few reasons for the acquisition of assets in a business are as follows:

5.5.1 Manual vs Automation

A job which is done by manual labour is more time-consuming and may not bring the desired quality. Automation can ensure both these qualities but requires consumption of huge funds at one stroke against receipts of cash profit in instalments in future. The business need to evaluate the value of investment at this stage with the additional cash inflows generated from the use of equipment before locking the funds in procurement of machinery.

5.5.2 Technological Developments

Rapid development in technology forces a business to acquire latest models of the equipment so as to keep the pace with the competitors. The cash flow generated with the use of new machinery can either be in the form of saving in cost (reduction in cash outflow) or incremental cash profit (increase in cash inflow).

5.5.3 Expansion

In the modern era no expansion worth mentioning can take place without the back up of machinery. Out of three M's—Man, Machinery and Material,—only man is living being and as such is constrained so far as stretchable limit is concerned to meet the requirements of expansion.

5.5.4 Replacements

Even in the ordinary course of business, replacement of assets is necessary due to these being worn out after certain years. A worn out machinery increases the cost of the product on the one hand and decreases its quality on the other. Hence, the need to acquire new assets.

5.5.5 Diversification

A business tries to diversify and develop itself into a conglomerate. By dealing in different products it reduces its risks and by becoming a conglomerate, it enhances its inherent strength. Diversification warrants acquisition of new assets.

5.6 ECONOMICS OF INVESTMENT

The decision to acquire or not to acquire the revenue-earning assets is very important for a business. The mechanics involved for taking such decisions may not be within the scope of this book but a broad outline of such mechanics can be mentioned here so as to appreciate the forecasting of investing activities in proper perspective. Such decisions lock in huge funds for long periods but the return is staggered to be received in distant future. In terms of cash flow there is cash outflow in one go but the inflow is spread for a number of years. Hence, the need to introduce a mechanism to evaluate both the cash flows.

The underlying idea of the whole mechanics is to compare the present value of future cash inflows with the value of investment. As is clear, rupee one today is more valuable than rupee one to be received after five years. Under the mechanics adopted, if the present value of the future cash flows equals or exceeds the value of present investment, the proposal of acquiring the asset is acceptable. The mechanism takes into consideration four factors:

5.6.1 Required Rate of Return

The required rate of return is the lowest rate which a business expects to earn on making investment. Basically, it is 'judgemental' rate. However, cost of capital can be one of the guiding factors for determining such a rate.

5.6.2 Cash Inflow

Cash inflow in such mechanics means additional earnings generated by the assets normally projected as increased cash inflow (annual basis). The streams of cash which flow into the business because of the asset put to use are discounted at the required rate of return, aggregate of which is compared with the total value of investment. The residual value of the asset is also discounted at the present rate.

5.6.3 True Commercial Life

True commercial life refers to the number of years an income-producing asset is reasonably expected to generate cash inflow. While determining the true commercial life, conservative approach is adopted, and in any case such life is shorter than the physical life of the asset. A few reasons for considering true commercial life less than a physical life are as follows:

— Techonological development may obsolete the machinery earlier than the expected life of the asset.

— Business may like to change its line of production or process to tailor its production to market requirements.

— Howsoever, one may apt for precision, there is always uncertainty inherent in the future streams of cash inflow. Shorter period will hedge these uncertainties to some extent.

— Present value of cash inflow of far off years is so low that it may not make any significant impact even if these are considered in the economics of investment proposals.

5.6.4 Investment

When a business procures a revenue-earning asset, it makes an investment. While calculating the value of investment total funds, including funds required to make it operative, are taken into account. A few elements are cost of machinery, transportation cost, installation and commissioning cost.

One interesting fact to be noticed in the case of investing activities is that from the point of view of cash budget outflows of cash are projected as investing activities but the cash inflows become part of operating cash receipts and are displayed under the operating activities. These receipts flow in to the business in the form of increased sales revenue. However, if the equipment is disposed of before or after expiry of its commercial life, cash so received is projected as inflow of investing activities.

The forecasting of investing activities depends on factors like level of present operating activity, anticipated growth rate and expected expansion. If the business is embarking on an ambitious expansion programme, the funds requirement for investing activities shall increase many fold. In the ordinary course of business also, there is a constant obsolescence of the fixed assets demanding substitutes. The funds for the investing activities shall, therefore, be required even if there is no expansion programme on the anvil. The cash budget takes care of the timings of release of funds which are dependent on terms of procurement. Ordinarily, some initial advance is paid at the time of initiation of procurement activities. Further payments are released on delivery of equipment and the balance payment after erection and commissioning of the equipment. Accordingly, the projection of cash expenditure should be displayed in the respective months. If the existing asset is to be disposed off, the expected cash realisation from its sales is to be shown as the receipts.

Some times a business constructs a property of its own. It can be an office building, factory or plant for its shop floor. The projection of cash expenditure for this should be calculated based on the CPM/

PERT charts. The project manager and the concerned finance personnel can provide the necessary details.

If the business is expected to acquire listed shares of a company, necessary provision for the funds requirement is made based on the quoted price in stock exchange or the negotiated price.

5.7 FORECASTING OF FINANCING ACTIVITIES

Profile of forecasted financing activities largely depend on the forecasted operating and investing activities. Providing faithful service, the financing activities are required to pump in and pump out cash as per the needs of operating and investing activities. In the accounting parlance these needs are reflected in the form of working capital and fixed capital. For the working capital, cash flow cycle reveals the time and magnitude of cash required for operating activities; and similarly cash required for fixed capital is indicated by investing activities. In addition to the requirements projected by operating and investing activities, forecasts for financing activities are also made to meet certain financial obligations related to financing activities. These include redemption of preference shares, debentures, bonds, repayment of fixed deposits and other borrowings. By and large estimation of these do not pose much problem because the organisation is well aware of the timings and amounts involved in these repayments much in advance. A few instances of financing activities are as follows:

5.7.1 Issue of New Shares

Issue of new shares bring influx of cash to the business. It is basically a management decision which is influenced by market conditions at macro level and business's own economics at the micro level. The important element to be observed from the point of view of cash budget is proper projection of the receipt of cash. Normally, only part amount is called for alongwith the application followed by additional amounts on the allotment of shares and call notices. In the cash budget these are required to be shown in the months in which the money is anticipated to be received.

5.7.2 Borrowings

A company may have to borrow funds to meet its fixed and fluctuating capital requirements. These borrowings can be anticipated based on the deficit periods projected by the cash flow cycle and also the fund requirements of the investing activities. Well laid out proposals based on the forecasted figures, to financial institutions submitted in advance, are likely to attract more favourable terms and conditions as against the ones which are put forward hurriedly for their vetting.

5.7.3 Dividend

Dividend is also an important item of financing activities. The declaration of dividend is a management decision which takes into consideration profitability, liquidity, solvency of the company and market environment at a particular point of time. In the cash flow projections, it should be ensured that outflow of cash is projected in the appropriate month of despatch of dividend warrants with due consideration to the statutory time period for the payment of dividend.

While on the issue of forecasting of financing activities, it is interesting to note that a prudent finance manager is capable of making the cash management an item of additional revenue to the organisation. This can be achieved by correctly estimating time and amount of funds to be borrowed well in advance which in turn help the organisation to obtain credit on the lower rates of interest and on the other hand, by investing the surplus funds judiciously and earning higher rates of interest.

5.8 MODEL OF CASH BUDGET — SHORT-TERM

Exhibit 5.3 displays a model of cash budget, The cash budget has been partitioned into four sections — receipt, payment, deficit/surplus and adjustment sections. In each section presentation of data has been classified on the basis of nature of activity, *i.e.,* operating, investing and financing. The format also provides for sub-totals activity-wise and period-wise. The sub-totals aggregate to totals both vertically and horizontally. Vertical totals indicate monthly cash inflows and outflows from all the three types of activities. Horizontal totals, on the other hand, display activity-wise cash inflows and cash outflows on annual basis.

The budget provides an overall view of cash receipts and cash payments for the budget period. The total cash receipts from operating activities are likely to be Rs. 2,17,50,000 (Sl No.1.1.0). As against this, the cash payments for operating activities are expected to be Rs. 1,85,50,000 (Sl No. 2.1.0). The business is likely to raise a total cash of Rs 1,80,00,000 on account of new shares and long term borrowings during the year (Sl No.1.3.0). The outflow of cash on account of financing activities is Rs. 1,15,00,000 only for re-payment of long term borrowings and payment of dividend (Sl No. 2.3.0). The business shall spend Rs. 84,00,000(Sl No. 2.2.0) in cash for purchase of fixed assets and its anticipated cash inflow from investing activities is Rs 7,00,000 only (Sl. No. 1.2.0).

Further analysis of individual section reveals the following:

Receipt Section

The major sources of cash receipts from operating activities are cash sales and collections from customers. During the month of

December, investing activities too , are likely to make small contribution of Rs 5,00,000 in the cash inflow on account of selling the plant owned by the business. It may be noted that the sale of plant may be on profit or loss. It has no bearing so far as preparation of cash budget is concerned. In the month of June the business proposes to raise capital amounting to Rs. 1,00,00,000 for liquidating its borrowings by issuing new shares. It is likely to receive Rs. 2,00,000 in the month of July on account of interest on the investments made in the securities. Subsequently in the month of January, a long-term loan amounting to Rs. 80,00,000 is raised to procure a plant.

Payment Section

It can be observed from the cash budget that monthly payments to suppliers are less than the monthly collections from customers except in the months of August, September and October resulting in the cash deficits during these months. Salary, wages and other cash expenses being mixture of fixed, variable and semi variable expenses change in sympathy with the increase and decrease in the sales, according to their nature. Payments involved in the investing activities are reflected in the procurement of a plant valuing Rs. 84,00,000 during January out of long-term loans amounting to Rs. 80,00,000. The balance Rs 4,00,000 is to be met from own generated resources. Similarly, repayments of long-term borrowings amounting to Rs. 1,03,00,000 are scheduled to be made out of the proceeds of new issues of shares amounting to Rs. 1,00,00,000, and the balance Rs. 3,00,000 from the available cash. The second item of payment from financing activities is dividend amounting to Rs 12,00,000. Receipt of interest and the profit generated by the business provides the source for the payment of dividend.

Deficit / Surplus Section

This section makes categorical display of deficits and surpluses for all the individual months of the budget period. The monthly balances are arrived at by taking into account the opening balances in the beginning of the month, the monthly cash receipts and cash payments. From the cash balances so forecasted, the amount of the desired monthly cash balance which in the present case is Rs 4,00,000 is deducted. The resultant figure is cash deficit or cash surplus for the month.

Adjustment section

This section equips the business to take advance actions for investment of short term surpluses and raising of money to meet the deficits. From April to July every month there is surplus which can be invested in short-term investments. During August to October the

Exhibit 5.3
CASH BUDGET

Period : April '95 to March '96
Basis : Monthly

Date : 15th March, 1995

(Rs. in thousands)

		April	May	June	July	August	Sept.	Oct.	Nov.	Dec.	Jan.	Feb.	March	Total
1.	CASH RECEIPTS													
	1.1 OPERATING ACTIVITIES													
	1.1.1 Cash Sales	300	400	500	600	300	200	150	300	600	650	650	700	5350
	1.1.2 Collection of Receivables	1000	1400	1800	2000	1100	800	700	1000	1200	1600	1800	2000	16400
	1.1.0 Sub Total	1300	1800	2300	2600	1400	1000	850	1300	1800	2250	2450	2700	21750
	1.2 INVESTING ACTIVITIES													
	1.2.1 Sale of Plant									500				500
	1.2.2 Receipt of Interest				200									200
	1.2.0 Sub Total				200					500				700
	1.3 FINANCING ACTIVITIES													
	1.3.1 Issue of New Shares			10000										10000
	1.3.2 Long-Term Borrowings										8000			8000
	1.3.0 Sub Total			10000							8000			18000
	Total: (1.1.0 + 1.2.0 + 1.3.0)	1300	1800	12300	2800	1400	1000	850	1300	2300	10250	2450	2700	40450
2.	CASH PAYMENTS													
	2.1 OPERATING ACTIVITIES													
	2.1.1 Suppliers	600	850	1100	1200	1600	1700	1200	600	1100	1500	1700	1800	14950
	2,1.2 Wages & Salaries	150	175	175	200	200	150	150	150	175	200	200	200	2125
	2.1.3 Other cash expenses	100	125	125	150	100	100	100	100	125	150	150	150	1475
	2.1.0 Sub Total	850	1150	1400	1550	1900	1950	1450	850	1400	1850	2050	2150	18550

	2.2 INVESTING ACTIVITIES													
	2.2.1 Purchase of Plant										8400			8400
	2.2.0 Sub Total										8400			8400
	2.3 FINANCING ACTIVITIES													
	2.3.1 Payment of Dividend				1200									1200
	2.3.2 Repayment of Long-term Borrowings			10300										10300
	2.3.0 Sub Total			10300	1200									11500
	Total: (2.1.0 + 2.2.0 + 2.3.0)	850	1150	11700	2750	1900	1950	1450	850	1400	10250	2050	2150	38450
3.	DEFICITS/SURPLUSES													
	3.1 Balance in the beginning	600	400	400	400	400	400	400	400	400	400	400	400	600
	3.2 Cash Receipts	1300	1800	12300	2800	1400	1000	850	1300	2300	10250	2450	2700	40450
	3.3 Cash Payments	–850	–1150	–11700	–2750	–1900	–1950	–1450	–850	–1400	–10250	–2050	–2150	–38450
	3.4 Forecasted Cash Balance	1050	1050	1000	450	–100	–550	–200	850	1300	400	800	950	2600
	3.5 Desired Cash Balance	–400	– 400	–400	–400	–400	–400	–400	–400	–400	–400	– 400	—400	– 400
	3.6 Cash (Deficit) /Surplus	650	650	600	50	–500	–950	–600	450	900	—	400	550	2200
4.	ADJUSTMENT													
	4.1 Short-Term Investments	650	650	600	50				350	900		400	550	4150
	4.2 Sale of Short Term Investments					500	950	500						1950
	4.3 Short--Term Borrowings							100						100
	4.4 Repayment of Short-Term Borrowings								100					100

Prepared by:

budget projects monthly cash deficits. The deficits for these months totals to Rs 20,50,000 whereas amounts available in short-term investment is Rs 19,50,000 necessitating a short-term borrowing of Rs. 1,00,000 during October. November is likely to yield a surplus of Rs. 4,50,000 out of which Rs 1,00,000 can be utilised for settling short-term borrowings and balance Rs 3,50,000 can be invested in short-term securities.

We shall study in details the various avenues open for the short term investment of surplus cash in Chapter 11 and the numerous sources available for raising money for short term in Chapter 12.

QUESTIONS

1. Explain the general factors which are taken into account while making short-term cash forecasting.
2. What impact do cash and credit sales have on the forecasting of cash receipts for a period?
3. How are cash flow projections influenced by discounts offered to customers.
4. Describe the various sources of developing a comprehensive list of expenses.
5. How shall the cash flow projections in respect of following expenses be made?

   a) Salary
   b) Freight & cartage
   c) Advertising and selling
   d) Insurance and
   e) Interest.

6. What factors are taken into account before taking a decision in respect of investing activities.
7. Explain the cash forecasting of financing activities. How can borrowings be projected for a cash budget?
8. Write short notes on:

   a) Semi-variable expenses
   b) Forecasting for sales returns and bad debts
   c) Adjustment section of a cash budget.

9. XYZ & Co. makes 20% of its total sales as cash sales and the balance 80% is on credit. As per the past trends it is expected that 60% of the credit sales will be realised in the month following sales, 30% in the second following month and the balance 10% in third following month. It is also felt that the bad debts are likely to be 1% of the credit sales. The business gives the following figures of sales:

1995	Rs.
October	1,00,000
November	1,10,000
December	1,25,000
1996	
January	1,50,000
February	1,60,000
March	2,00,000

Calculate the cash receipts on account of sales for the months of January '96 to March '96.

10. ABC & Co. provides the following information for the preparation of a cash budget for the period of October '95 to March '96:

	Oct.	Nov.	Dec.	Jan.	Feb.	Mar.
Sales	80,000	85,000	90,000	75,000	72,000	78,000
Purchases	32,000	34,000	35,000	31,000	30,000	31,000
Wages	10,000	11,000	13,000	10,000	9,000	9,000
Production overheads	12,000	13,000	15,000	10,000	9,000	11,000

A) Sales for the month of August, '95 and September, '95 are Rs. 78,000 and Rs. 80,000 respectively. Purchases from suppliers for September '95 are Rs. 32,000.

B) 25% of the total monthly sales is on cash basis.

C) The administration overheads are Rs. 5,000 per month.

D) The company allows two months of credit to customers and avails one month of credit from its suppliers.

E) During November '95 payment for dividend amounting to Rs. 20,000 is to be paid to shareholders.

F) The company proposes to acquire an equipment amounting to Rs. 50,000 in the month of January, '96 and for this a loan of Rs. 45,000 is expected to be raised in December, '95.

G) Also during December, '95 debentures amounting to Rs. 10,000 are scheduled to be liquidated.

H) In March, '96 a plant with a salvage value of Rs. 3,000 is expected to fetch Rs. 1000 when disposed off in the market.

I) Advance tax instalments amounting to Rs. 10,000 -each are to be deposited in months of December, '95 and March, '96.

J) Cash balance as on 30th September, '95 is Rs. 4,000 and the monthly desired cash balance is Rs. 10,000 for the budgeted period.

Prepare cash budget in proper format detailing separately the operating, investing and financing activities.

6

CASH BUDGET — LONG-TERM

6.1 INTRODUCTION

Long-term cash forecasts are spanned for a longer period as compared to short-term cash forecasts. Still 'period' is not the basic difference; the basic difference lies in the objective for which both these forecasts are prepared. Short-term cash forecasts aim at providing tactical control over a limited future period only, so as to identify two distinct situations — periods of cash shortages and periods of cash surpluses. The underlying idea is to ensure that the business meets its commitments whenever required and also surplus cash does not remain idle and infertile. Long-term cash forecasts, on the other hand, aim for two objectives, (a) ascertaining the financial consequences of the various strategic plans drafted by management for the growth and development of the organisation, and (b) choosing the pattern of financing so as to ensure adequate funds supply for implementing the plan selected by the business. The importance of long-term cash forecasts lies in the fact that no business can remain contented with its position of status quo. It has to plan for the future growth and development lest it ceases to be commercially viable and finds itself out-raced by its competitors. For this, it strategically chalks out various alternatives for its growth so that its resources could be utilised at the optimum level. Long-term cash forecasts are then prepared which assist the management in the selection of the alternative and also to provide guidance regarding fund mix for the financing of the selected alternative taking into account likely debt equity scenario consequent upon implementation of the alternative.

Aspirations of management are enshrined in the corporate plan. Long-term cash forecasts are invariably bound by them. Rate of growth envisaged by management after making 'SWOT' analysis under corporate plan is more relevant for the long term forecasts than for short-term forecasts. Any attempt at preparing cash forecasts other than based on the corporate plan will be a futile exercise.

Preparing long term cash forecasts without corporate plan is like driving a vehicle without choosing a destination.

6.2 PROCESS OF LONG-TERM CASH FORECASTING

Long-term cash forecasting is guided by broad brush approach. Rightly so, because any attempt to make itemised estimates of revenue and expense items like that under short-term forecasts shall be more in the realm of conjectures than realistic estimates. As the time frame of estimates is stretched further into future their precision gets diluted due to scores of unpredictable and uncertain factors in the longer time horizon. Hence, the need for having broad base estimates.

Long-term cash forecasts, therefore, are prepared by indirect method. Net Adjusted Income method is most appropriate for making long-term cash forecasts. The process involves preparation in two stages. In the first stage estimates are made for certain 'core data' which enables the preparation of annual forecasted profit and loss accounts and balance sheets, for a long period, say, five years. Under the second stage, from the figures so estimated cash movement for the period is traced out and is presented in a statement known as 'Forecasted Cash Flow Statement'. We now study these two stages in detail.

6.3 PREPARATION OF FORECASTED PROFIT AND LOSS ACCOUNT AND BALANCE SHEET

The first stage in long-term cash forecasting is to estimate data for the preparation of forecasted profit and loss account and balance sheet. The detailed exercise of estimating components of core data like sales, purchases, fixed assets, equity, loan *etc.* is outside the scope of this book. However, the following common factors merit consideration for preparation of such forecasts.

6.3.1 Past Facts

Actuals of the past can provide useful guidance for knowing future trend. An analysis of historical data shall reveal a significant relationship between figures appearing in the balance sheet, and profit and loss account prepared for the past period. To take an instance, gross profit ratio of the past few years when averaged out will indicate working profit level of the company. In the case of businesses engaged in seasonal activities, past facts can provide guidance of cost and revenue during both on and off seasons. However, the past should not be followed blindly. Nothing remains static in ever-changing world of business. So the past should be used for the analysis of historical facts subject to adjustments considering present capabilities, and judicious interpretation of future trends.

6.3.2 General Growth Rate

An organisation fixes a growth rate for achieving the goals targeted in its corporate plan. The rate so determined would depend upon a number of internal and external factors which the management would have to weigh. But appropriately rate should be a blending of idealistic and practical possibilities. Unless an idealistic rate is targeted, an organisation may find itself out of the race track with its competitors. On the other hand, if rate is too idealistic and unpractical, forecasting shall turn out to be merely a theoretical exercise devoid of any practical significance.

6.3.3 Inflation

Inflation is a reality of today. Long-term forecasts are more susceptible to this than short-term forecasts because of the longer time span for which the forecasting is carried out. Also, under long-term forecasts one has to provide for not only revenue items but also for the capital items involving heavy investments. So due allowance has to be given to inflation rate. Another dimension of inflation is volume-value relationship. It may be possible that the volume of cost and revenue may increase but due to the high inflation rate value may decrease.

The effect of growth rate and inflation rate while forecasting figures of sales is displayed in the Exhibit 6.1.

Exhibit 6.1
SALES PROJECTION

Year	Growth Rate	Sales Quantities	Unit Price (Rs.)	Price Increase	Revised Price (Rs.)	Sales Value (Rs.)
1	2	3	4	5	6	7
1996	4%	10400(10000×4%)	50.0	5%	52.5	546000
1997	4%	10816(10400×4%)	52.5	—	52.5	567840
1998	5%	11357(10816×5%)	52.5	5%	55.0	624635
1999	5%	11925(11357×5%)	55.0	—	55.0	655875
2000	6%	12640(11925×6%)	55.0	7%	59.0	745760

The business envisages a growth rate of 4% for the first two years followed by growth rate of 5% for the next two years and 6% for the final year. Provision for inflation has been made in the first, third and fifth year. Rates of inflation expected in these years are 5% for first and third year, and 7% for the fifth year. The important fact to be noticed here is that for the computation of yearly sales figures, effect of annual growth should be accounted for at the first place and impact of inflation thereafter. Application of these in reverse order will give misleading results.

6.3.4 Management Policies

Every astute management formulates its policies concerning liquidity, solvency and profitability oriented towards achievement of its corporate goals. For instance, on the production front, for maximising profit it may like to rationalise product mix following "pareto principle" of 80:20, thereby channelising 80% of the resources to 20% of the profitable products and brutally discarding items with low or nil margin. Also management may decide at a particular point of time to deepen its reservoir of cash-in-till to meet its speculative motive of capturing a "cash cow" unit in the market by cornering its shares secretly. Such decisions have an important role to play in long-term cash forecasting.

6.4 CONSTRUCTION OF FORECASTED CASH FLOW STATEMENT

Once the forecasted profit and loss accounts and balance sheets have been drawn out the next step is to make cash forecasts for the same period. This is done by constructing a forecasted cash flow statement which summarises sources of cash inflow and cash outflow of the business during that period. As stated above, the input for the construction of such statement is extracted from the comparative forecasted balance sheets, profit and loss accounts and any other relevant information available. The process of construction of the statement involves following adjustments in order to ascertain the quantum of cash inflow and cash outflow likely to occasion during the period.

6.4.1 Accrual to Cash

Forecasted profit and loss account and balance sheet incorporate figures based on the accounting method of accrual basis while forecasted cash flow statement portrays figures on cash basis for the same period. Preparation of forecasted cash flow statement, therefore, involves an exercise of conversion of figures from accrual to cash basis. Bolten summarises the whole process as "Items accrued and not collected or paid for in cash during the period are not reported in this statement, and those cash items which are hidden in the balance sheet and income statement because they are with accrued items are reported separately." This excercise is done by adopting Net Adjustment Income method.

6.4.2 Analysis of Balances

Forecasted cash flow statement quantifies the changes in the sources and uses of cash over a financial period by extracting the information from the balance sheet figures of the two consecutive years. An analysis of opening and closing balances of current and non-current accounts of both assets and liabilities is carried out (balance appearing in the previous year's balance sheet becomes the opening balance of the next year's balance sheet). Such analysis reveals cash flow on account of all the three classes of activities — operating, investing and financing. Cash flow movement for the three activities is extracted by the following manner:

Operating activities: by adjusting the figures of the profit earned during the year and analysing changes in the opening and closing balances in current assets (other than cash) and current liabilities.

Investing activities: by analysing changes in opening and closing balances of non-current assets.

Financing activities: by analysing changes in opening and closing balances of non-current liabilities.

6.4.3 Additional Information

In addition to this certain additional information concerning profit, current and non-current accounts, also help to determine cash flow movement during that period.

Exhibit 6.2 shows a forecasted profit and loss account and balance sheet alongwith forecasted cash flow statement constructed therefrom tracking the cash movement of individual items.

Exhibit 6.2 eloquently tracks down the changes in values of balance sheet items in terms of cash movement. Profit is adjusted with changes in current assets and current liabilities to arrive at the figure of cash generation from operating activities. The increase in the figures of capital and loan implies changes in flow of cash in the business on account of financing activities. Against these two sources of cash inflow, cash outflow is on account of investment in purchase of fixed assets. The net cash inflow tallies with the increase in cash from Rs 20,000 to Rs 1,20,000.

We now study in detail the cash flow movement arising from operating, investing and financing activities.

6.5 CASH FLOW FROM OPERATING ACTIVITY

The most dominating and regular source of cash is the one which is generated through operating activity and reflected in profit. The figure of profit mentioned in the profit and loss account and the actual cash flow generated during that period is likely to be different because the former is a calculated figure and the latter is a reality. However, with the help of certain adjustments one can arrive at the figure of the cash flow generation from the figure of profit displayed in the profit

Exhibit 6.2

BALANCE SHEET AND CASH FLOW MOVEMENT

(Rs. in thousands)

Forecasted Profit & Loss A/c for the year ending 31.3.97

Sales	530
Less Expenditure:	
Cost of good sold	325
Wages & salaries	75
Rent	15
Depreciation	25
Interest	10
Profit	80

Balance Sheet

	As at 31.3.97 (Forecasted)		As at 31.3.96		Increase	Decrease
Assets						
Cash		120		20	100	
Sundry debtors		330		270	60	
Stock in hand		50		40	10	
Prepaid expenses		10		8	2	
Fixed assets	300		250		50	
Less accumulated depreciation	75	225	50	200		25
Total		735		538		
Liabilities						
Sundry creditors		200		160		40
Expenses payable		5		3		2
Loans		100		75		25
Reserve		180		100		80
Capital		250		200		50
Total		735		538		

Forecasted Cash Flow Statement - 1996-97

Profit as per P & L A/C		80
Less increase:		
Sundry debtors	60	
Stock in hand	10	
Prepaid expenses	2	
		72
		8
Add increase:		
Depreciation	25	
Sundry Creditors	40	
Expenses payable	2	
		67
Cash from operating activities		75
Add increase:		
Loan	25	
Capital	50	
Cash from financing activities		75
Gross cash inflow (Sources)		150
Less cash outflow (Uses):		
Purchase of fixed assets		50
Increase in net cash inflow		100

and loss account. The Exhibit 6.4 details such adjustments made in the figure of net profit to arrive at the figure of cash flow generation during the period. The adjustments are explained as follows:

6.5.1 Basis of Accounting

Accounting profit is computed on accrual basis. Revenue is taken into consideration whether or not it is backed by cash and similarly expenditure is deducted from revenue receipt whether or not paid in cash. The adjustments, therefore, have to be effected by segregating the items of revenue and expenditure which occasion the movement of cash flow with the items which are not supported by flow of cash.

6.5.2 Non-Cash Expenses

A number of expense items represent merely book entries without any corresponding decrease in cash flow. The most commonly quoted such item is depreciation. To determine figure of profit, depreciation is reduced from revenue but since it does not in any way lower cash volume it has to be added to the profit figure for the purpose of determining total cash inflow.

6.5.3 Extraneous Profits and Losses

Revenues or losses which are not directly caused by business operations need be adjusted appropriately in the profit. The profit and loss account may include items showing the revenue profit arising on the sale of an asset. The cash sale value of an asset is projected in the statement as a separate source of cash receipt under investing activities. The actual income on account of sale of asset which has been taken into consideration for determination of the net profit is to be reduced therefrom. Conversely, the loss in such a transaction shall be added to the profit.

6.5.4 Analysis of Current Accounts

Increases and decreases in the current assets and current liabilities play a vital role in the flow of cash from operating activities. These are derived from the figures appearing in the comparative balance sheets. Such increases and decreases are adjusted in the net profit in the following manner to ascertain cash generation of a particular period.

(a) *Sundry Debtors:* Sundry debtors owe their existence to the sale made on credit. Profit and loss account consider the total sale whether in cash or credit as an item of revenue for calculating profit. Increase or decrease in sundry debtors shall provide information regarding actual amount of collections from debtors during the period. Increase in debtors would indicate that collections from sundry debtors are less than the sales revenue while decrease in debtors would mean that amount received from debtors is more than the sales revenue. Exhibit 6.2 shows that at the end of previous year sundry debtors were Rs 2.70 lakhs which escalated to Rs 3.30 lakhs at the end of the current year, *i.e.,* an increase of Rs 60,000. The profit calculation have considered total sales in cash plus credit as revenue for both the years whereas the business has been deprived of cash collections to the extent of increase in debtors. Therefore, profit figure is reduced to the extent of increase in debtors to know the actual inflow of cash from collections of receivables.

(b) *Closing Stock:* For the purpose of determining profit or loss it is not the value of purchases made during the year but cost of goods sold which is taken into consideration. Cost of goods sold is a derived figure. It is calculated by adding in the opening stock, purchases made during the year and reducing therefrom closing stock at the end of the year. Purchases, on the other hand, refer to cost of procurement made during the year. Increase in closing stock vis-a-vis opening stock, therefore, implies that purchases were in excess of cost of goods sold by that amount resulting in more cash outflow. Appropriately therefore, increase in closing stock is deducted from net profit and decrease in closing stock is added to profit. In Exhibit 6.3 we study three distinct cases under which all the figures remain constant except the figures of closing stock and the resultant figures of cost of goods sold.

Exhibit 6.3

CLOSING STOCK AND CASH GENERATION

(Rupees)

	Case 1	Case 2	Case 3
Opening stock	5,00,000	5,00,000	5,00,000
Purchases	45,00,000	45,00,000	45,00,000
Closing stock	(6,00,000)	(5,00,000)	(4,00,000)
Cost of goods sold	44,00,000	45,00,000	46,00,000
Sales	50,00,000	50,00,000	50,00,000
Profit	6,00,000	5,00,000	4,00,000
(Increase)/Decrease in stock	(1,00,000)	—	1,00,000
Cash generation	5,00,000	5,00,000	5,00,000

It is interesting to note that increase in cost of goods sold has inverse effect on the profit. It is reduced in identical proportion but cash generation which is influenced by factors like sales and purchases remains constant because there is no change in these components. Viewed from different angle, profit is concerned with the valuation of closing stock, but cash generation is immune to it.

(c) *Prepaid Expenses:* Accounts are prepared for a particular period, normally for an year. Accordingly, the expenditure is accounted for items relevant to that period only. However, there are certain expenses which have to be incurred for a period not synchronising with the period for which accounts are prepared. Suitable adjustment is, therefore, required to be made in the accounts by charging to the profit expenditure of the relevant period and showing the balance expenditure for the future period as prepaid expenses. A common instance is that of insurance which is paid in advance for a period normally different than a period for which the accounts are prepared. Increase in prepaid expenses indicate that actual cash outflow has been more than the expenses accounted for in the profit calculations whereas decrease in the prepaid expenses would reveal that the expenses which have been incurred in the past period have now been adjusted in the accounts. Therefore, increase in expenses is reduced from the profit, and decrease in prepaid expenses is added to the profit to arrive at the figure of cash generation during the period.

(d) *Accrual Basis:* There are certain items of income though not received in cash during the period, are considered for the purpose of determination of profit, on accrual basis. A few instances are interest accrued but not due, pre fixed incentives receivable from the government agencies and the likes. Increase in such accrued income implies that the cash inflow has been less than the amount shown in the profit and loss statement whereas decrease in accrued income implies that cash inflow has been more than the amount of income stated in the profit and loss account.

(e) *Sundry Creditors:* Creditors come into existence when business makes purchases on credit. The adjustment to be effected in the profit, therefore, is opposite to what is required to be made under sundry debtors. The increase in creditors means that payments to creditors are less than the purchases made and decrease in creditors implies that payments to creditors are more than the purchases made during the period. To determine the cash generation, adjustment is made by adding to the profit the increase in creditors and reducing from the profit decrease in creditors.

(f) *Increase in Expenses Payable:* Certain expenses remain outstanding at the end of the year. These expenses are considered in the profit and loss account since these pertain to the pertinent period but payment for these have not been released during the period. Increase in such expenses at the end of the year implies that cash outflow has been lesser by the amount of increase whereas decrease in such outstanding expenses shall imply that certain expenses which have been accounted for in the previous period have been paid during the current period. Therefore, increase in expenses is added to the profit whereas decrease is subtracted from the profit to calculate the cash flow generation of the period.

Exhibit 6.4 displays the cash flow generation through operating activities.

Exhibit 6.4

CASH FLOWS FROM OPERATING ACTIVITIES

The balance sheet of ABC Co. as at March 31, 1996 and forecasted balance sheet as at March 31, 1997 are as follows. The cash flow generation from the operating activities for the year 1996-97 can be determined with the help of these figures.

COMPARATIVE BALANCE SHEETS

	As at March, 97 (Forecasted) (Rs)	As at March, 96 (Rs)
Capital	10,00,000	10,00,000
Reserve & surplus	3,20,000	2,00,000
Sundry creditors	1,00,000	80,000
Expenses payable	10,000	15,000
	14,30,000	12,95,000
Fixed assets	9,10,000	8,00,000
Less depreciation	(1,90,000)	(90,000)
Sundry debtors	3,50,000	3,00,000
Prepaid expenses	15,000	20,000
Stock	2,00,000	1,75,000
Cash	1,45,000	90,000
	14,30,000	12,95,000

FORECASTED PROFIT & LOSS ACCOUNT FOR THE YEAR ENDING MARCH, 1997.

Sales		20,00,000
Expenditure:		
Cost of goods sold	13,55,000	
Operating expenses	3,00,000	
Depreciation	1,00,000	
Interest	50,000	
Other expenses	75,000	
		18,80,000
Profit		1,20,000

EXPECTED CASH GENERATION FROM OPERATING ACTIVITIES

Profit as per profit & loss account		1,20,000
Add:		
Depreciation	1,00,000	
Increase in creditors	20,000	
Decrease in prepaid expenses	5,000	
		1,25,000
		2,45,000
Less:		
Increase in debtors	50,000	
Increase in stock	25,000	
Decrease in expenses payable	5,000	
		80,000
Cash generated from operations		1,65,000
Less cash used for buying fixed assets		1,10,000
Increase in Cash		55,000
Add Opening Balance as on April 1 1996		90,000
Closing balance on March 31,1997		1,45,000

The expected profit during the year computed as per accounting norms is Rs 1,20,000. Depreciation being non-cash expenditure has been added to it. Increase in creditors which implies lesser outflow of cash vis-a-vis purchases made has been added along with decrease in prepaid expenses which too implies lesser outflow of cash. Conversely, amounts pertaining to increase in debtors and stock have been reduced from profit as the actual realisation and cost of goods sold are less than sales and purchases, respectively. Similarly, decrease in expenses payable involve additional outflow of cash as compared to the expenses charged to profit. So the total generation of cash from operating activities is Rs 1,65,000. Out of this generated cash, Rs 1,10,000 is to be utilised to buy some fixed assets. The net increase of cash expected during the year, therefore, is Rs 55,000 which when added to opening balance tallies with the closing balance of cash as at the end of the period.

6.6 CASH MOVEMENT FROM INVESTING ACTIVITIES

Changes in the non-current assets during a particular period provide information about cash movement occasioned by the investing activities. These changes primarily pertain to acquisition, disposition and amortisation of the non-current assets during a period. Acquisition and disposition of these assets result in the outflow and inflow of cash respectively, whereas amortisation being a book entry only, does not effect cash movement. However, a detailed analysis will be required to bring out hidden element of cash in the whole process of changes in assets. The analysis is based on the information provided by the following sources:

- Figures of opening and closing balances of gross block of assets and depreciation,
- Amounts of gains or losses from disposal of assets appearing in profit & loss account, and
- Any other information provided in this regard.

It is illustrated through Exhibit 6.5

Exhibit 6.5
CASH FLOWS FROM INVESTING ACTIVITIES

ABC Co. provides the following information in respect of purchases and sales of assets to determine cash inflow and outflow during the year 1996-97.

	March 31,1997 (Rs)	March 31,1996 (Rs)
Plant and equipment	2,10,000	2,00,000
Accumulated depreciation	65,000	60,000
Profit on sale of plant		4,000

During the year company is likely to sell plant which is appearing in the books of accounts valuing Rs 25,000. The accumulated depreciation identified with the plant to be sold is Rs 15,000.

The missing information in this exercise is with regard to inflow and outflow of cash on account of sale of existing plant and purchase of new plant respectively during the year. These can be traced as:

CASH INFLOW ON SALE OF PLANT AND EQUIPMENT

	(Rupees)
Gross value of plant & equipment to be sold	25,000
Less accumulated depreciation	15,000
Net value of the plant & equipment to be sold	10,000
Add profit on the sale of plant & equipment	4,000
Cash receipts on account of sale of plant & equipment	14,000

CASH OUTFLOW ON PURCHASE OF PLANT AND EQUIPMENT

Gross value of the plant & equipment at the beginning	2,00,000
Less gross value of plant & equipment sold	25,000
	1,75,000
Cash payment for purchase of plant & equipment during the year (balancing figure)	35,000
Gross value at the end	2,10,000

Thus, cash receipts from investing activities are Rs 14000 and cash payments in respect of these activities are Rs 35,000. The net cash consumption on account of investing activities is therefore Rs 21,000.

6.7 CASH MOVEMENT FROM FINANCING ACTIVITIES

Changes in non-current liabilities throw light on the movement of cash caused by financing activities of the business. Non-current liabilities relate to both owner's capital and borrower's funds. Variations in the share capital is an important item of financing activities which provide information regarding cash movement during the year. Variations may be due to fresh issue of equity shares or redemption of preference shares. The increase in share capital, however, need not necessarily involve cash movement because shares can be issued for consideration other than cash as well. Terms of issue, *e.g.*, whether issued at par or at premium, would also help to determine amount of cash inflow.

Another important source is debentures. Issue of debentures, redemption of debentures at par, discount or premium result in movement of cash. Conversion of debentures into capital, normally, does not involve any cash transactions and as such any variation in debenture and share capital on this score remains out of the purview of cash flow projections. Other important items of financing activities are long- term loans from financial institutions and issue of bonds. Changes in these also provide information regarding receipts and payments of cash during the particular period.

Exhibit 6.6 shows movement of cash on account of financing activities.

Exhibit 6.6
CASH FLOWS FROM FINANCING ACTIVITIES

M/s ABC & Co. provides the following information relating to financing activities. Cash receipts and cash payments during the year 1996-97 can be computed therefrom.

	March 31,1997 (Rs)	March 31,1996 (Rs)
Equity Capital	30,00,000	20,00,000
14% Bonds	8,00,000	10,00,000
12% Debentures	6,00,000	8,00,000
Share premium	14,00,000	5,00,000

Notes:
1. Shares are of the face value of Rs 10 each.
2. Face value of debentures is Rs 100.
3. 2,000 debentures are to be converted into shares @ 10 shares for 2 debentures.
4. During the year new shares are also to be issued.

Segregating the non-cash items, it is observed that conversion of debentures into shares does not involve cash movement. For the rest of the financing activities cash flow movement is as follows:

CASH INFLOWS — ISSUE OF NEW SHARES

		(Rupees)
(i) Equity capital as on 31.3.1997	30,00,000	
Less conversion from debentures	1,00,000	
	29,00,000	
Less Equity capital as on 31.3.96	20,00,000	
Cash receipts on issue of new shares		9,00,000
(ii) Share premium balance as on 31.3.1997	14,00,000	
Less balance as on 31.3.96	5,00,000	
Cash receipts on account of premium on new shares		9,00,000
Total cash receipts from financing activities		18,00,000

CASH OUTFLOWS - REPURCHASE OF 14% BONDS

Amount of 14% Bonds as on 31.3.97	8,00,000
Repurchase of Bonds during the year (balancing figure)	2,00,000
Amount of 14% Bonds as on 31.3.96	10,00,000

Connecting the missing link it transpires that the company during the year 1996-97 is likely to receive Rs 18,00,000 as total cash from financing activities on account of issue of 90,000 shares at a premium of Rs 10 per share. The company expects to purchase its own bonds from the market by spending Rs 2,00,000. The net inflow during the year in respect of financing activities therefore is Rs 16,00,000.

6.8 MODEL OF CASH BUDGET — LONG-TERM

Exhibit 6.7 shows a model of long-term cash budget. In the first stage forecasted financial statements for the year 1996-97 have been drawn. Forecasted profit & loss account shows a profit of Rs. 4,20,000. After making provisions for taxation and dividend the balance Rs. 2,90,000 is to be transferred to Reserve and Surplus. A study of the figures of comparative balance sheets indicates variations in the current assets and liabilities, fixed assets and long-term liabilities and capital. These variations help in projecting the cash flows on account of operating, investing and financing activities.

Exhibit 6.7

FORECASTED PROFIT AND LOSS ACCOUNT FOR THE YEAR ENDING 1996-97

		(Rupees)
Sales		30,00,000
Less		
Cost of goods sold	16,70,000	
Operating expenses	6,50,000	
Depreciation	80,000	
Interest	60,000	
Other expenses	1,20,000	25,80,000
Profit before tax		4,20,000
Less provision for taxation		60,000
Profit after tax		3,60,000
Less provision for dividend		70,000
Transfer to reserve and surplus		2,90,000

COMPARATIVE BALANCE SHEETS

(Ruppes)

	As at 31.3.97 (Forecasted)	As at 31.3.96
Capital	8,00,000	7,00,000
Reserve & surplus	8,40,000	5,50,000
Sundry creditors	2,00,000	1,10,000
Debentures	2,00,000	4,00,000
Provision for taxation	60,000	50,000
Provision for dividend	70,000	—
	21,70,000	18,10,000
Cash	35,000	1,70,000
Sundry debtors	4,00,000	3,20,000
Shares in cooperative society	—	30,000
Stock	3,85,000	2,30,000
Land	8,70,000	5,00,000

Plant & equipment	8,00,000	8,00,000
Less: Accumulated depreciation	(3,20,000)	(2,40,000)
	21,70,000	18,10,000

CASH BUDGET

PERIOD: 1996 - 1997 DATE: 15th Jan' 96

BASIS: YEARLY

(Rupees)

1. CASH GENERATION		
1.1 OPERATING ACTIVITIES		
1.1.1 Forecasted profit		4,20,000
1.1.2 Less : Corporate tax paid		(50,000)
1.1.3 Profit after payment of tax		3,70,000
1.1.4 Add adjustments on account of		
— Depreciation	80,000	
— Creditors	90,000	1,70,000
1.1.5 Less adjustments on account of		
— Debtors	80,000	
— Stock	1,55,000	
		(2,35,000)
1.1.0 Sub total		3,05,000
1.2 INVESTING ACTIVITIES		
— Sale of shares		30,000
1.2.0 Sub total		30,000
1.3 FINANCING ACTIVITIES		
— Equity Issue proceeds		1,00,000
1.3.0 Sub total		1,00,000
Total(1.1.0+1.2.0+1.3.0)		4,35,000
2. CASH REQUIREMENTS		
2.1 INVESTING ACTIVITIES		
2.1.1 - Purchase of land		3,70,000
2.1.0 Sub total		3,70,000
2.2 FINANCING ACTIVITIES		
—Redemption of debentures		2,00,000
2.2.0 Sub total		2,00,000
Total (2.1.0+2.2.0)		5,70,000
3. NET CASH GENERATION		
3.1 Cash (Deficit)/Surplus		(1,35,000)
3.2 Balance in the beginning		1,70,000
3.3 Desired balance		(2,00,000)
3.1.0 Total (3.1+3.2+3.3)		(1,65,000)
4. PLANNED FINANCING		
4.1 BORROWINGS		
— Financial institution		1,00,000
— Inter corporate deposits		65,000
		1,65,000

Prepared by:

The format of long term cash budget has four sections. The first section projects the expected cash generation from operating, investing and financing activities. The second section displays the anticipated cash requirements of these activities. The third section indicates the figures of net cash generation, positive or negative. The fourth section shows the arrangement of planned financing.

The business anticipates a profit of Rs. 4,20,000. Tax amounting to Rs. 50,000 provided for in the previous year is paid out of it and balance Rs. 3,70,000 is available as profit before working capital changes. After making necessary adjustments on account of increase and decrease in the current assets and current liabilities a figure of Rs. 3,05,000 is arrived at as net cash from operating activities. Sale of shares of co-operative society under investing activities and receipts of equity issue proceeds amounting to Rs. 30,000 and Rs. 1,00,000 respectively aggregates the total cash generation to Rs. 4,35,000 during the year. The second part shows cash requirements for investing and financing activities which totals to Rs. 5,70,000. The net result is cash deficit amounting to Rs. 1,35,000 during the year as depicted under section three. After adjustments of opening cash balance and desired closing cash balance a net deficit of Rs. 1,65,000 is indicated. Section four shows that a loan of Rs. 1,00,000 from financial institutions and inter corporate deposit of Rs. 65,000 are envisaged by the business to meet the deficit.

6.9 TOTAL CASH REQUIREMENTS OF A PLAN PERIOD

Long-term cash forecasts for the individual years can be planted in one statement so as to provide overall view of total cash requirements of a plan period . Exhibit 6.8 shows one such statement incorporating yearly projections of five-year plan period from 1996 to 2000. This will give an overall picture of generation of cash from all the activities and also flash signals for the looming cash flow problems likely to be encountered during the plan period.

Exhibit 6.8

STATEMENT OF CASH REQUIREMENTS FOR A PLAN PERIOD

(Rs. in lakhs)

	1996	1997	1998	1999	2000
Forecasted profit	50	54	60	67	75
Less Corporate tax	(25)	(27)	(30)	(33)	(37)
Profit after tax	25	27	30	34	38
(Increase)/Decrease on account of					
— Depreciation	10	12	16	21	26
— Debtors	(5)	(7)	(10)	(19)	(26)
— Creditors	4	5	7	11	14
— Stock	(2)	(3)	(4)	(6)	(7)
Cash generation from operating activities	32	34	39	41	45
Cash requirements for investing activities					
— Purchase of plant	—	(50)	—	—	—
— Purchase of building	—	—	(60)	—	—
— Investment in joint venture	(35)	—	—	—	—

Cash requirements for financing activities					
— Repayment of bonds	—	—	(5)	(25)	(25)
— Repayment of long-term borrowings	—	—	—	(23)	(16)
—Dividend	(2)	(3)	(3)	(4)	(5)
TOTAL CASH REQUIREMENTS	(5)	(19)	(29)	(11)	(1)
Planned financing					
— Cash in hand including cash equivalents	1	1	1	1	1
— Sale of long-term investments	4	—	—	—	—
— Borrowings	—	18	28	—	—
— Equity capital	—	—	—	10	—
TOTAL PLANNED FINANCING	5	19	29	11	1

The first part of the statement as shown in Exhibit 6.8 is indicative of total requirements for a long-term duration in respect of the operating, investing and financing activities. Statement starts with forecasted profits which when adjusted provide information regarding cash generation from operating activities. This is followed by cash needs on account of investing activities. Also, the business requires cash for repayment of loans and bonds as detailed under financing activities. One regular item which appears in financing activity is payment of annual dividend. The second part of the statement portrays the planned financing for all the individual years of cash requirements. At times the company may have to go for borrowings to raise additional capital. For the first year the cash requirement is for Rs 5 lakhs and the need has arisen because heavy investment is made in joint venture. Part of the requirement is met by the cash generated by the business and the balance is supplemented by sale of long-term investments. The investment in joint venture consumes the cash generated from operating activities and further cash requirement is met by selling long-term investments. The second and third years witness a heavy investment in purchase of plant and building. The business would be raising borrowings for the procurement of fixed assets. The procurement of these fixed assets is as per the growth rate expansion provided in the corporate plans. In the fourth year the business is obliged to meet its contractual obligations of repayment of bonds and borrowings amounting to Rs 25 lakhs and Rs. 23 lakh respectively. These payments are made out of the cash generation of the year and issue of equity capital of Rs. 10 lakh. In the final year of long-term forecasting, the business is making higher profit and greater generation of cash which can help it to redeem second tranche of bonds. The balance amount can be utilised for liquidating long-term borrowings to the extent of Rs 16.00 lakhs. Dividend has been increasing gradually for compensating the shareholders for the additional revenue generated from the growth of the business.

It may be observed that the thrust of the statement is targeted towards meeting long-term cash requirements and the arrangements of the requisite finance for the next five years. It is possible that during a particular year cash deficit may be encountered when the short-term cash needs become more than Rs one lakh. But that will be taken care of by the short-term cash forecasts which may provide for overdrafts from bank for the requisite period. Long-term cash forecasts will not focus for such day-to-day cash requirements but will concentrate on strategic cash requirements required for longer duration.

QUESTIONS

1. What are the primary objectives of long-term cash forecasting?
2. How the general growth rate and inflation rate affect the forecasting?
3. Explain the long term cash forecasting of operating activities?
4. How cash forecasting on long-term basis is done for investing activities.
5. Describe the method of making long-term cash forecasts for financing activities.
6. Write short notes on:
   - (a) Accrual and cash basis system on accounting.
   - (b) Analysis of opening and closing balances for extracting cash movements.
   - (c) Closing stock and cash generation.
7. ABC & Co. has drawn the following balance sheets based on the forecasted figures for the years 1995-96 and 1996-97.

BALANCE SHEET

(Rupees)

	As at 31.3.97	As at 31.3.96
Capital	55,000	50,000
Reserves	28,000	20,000
Loan	10,000	—
Creditors	16,000	14,000
	1,09,000	84,000
Land	40,000	40,000
Plant	20,000	15,000
Stock	14,000	10,000
Debtors	22,000	17,000
Cash at bank	13,000	2,000
	1,09,000	84,000

Prepare a cash budget for the year 1996-97.

8. The forecasted sales of XYZ & Co., for the year 1996-97 is expected at Rs. 22,50,000. The purchases during the year are estimated at Rs. 12,52,500. The expenses are expected to be; operating expenses Rs. 4,87,500, depreciation Rs. 60,000, interest Rs. 45,000 and other expenses Rs. 90,000. The balance sheets as at March 31, 1996 and March, 31, 1997 (forecasted) are as below:

BALANCE SHEETS

(Rupees)

	As at 31.3.1997	As at 31.3.1996
Land	6,52,500	3,75,000
Plant and Equipment	6,00,000	6,00,000
Accumulated Depreciation	(2,40,000)	(1,80,000)
Investment	—	22,500
Stock	2,88,750	1,72,500
Receivables	3,00,000	2,40,000
Cash	26,250	1,02,500
	16,27,500	13,32,500
Capital	6,00,000	5,00,000
Reserve & surpluses	6,30,250	4,12,500
Bonds	1,50,000	3,00,000
Payables	1,50,000	82,500
Taxation — provision	47,250	37,500
Dividend — provision	50,000	—
	16,27,500	13,32,500

Assuming an income tax rate of 15%, dividend 10%, and desired cash balance of Rs. 1,50,000, prepare a cash budget for the year 1996-97 by adopting Net Adjusted Income Method.

7

CASH MANAGEMENT TECHNIQUES

7.1 INTRODUCTION

Cash management techniques aim at acceleration of cash inflows and deceleration of cash outflows. This is done through speedy collection of accounts receivables and by delaying disbursements of accounts payables. In Chapter 2, we observed that cash flow cycle is a constant process of generation-consumption-generation of cash. Generation of cash can be increased by speedy collections. Consumption can be effectively optimised by slowing disbursements. In this chapter, we shall study the various techniques which are adopted to quicken the pace of cash collections and slow the process of cash disbursements.

7.2 SCOPE OF CASH MANAGEMENT TECHNIQUES

As stated above, these techniques cover both payables and receivables and have immense impact on the cash flow cycle. Exhibit 2.3 in Chapter 2 shows the steps involved in the cash flow movement. Borrowing the basic data from the Exhibit 2.3, the steps are divided into four phases as displayed in Exhibit 7.1.

The first phase relates to payables and have four steps A1 to A4. The activity starts with the placing of order for the materials which are received after ten days (A1 - A2). Credit period of 10 days has been allowed by the supplier (A2 - A3), after the expiry of which cheque is despatched. Another 4 days are consumed in the mailing time, cheque processing time and clearance by the bank (A3 - A4). In the mean time, second phase has already started on the receipt of the materials. The materials are then processed for production, the processing time being 30 days (B1 - B2). This ends the second phase and the third phase starts. This phase covers wait-in-time for the inventory to be sold (C1 - C2). Then follows phase four which is activated by the sale of goods on credit of 40 days (D1 - D2). The payment despatched by the customers after 40 days consumes 2 days in the mail (D2 - D3) and another two days for internal processing of cheques by the business for presentation to bank (D3 - D4). Finally, the bank takes two days for clearance (D4 - D5).

Cash management techniques are concerned with A2, A3, A4 and D2, D3, D4 and D5.

Exhibit 7.1
PHASES OF CASH FLOW MOVEMENT

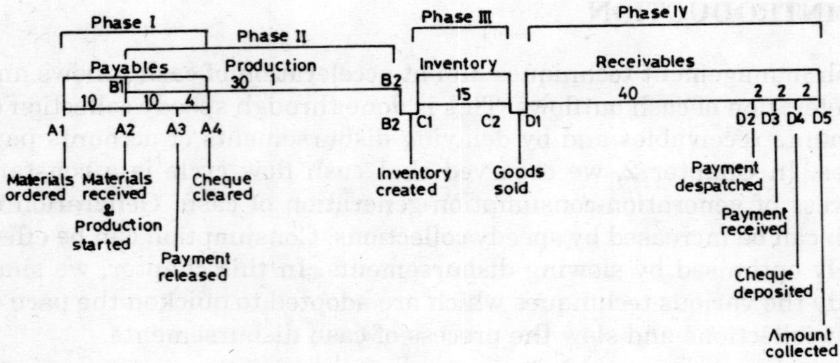

7.3 PARTIES TO CASH MANAGEMENT TECHNIQUES

The techniques require active participation by the three parties — business, bank and customer/supplier. The business has to gear up and infuse necessary motivation in its personnel to accelerate collections and slow the disbursements. All the techniques do not have universal application. A business will have to make choice for one which is most suitable for its requirements. A combination of techniques can also be adopted and a model can be tailored befitting to the needs of the business.

The second party is the bank. Most of the techniques require a fully developed automated banking infrastructure. Banks, as a matter of fact, play a commanding role in the contemporary cash management strategies and many steps involved in these techniques are under the control of the banks. The developed countries have very advance banking systems. Many of the techniques which are applicable in these countries are not prevalent in developing countries. The developing countries have, however, developed some substitute indigeneous models as explained later in the chapter.

The third party involved in the cash management strategies is the customers or the suppliers. These techniques solicit active participation of suppliers/ customers. They are at the other end of the channel and unless they cooperate these techniques cannot be made effective.

Before we proceed further we define here a term which is likely to be used very often and play a critical role in the operation of cash management techniques. It is known as Float.

7.4 FLOAT

A business at times deals with two balances associated with its bank account. One, the balance appearing in its own books of accounts and the other the actual cash balance as displayed in books of the bank. The reasons for the difference in these two balances can be many. The two most prominent reasons are:

— Cheques presented by the business but not yet collected;

— Cheques issued by the business but not yet presented.

The sum total of these two is known as 'Float'. The former is known as Collection Float and the latter as Disbursement Float.

7.4.1 Collection Float

The collection float is represented by the aggregate of the amounts of the cheques which have been deposited in the bank but are in the process of collection by the bank. As soon as the cheques are deposited in the bank, the amounts are debited to the bank account appearing in the books of the business. But the bank accords the credit to its customer when it realises the amounts from the banks of the customers. The time lag in the two results in the difference of balances known as Collection Float.

As a matter of fact collection float is part of overall "Deposit float", which additionally covers mailing float and processing float. Mailing float accrues due to time lag involved in the issue of cheques by customers and their receipts by the recipients. Processing float is on account of time taken by the business for processing the cheques for presentation to the bank.

Close monitoring of all the three is important for speedy collection of receivables.

7.4.2 Disbursement Float

Disbursement float is sum total of all the cheques which have been issued to suppliers but are in the process of being presented to the bank for payments. The bank account in the books of the business is credited as soon as cheques are drawn on it and sent to suppliers but the bank would debit the account of its customer only on the receipt of the cheques from the bankers of suppliers. The difference between the two balances is known as Disbursement Float. The disbursement float is used as an item for delaying payments by adopting the technique of 'riding the float' as explained later in the chapter.

Cash management techniques fall into two functional areas: accelerating collections and decelerating disbursements. In both the areas efforts are made to exploit their respective floats to the maximum. Collection float assists in quickening the pace of cash inflow and disbursement float helps the business in delaying the cash outflow.

7.5 ACCELERATING COLLECTIONS

Credit to customers is inevitable. No business can function without it. The business, however, can adopt such policies which ensure early retrieval of cash from customers. We have seen earlier that discount is one such strong pursuasive factor and a business following a policy of offering discount will get early payments from customers. In addition to such policies, there are some cash management techniques which accelerate speedy collection of receivables. The important cash collection techniques are as follows.

7.5.1 Concentration Banking

Normally, the customers of a business are required to despatch their remittances to the head office. This way cash is pooled and disbursed centrally facilitating effective cash control and efficient monitoring. But if the size of the business is very big and customers scattered over a large area, considerable time will be consumed in raising bills and processing cheques. To avoid this and reduce the deposit float, the system of concentration banking is adopted.

Under this system cash collection is centralised by the receipts from decentralised cash collection centres. Normally, local sales offices are saddled with the additional responsibility of collecting receipts from customers located in the geographical areas falling under their purviews. Cheques so collected are deposited in the local bank accounts serving the concerned sales offices. The local banks are instructed to keep a predetermined limited amount with them and transfer the balance to a central or 'concentration' bank account on daily basis. All the disbursements are effected through this central bank account. Exhibit 7.2 shows the operation of concentration banking.

The advantages of concentration banking stem from both of its operational wings—decentralised billling and cash collection, on one hand and centralised pooling of cash, on the other. The foremost ad-

Exhibit 7.2
CONCENTRATION BANKING

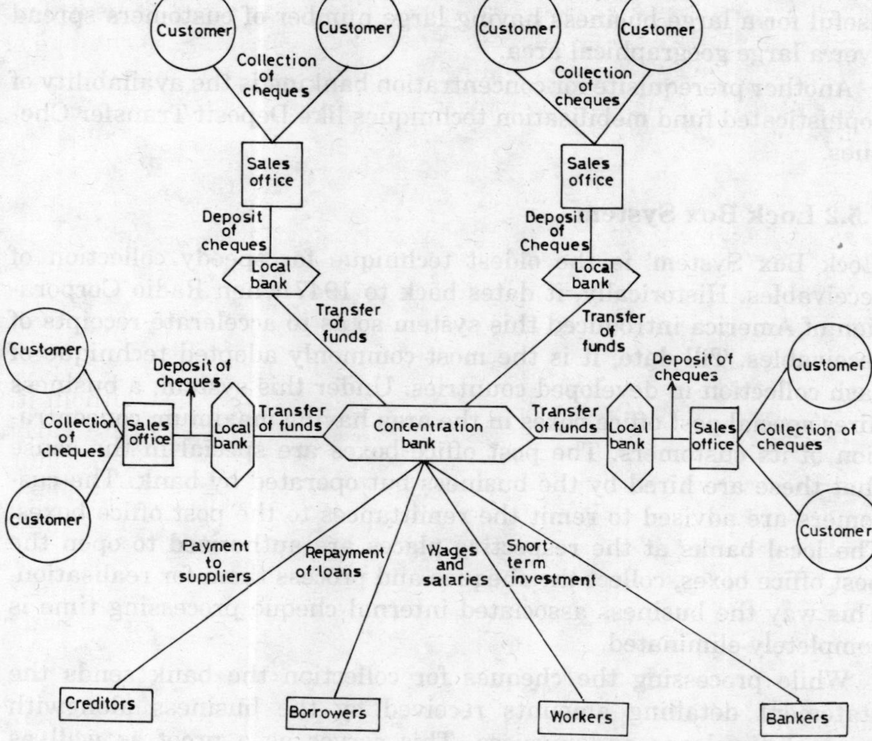

vantage of concentration banking is drastic reduction of mailing time due to close proximity of customer with sales/collection centre and that of sales/collection centre with the bank. As a result of which the saving is effected in the following deposit float:

— time involved in sending a bill to the customer
— time involved in despatch of a cheque from the customer to sales/collection centre
— time involved in sending the cheque to bank
— time involved in processing the cheque as the cheque belongs to local clearing.

Another important advantage of concentration banking is efficient 'warehousing' of cash. The funds are pooled at one place in a central bank account allowing business to make the adroit use of these funds. The funds can be disbursed as per the priorities laid down by the business and idle funds can be parked for earning interest. Pooling of funds from scattered collection centres aggregate to a sizeable amount and the banks are not reluctant to accept such funds even for a very short period.

Concentration banking for its operation involves a number of units of banks which naturally add to its costs. The system, therefore, should be introduced after making proper cost-benefit analysis. It is useful for a large business having large number of customers spread over a large geographical area.

Another prerequisite for concentration banking is the availability of sophisticated fund mobilisation techniques like Deposit Transfer Cheques.

7.5.2 Lock Box System

'Lock Box System' is the oldest technique for speedy collection of receivables. Historically, it dates back to 1947 when Radio Corporation of America introduced this system so as to accelerate receipts of receivables. Till date, it is the most commonly adopted technique of cash collection in developed countries. Under this system, a business hires special post office boxes in the area having maximum concentration of its customers. The post office boxes are special in the sense that these are hired by the business but operated by bank. The customers are advised to remit the remittances to the post office boxes. The local banks at the respective places are authorised to open the post office boxes, collect the cheques and process them for realisation. This way the business associated internal cheque processing time is completely eliminated.

While processing the cheques for collection the bank sends the statement detailing amounts received by the business alongwith original envelopes and invoices. This serves as a proof as well as record for according necessary accounting treatment to the receivables. This way, both the collection process and accounting process function simultaneously. Exhibit 7.3 shows the operation of Lock Box System.

Selection of city, bank and post office box is an important factor since all the activities are associated with them. Ideally, the city should be large enough to have its own clearing house with automated facilities like MICR. But most important is its geographical location. It should be in close proximity of the places from where the receipts are originating. Bank performs the pivotal role in the system. It intercepts the mail and simultaneously acts on two fronts — sends the cheques for processing and sends the invoices, photo copies, and statements of receipts to the business. It is, therefore, necessary that the bank selected should be a reputed one having good track record of efficient service. Preferably, the bank should have computer base so as to facilitate direct interface between lock box receipts and automated accounts receivable system. If possible, the bank which is patronised by most of the customers should be selected. It would drastically reduce the bank associated processing time for the clearance of cheques. Post office box selected should be one which has clear ap-

Exhibit 7.3
LOCK BOX SYSTEM

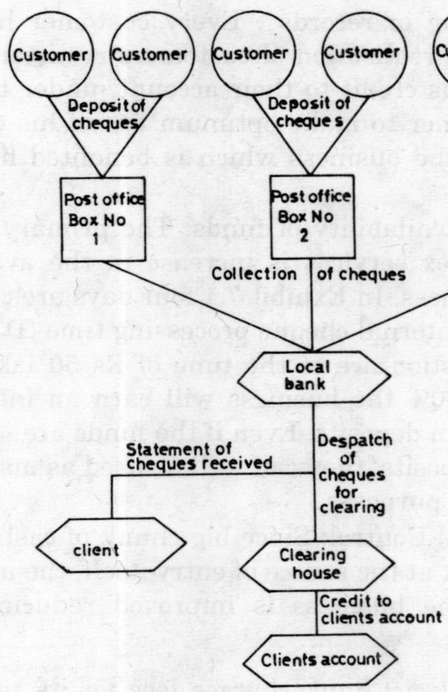

proach and easy accessibility as the bank may have to empty the box a number of times a day.

(a) *Advantages:* The advantages of lock box system have made it a favourite technique of cash management. These are explained below:

(i) Reduction in the mail processing time: The lock box system follows the basic principles of concentration banking — collections through decentralised units. But it is superior to concentration banking in one way that it has the minimum mail processing time. The customers are required to send remittances directly to post office box which are handled by the bank. This reduces the business associated mail processing time.

(ii) Reduction in the cheques collection time: The bank itself initiates the cheques collection process. As a result, the time involved in the presentation of cheques by the business to bank is completely eliminated. Besides, the bank empties the post office box a number of times a day quickening the pace of cheques collection.

(iii) Reduction in receivable processing costs: A business has to engage dedicated staff to handle manual opening, sorting and making necessary endorsements in the records. The cost on this account is subnstantially reduced when the bank handles these activities because the bank specialises in high volume lock box processing and enjoys the economy of scale.

(iv) Constant updating of records : Every customer has a credit limit. Accelerated realisation of customers remittances and almost simultaneous credit to their account, under this system, enable the customer to make optimum use of his credit limit. Ultimately it is the business which is benefited by increased sales.

(v) Increase in the availability of funds: The primary motivation for use of lock box services is increase in the availability of funds to the business. In Exhibit 7.1 four days are consumed in the mailing and internal cheque processing time (D3-D4-D5). If the funds in question are to the tune of Rs 50 lakhs and the rate of interest 10% the business will earn an interest of Rs 5479 on short-term deposits. Even if the funds are not intended for short-term deposits, they can well be used as margin money and other similar purposes.

(vi) Improved Internal Control: Since big chunk of cash is handled by outside agency, at the source of entry itself, the internal control system of the business is improved reducing the possibilities of frauds.

(b) *Cost-Benefit Analysis:* Bank charges fees for its services. The business must weigh the gains from lock box system with costs charged by the bank. Gains must include all types of savings — in opportunity costs, clerical costs and the likes. Should it find gains more than costs only then the system should be introduced.

Limitations

In this system the remittances are directly handled by the banks. The business cannot verify the amount till it is notified by bank and/or cheque is realised. It thus can take up the matter with the customer much later incurring additional time and expense. Besides this, some times too much efficiency in the realisation of cheques becomes an irritant factor for customers who loses otherwise due float to them. A successful business cannot annoy its customers. Finally, lock box system, too, because of the heavy magnitude of operation is suitable for a large organisation having battery of customers spawned over a vast geographical area.

7.5.3 Pre-Authorised Cheques

Pre-authorised cheques (PAC) is also an important method of accelerating the cash collection. In this system an arrangement is entered into among the parties involving the business, its customers and the banker. The arrangement authorises the business company to raise a demand for a predetermined amount on a predetermined date on the bank of the customer. The bank accepts the demand as if it is a mandate from the customer himself. The demand deposit instrument so raised is known as PAC. Some times the business company authorises its bank to do this job. Complete details of customers alongwith their banks and account numbers are supplied to the bank. The bank raises the PAC on the specified dates on the bank of the customer and credits the amount to the business company on the realisation of demand deposits.

The system of PAC is normally applied where the payments to be received are repetitive in nature and amount is fixed one. Examples are, insurance payments, rent payments, payments on account of loan instalments where monthly equated instalments are determined in advance. However, some times in order to overcome the limitation of variability eleven instalments are paid for a fixed amount and the balance amount is adjusted in the twelfth instalment.

The advantages of PAC are two-fold. Acceleration in receipts collection and reduction in cost. It eliminates certain activities necessary for the collection. The business need not send a reminder, thereby eliminating postal float associated with raising of invoices. Even the postal float associated with receipt of cheques from customer is saved. In case bank has been authorised to raise PAC the float associated with cheque processing by the business itself is also eliminated. PAC system has direct impact on the reduction of cost as well. Costs involved in sending notices and postage expenses are saved. Also clerical costs involved in processing mail on the receipts of cheques are reduced. Probably, the most important advantage is the certainty involved in the receipt of money adding much needed accuracy to cash inflow projections.

7.5.4 Pre-authorised Debits

Pre-authorised debit (PAD) is one of the latest techniques for the acceleration of cash inflow. It is an 'automatic system' and warrants good deal of automated infrastructure for its operation. Under this system, on a pre-determined date the bank of business company automatically debits bank of the customer with the due amount. The bank has already been authorised by the customer to honour such debits. There is no movement of any document, script or cheque. Merely a computer entry is highwayed. This "paperless" operation is better than pre-authorised cheque system in the sense that even the use of demand deposit instrument is eliminated. This results in the reduction of cost of printing of demand deposit note, banker's charges *etc.*

The advantages of this method are identical to the advantages of

PAC system; elimination of postal float, processing float and resultant saving in cost. Also, costs associated with forgotton remittances and delayed payments are reduced.

However, the customers object to this system because of its machine operated harsh approach under which they do not buy any float due to automatic transfer of funds. Exposure to computer error is also considered as a weak point.

7.5.5 Pay Order by Bank

This is a popular technique in developing countries like India. In this, instead of the cheque the business insists for payment by pay order by a bank. Pay order is a banker's cheque. In order to facilitate early clearing, the bank draws on another branch in the different city a pay order for the desired amount. Procedurally, it is presented in the same way as cheque and credit accorded through local clearing of the city. The bank charges for the issue of pay order which becomes additional cost to be borne either by customer or the business. Of course, an additional advantage is guaranteed payment since the cheque is issued by the bank.

7.5.6 Post-Dated Cheques

This is indigenous version of pre-authorised cheques. If the payments to be released have a definite amount and definite periodicity the payer sends post-dated cheques to the payee. The relevant cheques are deposited at the scheduled time. It has the benefit of reducing postal float tremendously since this float is involved only once.

7.5.7 Letter of Credit

Letter of credit has got unique features making it favourite instrument in the commercial world specially in international trade. The basic advantage is that of guaranteed payment in case the order is executed as per the terms. As an additional advantage it acts as a cash management tool also. The business can get instantaneous payment of full amount or as agreed with the customer through the bank, against delivery of despatch documents. It need not wait till the goods reach the customer. Sometimes even before the despatch of the goods the bank provides advance against the letter of credit.

7.6 DECELERATING DISBURSEMENTS

Techniques involved in slowing release of payments to suppliers is as effective an instrument of cash control as methods involved for accelerating collection of receivables. Both the techniques are concerned with reducing the cash requirements of the business. They constitute two sides of the same coin.

There are several techniques to delay the payment of account payables.

7.6.1 Not Sooner than Due

Trade credit is interest free financial accommodation provided by the supplier. Business must acquire maximum benefit out of it. If the supplier has agreed for terms of "2/20 net 40 days" it will be uneconomical to release payment after 15 days. The business will be incurring opportunity costs of five days. Considering amount involved as Rs 50 lakhs and rate of interest as 10%, the opportunity cost in this case will be Rs 6,849. However, the payment should not be delayed beyond the period of discount otherwise it will stand to lose the amount of discount resulting in more cost and outflow of cash. And if the payment is delayed beyond credit period the business is likely to lose its credibility also.

In addition to contractually due payment there are certain payments which are due statutorily *e.g.* payment on account of advance income tax, deposit of provident fund dues, dividend payments *etc.* The business will do well to release these payments during last days of the permissible period.

7.6.2 Centralisation of Disbursements

The basic objective of conservation of cash resources is to optimise its utilisation. This can well be achieved by concentrating the entire funds of the business at one place and making centralised disbursements therefrom. We have already seen the advantages of pooling of cash resources at one place under concentration banking from where the payments can be made to all the suppliers of the business. Centralised disbursement as a matter of fact, is second leg of concentration banking functioning under the overall system of cash control.

All payments, under this system, are released from the centralised disbursement account, normally operated at corporate office. The business thus achieves its objective of slowing of disbursements. With the customers scattered in far-off places, issue of cheques from corporate office will consume more postal time. Secondly, the funds can be released as per decided priorities. This covers decisions with regard to availing cash discount, getting benefits of lower prices or adhering to disbursement schedules chalked out earlier. Lastly, centralised disbursement enhances the investment value of cash reservoir available with the business. Under the decentralised payment system, the requirements of minimum balances at various places shall deprive the business to maximize its return from short-term investments. It will increase clerical costs also.

All this has made the centralised disbursements as most effective instrument for the control of cash outflow.

7.6.3 Riding the Float

Earlier, we have defined Disbursement Float as sum total of cheques issued by the business but not yet presented to the bank. If the business has issued cheques amounting to Rs 10.00 lakhs but the bank has encashed cheques worth Rs. 6 lakh only, then there exists a disbursement float of 4.00 lakhs. This float continues till the time the bank receives cheques from the suppliers bankers and debits the account of the business after making payments. A prudent finance manager makes use of this gap amount by temporarily using these funds for other purposes. This is known as 'riding the float' or 'playing the float'. Exhibit 7.1 shows that three steps are involved in the Disbursement Float. The steps are: (a) mailing time, (b) cheque processing time associated with the supplier, and (c) collection processing time with the bank.

Some of the ways of 'playing the float' are as follows:

(a) *Payment from a Remote Bank:* The float can be increased by issuing cheques from a distant bank located far away from the bank of the supplier. For example, cheques for a supplier from Cochin can be issued from a bank at Shillong. This way the float associated with the postal time as well as with that of cheque collection will be substantially increased. There are certain limitations in the use of this method. First, the practice of releasing funds from different places clashes with the principles of centralised disbursements. Secondly, with automation involving highly proficient computers, wire transfer *etc*., effectiveness of this technique has diminished.

(b) *Delayed Post Marks:* The cash discount is normally linked with the date of despatch by the business and not with the receipt of cheque by the supplier. The date of despatch is evidenced from the postmarked dates. If a business post marks a cheque on Friday and get it mailed on Monday, it is likely to get three additional days' float and enjoy discount as well. This technique, however, has the risk of losing business creditability with the supplier, if followed persistently.

(c) *Study of Encashment Pattern:* A proficient finance manager can make a study of encashment pattern of cheques issued in the past and find out general trend. A business deals with wide variety of suppliers — some of them very efficient while some others not so efficient. Their efficiency is reflected in their own cheque processing time. An analytical review can indicate the actual float which is likely to be available with the business. Likewise, it is experienced that all the employees whom the salary payments have been made do not rush to the bank immediately for encashment; some delay by a few days, lengthening the float availability.

Playing the float is a very sensitive cash control instrument and requires very cautious and deft handling by the finance manager. In this case, the attention is focussed on the balance as appearing or likely to appear in the bank and not in its own ledger account. The balance in the bank is not under the direct control of the business and warrants a close monitoring for successfully exploiting the time gap. Any miscalculation may land the business in difficulties. It may end up incurring more costs for the overdraft perforce availed due to non-availability of funds at the time of presentation of cheques or the business may find its cheques being dishonoured exposing it to all sorts of legal and commercial complications.

7.6.4 Payment Through Draft

This is yet another technique prevalent in advanced countries, particularly in U.S.A. It is used for slowing disbursements. Draft is a cheque like instrument but unlike the cheque it is drawn on the issuer instead of on a bank. Procedurally, a draft is presented to bank for collection like a cheque. The bank does not debit the account of the business on its presentation. Rather it sends it to issuer for confirmation. The business gets additional time for transferring the funds so that the draft is honoured. This results in lengthening of the float and also enables the business to keep a nominal amount in the bank till the time a draft is presented. Banks are not very enthusiastic about this practice. They have to handle draft processing and cooperate till the arrangement of funds are made by the business. They normally insist for retaining some respectable balance with them.

7.6.5 Special Disbursement Account

This is a dedicated account meant for disbursements only. Under this system, one central account is operated for catering to the requirements of a number of special disbursement accounts. As and when need arises, specific amount is transferred from central account to special disbursement account. If the central account and special disbursement account are in the same bank, then the disbursement account will have zero balance at the end of the day. It is also known as "Zero Balance Account". If the disbursement accounts are spread over a large area, there may be overdraft for one day in special disbursement accounts. Some of the benefits under this system are:

- It is excellent blending of centralised pooling of cash and decentralised disbursements.
- Dealing with only the centralised cash account is easy and convenient.
- Disbursements being decentralised, good deal of autonomy at the unit level is ensured.
- There is no requirement to maintain minimum cash at various scattered bank accounts.

— It achieves the objective of lengthening of float.

While dealing with cash management techniques a cautious approach is recommended. Some of the techniques extract speedy collections from the customers while some other slow payments to suppliers. Abrasive application of these techniques may antagonise the parties if they are deprived from enjoying float which they are otherwise entitled to. It may be wrong policy to follow. No business can flourish with disgrunted business associates. It is, therefore, imperative that these techniques should be deployed truthfully and tactfully.

QUESTIONS

1. Explain the basic concept of the cash management techniques.
2. Who are the parties to the cash management techniques?
3. Define float. Describe collection and disbursement floats.
4. What do you understand by concentration banking?
5. Explain lock box system with special reference to its merits and limitations.
6. Describe pre-authorised cheques and pre-authorised debits as techniques of cash management.
7. Explain centralisation of disbursements and special disbursement accounts as techniques engaged for slowing down the release of payments.
8. Explain the term riding the float. What are the various ways of riding the float?
9. Write short notes on:

   a) Letter of credit
   b) Not sooner than due
   c) Post-dated cheques

10. A business has an annual credit sales of Rs 30,00,000. Its purchases on credit are to the tune of Rs 18,00,000. After adopting the techniques of concentration banking and special disbursement accounts, it is successful in early collection of receivables by two days and delay of payments to suppliers by one day. The total days in an year are 360 and interest rate prevalent in market is 10%. Calculate the annual savings on account of:

    a) Acceleration of receivables
    b) Decelaration of payments

11. A company provides the following informations:

    a) Average daily collection against receivables are Rs 3,00,000.
    b) Average period of total deposit float is 6 days.
    c) The prevalent rate of interest on short term deposit is 10 %.

    The Company intends to opt for lock box system of cash management technique. A study made by it in this regard reveals that the cost-benefit of this technique will be as follows:

Benefits — saving of float by 4 days
Cost — bank's charge of Rs. 20,000/- per annum and retention of a compensating balance of Rs. 1,00,000.

Examine whether the business should go for adopting the lock box technique of cash management or not?

8

LIQUIDITY AND EFFICIENT USE OF CASH

8.1 INTRODUCTION

A business owns two types of assets — current and fixed.

Current assets like inventory and debtors are meant to be 'used up' and fixed assets like buildings and machinery are required to be 'used in' in the ordinary course of business. The former are converted into cash and the latter are amortised during a given period. Among the current assets as well, the time and cost involved in the conversion into cash is not same. Some can be readily encashed with minimum cost while some others require long time and heavy discount for encashment. This time and cost is a measure of their liquidity or nearness to cash. Liquidity, thus, can be defined as the ability of a business to convert its assets into cash incurring minimum cost and time. Every business strives to convert its current assets into cash at the first available opportunity so that cash so acquired can be used for acquisition of new such assets for quick conversion into cash again, and so on. This process of rapid generation and active utilisation of cash becomes the index of the efficiency of the business. Any flaw in this will thoroughly jeopardise the cash flow cycle of the business and the business is said to land in liquidity problems. So important is liquidity in a business that some writers have described cash management as management of liquidity for a business. They maintain that businesses often encounter liquidity problems and only those survive which surmount them successfully. We shall now examine the various facets of a liquidity problem.

What is a liquidity problem; how to recognise it; what are its symptoms; does it crop up suddenly or gradually? These are some of the questions, answers to which shall throw light on cash flow problems. A cash flow problem is symbolised by the situation of cash crunch. A business finds itself handicapped to meet its cash commitments. The reasons responsible for such a predicament can be many, and can be identified with the symptoms they generate. Like symptoms of a disease these start manifesting themselves at an early stage flashing clear warnings. Barring some cases where the onslaught of cash flow problems is sudden leading to an immediate liquidity crisis, normally it takes considerable time for these problems to grow and develop into critical stage. The situation becomes non-retrievable only if early warnings remain unattended. Indeed, lofty attitude of management is considerably responsible for throwing the business into the liquidity crisis.

8.2 SYMPTOMS OF A LIQUIDITY PROBLEM

A common symptom of liquidity problem is inability of a business to make payment to its creditors. If a business fails to release payments within the stipulated period it loses, first, the opportunity to avail cash discount, and secondly, its own credibility. If the cash crunch is persistent the business must take action to provide lubrication in the form of additional cash lest creditors petition for its bankruptcy.

Another symptom is excessive borrowing. The debt equity ratio need to be rational as per the nature of a business. High debt may lead to the business getting trapped in the mire of usuary.

Yet another symptom of looming liquidity crisis is existence of relatively low or in some cases negative working capital. Working capital is determined by reducing current liabilities from current assets. This is meant for day-to-day running of the business. Reasons of low working capital can be many - excessive payables, stock piling of obsolete and difficult-to-sell items, huge bad debts are few such instances. Alternatively, a business may be utilising suppliers credit or overdraft from bank for financing fixed assets. Whatever be the reason, one thing is certain, if the situation continues, the business is likely to suffocate and die.

Finally, over-trading is also responsible for the liquidity crisis. When a business overacts and increases its turnover too much in too little time it finds itself trapped in cobweb of cash flow problems. Turnover increases, production increases, stock increases, debtors increase but cash does not keep pace with them. The result is heavy payables to creditors, wages and even for statutory requirements like excise and taxes. Sales are increased by offering liberal credit terms and reduced profit margin but creditors may not provide identical favourable terms nor the wages and other costs can be availed on credit. The net effect is cash drought in the business. If the malady is not cured in time, the whole of cash will be drained out of the business leaving it as a lifeless body ready for burial.

8.3 LIQUIDITY IN VARIOUS SEGMENTS OF BUSINESS

Cash is an omnipresent phenomenon in the business. A business encompasses activities of all disciplines — purchase, production, personnel, marketing and finance. The origin of problem may be in any of these departments of the business but its ultimate manifestation will be in the form of a liquidity problem. Cash flows in the arteries of all these business organs. Any blockade in these arteries may lead to cardiac arrest of the business. We shall now see how cash flow is influenced by the problems in the individual segment of a business leading to liquidity crisis engulfing the whole business.

8.3.1. Purchase

Procurement policies or better known as material management play an important role in determining cash flow in a business. In construction and some manufacturing industries material cost may constitute 60% to 70% of the total cost. The motto of efficient material management is - right material in right quantity at right time for a right price. Any component of the equation if not right will affect cash flow substantially. If the material is not acquired at a right price the cost of production will go up reducing the profit margin. Cash will be effected first at the beginning in the form of excessive outflow of cash on account of high price paid, and subsequently at the end with reduced inflow of cash owing to reduction in the profit margin.

8.3.2 Production

Production covers the complete line starting with inputting of raw material, processing it and finally getting output in the form of finished product. Every stage of production line has its impact on cash flow. An inefficient inventory-turnover ratio may be the result of huge stock-piling. Blocking of funds in the unduly large stock will disturb the smooth operation of cash flow cycle warranting additional cash injection from outside sources. Higher interest burden on account of funds so raised will reduce margin of profit culminating in less cash inflow. On the other hand, repayment of principal and interest in cash will inflate cash outflow. Similarly, inefficiencies in the production process cycle shall increase production cost ultimately affecting the cash flow. Production process, in addition to material cost, has fleet of other elements of costs. These cost elements have a tendency to shoot up unless kept under a tight control. Rise in these expenses shall curtail profit and cash inflow. On the cash outflow front, the impact will be direct and visible because most of these items are of a nature which necessitate immediate cash payments.

8.3.3 Personnel and Administration

Much of the personnel and administration expenses are in the nature of fixed or semi- variable overheads. These expenses have the tendency of rising unobstrusively, eroding the profit margin silently. Being in the nature of fixed overheads cash outflow for these expenses is a commitment with the definite periodicity irrespective of the fact whether the commensurative cash inflow is generated or not. An example is excessive wage bill due to over staffing which has to be paid invariably in cash at the month end,whether there is profit or not. Similarly, administrative expenses, *e.g.,* telephone, telex, E-Mail *etc.,* can shoot up without being noticed unless these are kept under constant vigil and controlled efficiently failing which cash outflow will witness an unending increase.

8.3.4 Marketing

The success of marketing is reflected in sales. Reduction in sales has disastrous effect on the cash flows. There can be many reasons for the decline of sales. If the price is inaccurately fixed, sales are adversely affected. The cut throat competition in the market necessitates fixation of competitive price. An over-priced product will face reduction in turn-over followed by possible complete extinction from the market. Lower sales reduce the quantum of contribution (Contribution is the difference between sales and variable cost) with the result even recovery of fixed overheads becomes difficult. Profit margin is reduced and so is cash inflow. Reduction of sales will, as it is, truncate inflow of cash from receipts accruing from sales. The end-result of all this will be liquidity crisis.

8.3.5 Finance

Finally, the management of finance which covers cash management as well, has a decisive role in liquidity issue. Financial management covers all issues concerning finance, capital structure, investment decisions, fixed assets, working capital management, *etc.* For example, a business is expected to have proper capital gearing reflected in an appropriate debt equity ratio. A distorted structure, *e.g.,* heavy debt will increase interest and resultant cash outflow. Similarly, heavy sinking of funds in fixed assets will disturb parity between fixed capital and floating capital causing avoidable cash scarcity in the business. Besides, inefficient working capital management too can distort the *inter se* relationship of cash and other current assets resulting in unduly blocking of large funds in debtors, inventories *etc.,* ultimately forcing business to pump more cash at a high cost.

From above discussion, it is clear that the problems may crop up in any of business segments but once it gets mildewed it becomes a liquidity problem. For a successful business efficient management of all of its segments is imperative. Inefficient handling of one segment will have a chain effect on all other segments ultimately adversely affecting its liquidity. An effective and efficient overall management of a business alone can insulate it from cash flow crisis.

8.4 MEASUREMENT OF LIQUIDITY

The following measures are commonly adopted to measure the liquidity strength of a business.

8.4.1 Current Ratio

This is the most popular method of measuring the liquidity of a business. It is the ratio of total current assets to current liabilities and is calculated as:-

$$\text{Current ratio} = \frac{\text{Current assets}}{\text{Current liabilities}}$$

Current assets as explained in the introductory section of the chapter are those assets which are consumed in ordinary course of business. These are to be converted into cash within a short period of time, normally, not exceeding one year and include cash and bank balance, cash equivalent (short-term investments), inventory, debtors and pre-paid expenses. The current liabilities represent all obligations maturing within a year. These include trade creditors, bank credit, taxation provisions, dividend payable and outstanding expenses. Exhibit 8.1 shows simplified balance sheets of two companies for calculation of current ratio of the individual companies.

Exhibit 8.1.

BALANCE SHEET AS AT March 31, 1995

	ABC Company (Rs)	XYZ Company (Rs)
Share Capital	2,00,000	2,00,000
Reserves	75,000	50,000
Trade creditors	20,000	65,000
Outstanding expenses	4,000	15,000
Provision for dividend	10,000	30,000
Provision for taxation	26,000	50,000
	3,35,000	4,10,000
Fixed assets	1,10,000	1,30,000
Inventory	20,000	65,000
Trade debtors	75,000	1,65,000
Pre-paid expenses	5,000	10,000
Short-term investments	40,000	15,000
Cash & bank balance	85,000	25,000
	3,35,000	4,10,000

The Current Ratios of both ABC and XYZ Companies shall be:

	ABC Company	XYZ Company
Current Ratio:	$\frac{\text{Rs. } 2,25,000}{\text{Rs. } 60,000}$ = 3.75:1	$\frac{\text{Rs. } 2,80,000}{\text{Rs. } 1,60,000}$ = 1.75:1

The ABC Company has a better ratio of 3.75 as compared to XYZ Company which has a ratio of 1.75 though the total current assets of the latter are more in absolute terms. But it is the relative strength of the current assets vis-a-vis current liabilities which as measured by current ratio, is important as compared to absolute figures of current assets or current liabilities. As a conventional rule, a current ratio of 2:1 (current assets twice the current liabilities) is considered a satisfactory ratio. The Company XYZ does not qualify this test and, therefore, can be said to have lesser safety margin for its creditors. The higher the ratio better the cushion. However, this standard of 2:1 cannot be applied universally. Much depends upon the components going into current assets and liabilities. A company having heavy current assets mainly consisting of difficult-to-sell inventory or difficult-to-realise-debtors may find difficulties in meeting its obligations towards current liabilities though ratio is more than 2:1. Further, current ratio does not throw light on efficient usages of cash within the framework of current assets. We shall study this in a later section related to efficient usage of cash. The current ratio, thus, is a 'quantitative' rather than 'qualitative' index of liquidity.

8.4.2 Quick Ratio

This ratio is also known as "acid test" ratio. It is a refinement over current ratio and attempts to cope with inadequacies of current ratio. Current ratio considers all the components comprising current assets on the 'identical' footing so far as their convertibility into cash is concerned; which is not so. The time and cost involved in converting inventory into cash is certainly much more than converting cash equivalents (short-term investments) into cash. Quick ratio thus considers only those assets which can be readily and easily converted into cash to meet the current liabilities. The ratio is expressed as

$$\text{Quick ratio} = \frac{\text{Quick assets}}{\text{Current liabilities}}$$

Quick assets consist of cash, cash equivalents (short-term investments) and trade debtors. Inventories and prepaid expenses are not considered. Inventories are excluded because it takes much time to convert raw material into work-in-progress and then into finished product to be sold in the market. Even, inventory of finished products is not readily saleable and requires much time and effort before it can be exchanged into cash. Prepaid expenses are excluded because they cannot be converted into cash. Referring to Exhibit 8.2., we find that quick ratio of ABC Company and XYZ Company are:

Exhibit 8.2.

	ABC Company	XYZ Company
Quick Ratio	$\frac{\text{Rs. } 2,00,000}{\text{Rs. } 60,000}$ 3.33:1	$\frac{\text{Rs. } 2,05,000}{\text{Rs. } 1,60,000}$ 1.28:1

The quick ratio of ABC Company is 2.5 times more than that of XYZ Company. Conventionally the quick ratio of 1:1 is considered satisfactory as a company having, such ratio is capable of meeting all current claims. A very high ratio like that of ABC Company indicates a highly liquid position of the company. But it appears that the company is not very much concerned with high cost it is incurring to acquire such a highly liquid state. Certainly its cash resources do not seem to be properly exploited. We shall study this aspect later under efficient usage of cash.

8.4.3 Defensive-Interval Ratio

The current and acid test ratios provide information regarding ability of a business to meet its current liabilities which have already been obligated. The liquidity strength should also be measured by gauging the ability of a business to meet the projected daily expenditure from its operations. The defensive interval ratio provides such a measure by establishing the relationship between quick assets and the projected daily cash requirements. The ratio is calculated as follows:

$$\text{Defensive-interval ratio} = \frac{\text{Quick assets}}{\text{Projected daily cash requirements}}$$

Projected daily cash requirements are computed as:

$$\frac{\text{Projected cash operating expenditure}}{\text{Number of days in a year}}$$

Projected cash operating expenditure is determined by taking into consideration past actuals and future trends. It includes cost of goods sold and all selling, administrative and other miscellaneous expenses. It is pertinent to note that only those expenses which are payable in cash are considered. Thus, depreciation though an important element of cost of goods sold is not considered in the compilation of projected cash operating expenditure. Quick assets, as explained above, include current assets excluding inventory and prepaid expenses.

Defensive-interval ratio measures in terms of number of days, the quick assets of the business can enable it to operate without resorting to future revenue. We explain this by an illustration.

The projected cash operating expenditure of a business for the next year is Rs 5,40,000. Its quick assets amount to Rs 90,000. The defensive-interval ratio is:

$$\text{Projected daily cash requirements} = \frac{\text{Rs.}5{,}40{,}000}{360*} = \text{Rs. } 1{,}500.00$$

$$\text{Difensive-interval ratio} = \frac{90{,}000}{1{,}500} = 60 \text{ days}$$

---

*It is usual to consider number of days in a year as 360.

The defensive-interval of 60 days means that the business has liquid assets which are sufficient to meet its operating cash requirements for 60 days without resorting to next year's revenues. The higher ratio will indicate a better cash cushion available to the business and to that extent reflect the safety margin in determining its ability to meet its basic operational obligations.

8.4.4 Debtors Turnover Ratio

This ratio determines the velocity of debtors i.e. number of times on an average the debtors turn over in an year. This is found by dividing credit sales by average debtors.

$$\text{Debtor turnover} = \frac{\text{Credit sales}}{\text{Average debtors}}$$

Higher the ratio better it is. It shows the speedy collection of receivables. This ratio is explained in detail in Chapter 9 relating to Management of Receivables.

8.4.5 Inventory Turnover Ratio

This ratio is computed by dividing cost of goods sold by average inventory. This way the velocity of average inventory vis-a-vis cost of goods sold is determined. The ratio is,

$$\text{Inventory turnover} = \frac{\text{Cost of goods sold}}{\text{Average inventory}}$$

A low ratio is a pointer towards stock piling of difficult-to-sell items, whereas a high ratio is indicative of fast selling items.

The ratio is explained in detail in Chapter 10 relating to Inventory Management.

8.5 EFFICIENT USAGE OF CASH

Liquidity does not mean over stocking of cash. Be it so maintaining liquidity will impose extra burden on the business in view of opportunity cost inherent in carrying excess cash. Liquidity aims at ensuring availability of cash as and when it is needed by the business. This is dependent on the two interconnected factors. One, conversion of convertible assets with minimum cost and time, and second, efficient usage of cash. We have already discussed the first in the early section of the chapter and shall also study in detail in ensuing chapters pertaining to management of receivables, and inventory. We examine below role of efficient usage of cash in maintaining liquidity and overall cash management.

The cardinal principle of prudent cash management is holding of optimum cash in the business - neither more nor less. Both cash surpluses and cash deficits have their own set of costs as explained in Chapter 2. It, thus, becomes a matter of paramount importance that the cash maintained in the business is used most effectively and efficiently. This can be ensured by measuring the efficiency of cash usage and taking necessary corrective measures.

8.6 MEASURING THE EFFICIENCY OF CASH USAGE

A few important ratios which help to measure the efficiency of cash usage are explained below:

8.6.1 Cash in Current Assets

The two ratios, current ratio and acid test ratio, outlined in the preceding paragraphs measure the short-term liquidity of a company but these do not throw any light on the quantum of optimum cash required by a business. At best, these ratios indicate an overall picture of the company's current liquidity alongwith its short-term solvency. A current ratio of 3:1 may indicate somewhat excess liquidity. But an astute cash manager wants to know the further details of this excess so as to analyse the components responsible for the excess. He is primarily concerned to figure the component of cash balance in the excess. This can be done by determining first the optimum cash needed to run business operations and then by comparing it with the actual cash balance. The ratio of the cash balance to that of total current assets provides necessary guide to assess the likely cash balance requirements of a business on a broad basis as against the more detailed cash budgets. The ratio is expressed as:

$$\text{Cash in current assets} = \frac{\text{Cash balance}}{\text{Current assets}} \times 100$$

Suppose a Company has cash balance of Rs 50,000 and total current assets of Rs 5,00,000, then its ratio of cash to total current assets is 10%. This ratio when compared with the previous year's ratio can give an indication of the efficiency with which the cash has been used in the operation of the business. Similar comparisons can be made with the ratios of other units in the same industry. If it transpires that ratio should be in the range of 6% to 8%, the company will have to do further analysis to know the basic reasons of high ratio. It is possible that suppliers have curtailed the credit to the company due to late payments or company's nonchalant attitude towards cash management has resulted in the stockpiling of idle cash. The ratio, thus, provides an indication of potential problems; further probe is required to determine the cause and corrective action. Broadly, a company can take three steps to improve the ratio. First, compare the ratio with those of the previous years. Secondly, compare the same with that of other units in the same industry. The ratios of the other firms in the same industry shall provide some guide as to what the efficient ratio is under the prevalent circumstances. Thirdly, experiments can be made for testing the effects of reduction in cash balances on the business operations. This way the company will be successful in finding out minimum cash balance required for running the operations. In Exhibit 8.1., we observe that ABC Company has current assets valuing Rs 2,25,000 while those of XYZ Company stands at Rs 2,80,000. The cash balances including cash equivalents (short term investments) of these two companies are Rs 1,25,000 and Rs 40,000, respectively. The cash in current assets of the companies, therefore, is:-

	ABC Company	XYZ Company
Cash in current assets	$\dfrac{1,25,000 \times 100}{2,25,000}$	$\dfrac{40,000 \times 100}{2,80,000}$
	= 55%	= 14%

The cash represents 55% of total current assets in the case of ABC Company and 14% for XYZ Company. It may be recalled that current ratios of the companies were 3.75 and 1.75, respectively. Even quick ratio of 3.33 of ABC Company was much higher than 1.28 of XYZ Company. But so far as efficiency of cash usage is concerned, it is clear that XYZ Company though less liquid than ABC Company is successful in making efficient usage of cash whereas ABC Company is burdened with gross misuse of cash.

Like all other ratios, this ratio also has its own limitations. The ratio considers in its computations cash balance and balance sheet values of current assets as on a particular day. Excessive cash on a day need not necessarily indicate irresponsible stockpiling of idle cash. Cash might have been accumulated to meet a specific need, such as purchase of equipment or controlling shares of another company. Also, this ratio is related to all current assets. Changes in the level of ratio may not conclusively prove that anything has gone wrong with cash. The change may be owing to the changes in the values of other current assets. A change in inventory without corresponding change in the level of cash will decrease the ratio indicating an efficient use of cash. This will be misleading if the inventory has increased due to reduction in sale. It is, therefore, necessary that cause of change is identified before any conclusion is drawn. Subject to these limitations, this ratio reveals the efficiency of cash usage based on the gross working capital (total current assets) of the company.

8.6.2. Cash Turnover to Sales

Another important ratio to measure the efficiency of the cash usage is ratio of volume of sales in a period to the opening cash balance of that period. This ratio measures velocity of cash balance in terms of sales. The ratio is expressed as:

$$\text{Turnover of cash in sales} = \frac{\text{Sales for a period}}{\text{Initial cash balance}}$$

This ratio represents the number of times the initial cash balance is turned over in terms of sales effected during a period. For a given level of sales a high rate of turnover will indicate a small cash balance which implies an effective usage of cash. For example if sales of a particular period is Rs 20,00,000 and initial cash balance Rs 2,00,000, the velocity of cash is 10 times. However, if the sale continues to be Rs 20,00,000 but the initial cash balance is reduced to Rs 1,50,000, the velocity of cash will increase to 13 times.

A company which can increase the velocity of cash passing through its operations can expand its sales without needing extra cash. Alternatively, it can decrease the amount of cash in hand if sales are not growing. In both the cases profits are increased. It may possibly increase its production and sales without increasing its working capital resulting in reduction of costs and increase of profit. In the above example by increasing velocity from 10 times to 13 times, the company has saved Rs 50,000 alongwith the opportunity costs associated with it. Efficient usage of cash is explained by another example:

	Company A	Company B
Sales for period	Rs 4,00,000	Rs 3,25,000
Initial Cash Balance	Rs 45,000	Rs 20,000
Cash velocity	8.88	16.25

Assuming that the companies are in the same discipline having almost identical product mix, the figures clearly show that company B is more efficiently managed from cash point of view. Its turnover is lower by less than a quarter than that of Company A but it is managing with less than half the cash required by Company A to run its business operations. Once again, there is no universal standard with which to measure the turnover of cash in sales. Each Company has to determine its own ratio by examining its historical records and comparing it with the industry average.

This ratio too has its own limitations and should be relied upon after due analysis of reasons of variations. A higher velocity cash turnover ratio can occur because of low cash balance. This low cash balance may not be result of efficient cash arrangement but due to liquidity crisis - a product of inefficient cash management. It will, therefore, be dangerous to infer conclusion without going into details.

8.6.3 Cash Turnover in Total Funds

Another important ratio to test the efficiency of cash management is the ratio of initial cash balance to the total fund flow during a particular period, say, an year. It measures the ratio of turnover of cash in the total fund flow movement during a given period. The ratio is expressed as:

$$\text{Cash turnover in total funds} = \frac{\text{Total fund flow}}{\text{Initial cash balance}}$$

Initial cash balance refers to the cash available in the beginning of the period whereas total fund flow is the aggregate of the sources and uses of funds during the period. This ratio can be explained by a simple example illustrated below:

Exhibit 8.3

ABC & COMPANY LTD.

	Balance Sheet as at		Fund flow movement	
	31-03-1994	31-03-1995	Sources	Uses
Share Capital	8,00,000	10,00,000	2,00,000	
Reserves	2,25,000	3,25,000	1,00,000	
Loans	3,00,000	4,00,000	1,00,000	
Current liabilities	2,00,000	2,75,000	75,000	
	15,25,000	20,00,000		
Fixed assets	9,00,000	12,00,000		3,00,000
Stock	2,50,000	3,00,000		50,000
Debtors	2,75,000	3,50,000		75,000
Bank	1,00,000	1,50,000		50,000
	15,25,000	20,00,000	4,75,000	4,75,000

In the example given above the total fund flow movement during 1994-95 is sum total of both sources and uses of funds, *i.e.,* Rs 4,75,000 + Rs 4,75,000 = Rs 9,50,000. The initial cash balance is Rs 1,00,000. Therefore, the rate of turnover of cash during the year is,

$$\frac{9,50,000}{1,00,000} = 9.5 \text{ times}$$

Since the sources and uses of funds cover the entire activities of a business, this ratio can be used to gear the level of cash balance to the company's total operations. The ratio will throw light on the efficiency with which cash has been utilised in the total movement of funds. In case initial cash balance remains same but inventory increases, say, by Rs 1,00,000 with a corresponding increase in current liabilities, the ratio will increase to 11.5 times indicating thereby better utilisation of cash resources. Again to gauge the appropriateness of the ratio, comparison should be made with the other units of the industry. And if the ratio is considered satisfactory, then the projected ratio of cash velocity to total funds may be taken into acccount while drawing up cash budget for the future period..

8.7 RATIOS OF OPERATING CASH FLOW

The ratios discussed above measure the efficiency of overall cash management. We now discuss in more details some ratios related to operating cash flow. Operating cash flow plays a dominant role in the overall cash flow movement of a business. It is the major source of cash inflow. In Chapter 6, we dealt with this subject in detail. To recapitulate, operating cash flow is cash generated in a business through operating activities. It can be measured by making suitable adjustments in the profit earned during a period. The profit which is calculated based on the accrual system of accounting is adjusted to arrive at the actual figure of cash inflow generated on account of profit so computed.

Operating cash flow constitutes an important part of total cash movement occasioned during a period. Profit, the source of operating cash flow, is a product of multiple factors and strictly does not fall under the domain of cash management. But the quantum of cash generation through profit is, to a great extent, result of efficient cash management. Operating cash flow is directly influenced by the efficiency of cash flow cycle which, in turn, is key to the efficient cash management as explained in detail in Chapter 2. Below we discuss a few ratios concerning operating cash flow as a part of efficient cash management.

8.7.1 Operating Cash Flow to Sales

This ratio is expressed as:

$$\frac{\text{Operating cash flow} \times 100}{\text{Sales}}$$

The ratio establishes the relationship between operating cash flow and sales. A high ratio indicates that substantial portion of sales is on cash basis which is a sign of sound cash management. A low ratio may, on the other hand, warrant detailed analysis.It is possible that the business has disproportionately high figure of credit sales and is indulging in overtrading.

8.7.2 Operating Cash Flow to Capital Employed

The ratio is expressed as follows:

$$\frac{\text{Operating Cash Flow}}{\text{Capital Employed}} \times 100$$

This ratio portrays the return which a company gets in the form of additional cash from its operating activities by deploying certain amount of capital in the business. It measures the efficiency with which capital is utilised to earn cash profit, and to that extent is index of the prudent cash management.

8.7.3 Operating Cash Flow to Shares

Another ratio measures the operating cash flow vis-a-vis number of shares in a company. This ratio is calculated as:

$$\frac{\text{Operating Cash Flow}}{\text{Number of Shares}}$$

This ratio measures operating cash flow per share. The ratio on its own may not be useful for drawing any inference. It needs to be compared with the other units of the industry provided the face values of the shares of these units are identical. A higher ratio indicates better utilisation of cash resources.

8.7.4 Operating Cash Flow to Employees

Yet another ratio establishes the relationship between operational cash flow and number of employees. The formula for this ratio is:

$$\frac{\text{Operating Cash Flow}}{\text{Number of Employees}}$$

This ratio measures the level of operating cash flow generated by a set of employees. The ratio can be considered as high or low when compared with other units of the industry.

8.7.5 Debt Affordability Ratio

This ratio throws light on the capacity of the company to service its fixed interest on borrowings in terms of operating cash flow. This ratio is known as Debt Affordability Ratio and is expressed as:

$$\text{Debt affordability ratio} = \frac{\text{Operating cash inflow}}{\text{Financial cash outflow}}$$

Where operating cash inflow is operating cash flow before any charge on account of interest and financing, financial cash outflow is the amount of interest payments on the long-term loans. The ratio shows how many times the interest charges are covered by operating cash flow. From the point of creditors larger the coverage greater the capacity of the company to meet its obligations out of cash generated from the operating activities. If the ratio is abnormally low the company will have to borrow money to meet its commitments of payment of interest to creditors.

We observed that operating cash flow is generated through profit; and profit, to a great extent, is dependent on the aggressive sales programme, among other things. But sales do not bring instantaneous cash. It gets converted into receivables which in turn are converted into cash after some time lag. In the meantime, in order to continue production cycle new materials are to be procured. There is, therefore, a need for working capital to run the business.

Working capital management has a direct bearing on the operating cash flow generations. An efficient working capital management will result in higher generation of cash flow. Proficiency in working capital management can be achieved by managing all its components in most effective manner. In the ensuing chapters, we deal with the most important components of working capital—Management of Receivable and Inventory Management.

QUESTIONS

1. Define Liquidity. Describe its importance in a business.
2. What are the symptoms of a liquidity problem?
3. How is liquidity position effected by the activities of the various departments of a business?
4. Explain current ratio as an instrument of measuring liquidity.
5. Explain defensive interval ratio.
6. Describe the cash in current assets ratio as a tool to measure the efficient usage of cash.
7. How does cash turnover in sales help to measure efficient usage of cash?
8. Explain the cash turnover in total funds ratio for gauging the efficiency of cash usage in a business.
9. Write short notes on:

   (a) Quick ratio
   (b) Operating cash flow to sales ratio
   (c) Operating cash flow to capital employed ratio

10. The current assets and current liabilities of ABC are Rs. 20 lakhs and

Rs. 10 lakhs respectively as on date. It intends to incur the following transactions. Calculate the impact of each transaction individually and also total impact of all the transactions on the current ratio of the company.

(a) A new machinery costing to Rs.7 lakhs is purchased on cash basis.

(b) A term loan of Rs.15 lakhs for a period of 5 years is obtained from a financial institution to purchase an equipment of equivalent amount. A bank guarantee of Rs. 2 lakhs is provided to the financial institution. The bank insists for 100% margin for the issue of bank guarantee.

(c) A dividend of Rs. 3 lakhs is paid. Tax deducted at source on this, amounts to Rs. 0.60 lakhs.

(d) Inventory worth Rs. 6 lakhs is purchased against which a bank finance of Rs. 4 lakhs is obtained.

11. A summary balance sheet of XYZ & Co is as follows:

Balance Sheet as at March 31, 1996

	Rs.		Rs.
Share Capital	500000	Fixed assets	275000
Reserves	187500	Stock	150000
Creditors	60000	Debtors	187500
Provision for dividend	25000	Prepaid expenses	12500
Provision for taxation	65000	Cash & bank balance	212500
	837500		837500

The Company estimates that its cash operating expenditure for the next year shall be Rs. 27,00,000

Calculate the following rate of —

(a) Current ratio
(b) Quick ratio
(c) Defensive-interval ratio
(d) Cash in current assets ratio

12. The Balance Sheet of XYZ & Co. are as follows:

Balance sheet

	As at March 31,1995	As at March 31,1996
	Rs.	Rs.
Share Capital	7,00,000	10,00,000
Reserves	3,37,500	4,87,500
Debentures	3,00,000	4,50,000
Term loan	1,50,000	1,50,000
Outstanding expenses	1,12,500	1,68,750
Sundry creditors	1,87,500	2,43,750
	17,87,500	25,00,000
Fixed assets	8,50,000	13,00,000
Inventory	3,75,000	4,50,000

Prepaid expenses	1,12,500	1,25,000
Debtors	3,00,000	4,00,000
Short term investments	60,000	70,000
Cash	90,000	1,55,000
	17,87,500	25,00,000

Additional information provided by the company is as follows:

(a) Sales for the year 1995-96 is Rs. 27,00,000

(b) Operating cash flow during the year 1995-96 is Rs 2,00,000

You are required to calculate:

(i) Current ratio

(ii) Quick ratio

(iii) Debtors turnover ratio

(iv) Inventory turnover ratio

(v) Cash turnover to sales ratio

(vi) Cash turnover to total funds ratio

(vii) Operating cash flow to capital employed ratio.

9

MANAGEMENT OF RECEIVABLES

9.1 INTRODUCTION

Sales on credit is an inevitable necessity in the business world of today. No business can exist without selling the products on credit. The basic difference between credit sales and cash sales is the time gap in the receipt of cash. The customer starts enjoying the goods immediately on receipt but makes payment after the credit period. As a matter of fact it implies utilisation of sellers cash by the buyers; a kind of interest-free loan to customers. From the point of view of business, selling on credit constitutes an investment. The business invests money in credit sales to earn more money by increasing sales. An investment is always guided by the cost and benefit analysis so as to maximise return. The return on investment is maximum when the amount of investment is optimal and the optimal point is determined through cost and benefit analysis.

9.2 COST AND BENEFIT ANALYSIS

The primary objective of investment in trade debt is to increase profit by expanding sales. It is a marketing tool, rather a marketing force to attract new customers and retain old customers. By constantly increasing its sale and profit the business carves out a bigger niche in the market and elevates its status among the competitors. As a corollary to it, higher level of operations bring economies of scales. The business can face market forces of inflation and recession with greater confidence. But a note of caution; it is possible that an over-zealous business may get itself trapped in the whirl of overtrading. The sale may increase tremendously; the profit also follows but the cash flow does not match with the expansionary pace. In such an eventuality the business will continue to generate funds and keep on financing credit sales till it has no cash to meet its own liabilities. Therefore, it is necessary that credit sales should be financed upto an optimum level only. Such a level is determined by comparing benefits of the additional credit sales with the increase in cost owing to such incremental sales. A trade-off between costs and benefits will determine the optimum level. We have studied the benefits of credit sales above. Now we study various kinds of costs which have to be incurred to affect sales on credit.

(a) *Collection Costs:* First in the list is Collection Costs. A business has to engage additional staff for the management of receivables. Broader the canvas of trade debt, higher the cost of collection. The customers have to be constantly chased to ensure receipt of money as per schedule. Reminders have to be sent, telephone calls to be made, their queries, if any, have to be attended. In addition to these, lot of credit information is required to be gathered from internal and external sources.

(b) *Capital Costs:* The production and selling costs can be described as capital costs pertaining to credit sales. Funds are required for the purchase of materials, payment of wages, incurring of overheads immediately, whereas receipts against them are deferred till collection from debtors. It is not an uncommon phenomena for a business to raise overdraft so as to finance credit sales. Even if a business finances credit sales out of its own generated funds it bears costs in the form of opportunity costs. It could have invested these funds more profitably elsewhere.

(c) *Delinquency Costs:* Another kind of costs are described as delinquency costs. In a business there is always a category of customers who do not settle their accounts despite reminders. Lot of prodding is required to persuade them to pay. Repeated letters, telexes, faxes are sent. It is then followed by personal contacts. Costs incurred on these accounts are known as delinquency costs.

(d) *Default Costs:* Finally, the default costs. Cash sales are riskless. Credit sales on, the other hand, have got an element of futurity and future always have an inherent risk in it. In the credit sales this risk is in the form of bad debts. A liberal credit policy will increase sales, profit and also instances of bad debts. A bad debt is known as default cost. It constitutes a heavy drain on the cash flow of a business since it encompasses all types of costs; capital costs, collection costs and delinquency costs.

As stated above, optimum level of credit sales is determined by a trade-off between benefits and costs. It is pertinent to note that this trade-off should be with regard to incremental benefits and costs only, *i.e.,* costs and benefits accruing from additional sales. The optimal level is that point where profit generated by additonal investment in credit sales matches with the additional cost incurred because of such credit sales. Some scholars, however, opine that matching of such incremental profit should be done with the rate of return which a business expects on its funds rather than with additional cost of incremental sale.

9.3 CREDIT POLICY AND CASH FLOW

The credit policy followed by a business is crucial to its cash flow. A liberal or loose credit policy is expansionary in nature. It increases sales and profit but require relatively more cash to be tied up with the customers for a longer period. The ultimate effect is deceleration in the cash inflow. On the other hand, consumption of cash is immediate. A business is required to make payments to suppliers for the additional procurement of materials and disbursement of wages resulting in acceleration of cash outflow. The time gap between the sale of goods and receipt of cash increases, necessitating additional pumping of cash so that cash continues to flow smoothly in its orbital track. We have studied the circular flow of cash in Chapter 2. Another impact is depletion of cash from the cash flow movement due to bad debts. However, on the positive side, volume of cash running in the operating cycle increases due to increase in volume of sales.

A stringent and tight credit policy restricts trade debts to the limited few who have been screened well. It shortens the 'time gap' and there is lesser evaporation of cash due to bad debts. But the cash flow volume remains at low ebb due to lesser sale and fewer customers. Operational level of business remains at a lower plateau.

Let us now see determinant elements of a credit policy.

9.4 ELEMENTS OF CREDIT POLICY

There are three elements of a credit policy — Credit standards, credit terms and collection policies.

9.4.1 Credit Standards

It refers to the laid down criteria permitting sales on credit. Credit standards can be liberal or tight. Liberal standards shall expand sales. More cash will be required for incremental production and administrative costs. Increased cash outflow will also be there to meet additional collection costs and delinquency costs. Instances of bad debts shall be more. Average collection period may also swell because less creditworthy customers may get entry in the business who are habitual in delaying payments and unhappily old customers may also follow suit. The *inter se* relationship of cash and sundry debtors may be adversely affected. Exactly the opposite happens when credit standards are tightened. It is necessary that the standards should be fixed after rational judgement based on costs and benefits analysis as explained earlier.

9.4.2 Credit Terms

These refer to the terms and conditions in respect of payments which are agreed with the customers as a part of commercial deal. The two important components of credit terms are credit period and the cash discount.

We have already studied credit terms and cash discount in Chapter 5. To recapitulate briefly,these terms are expressed in an equation covering credit period, rate of cash discount and discount period. The equation runs as "2/15 net 40". This implies that permitted credit period is 40 days but if a customer pays by 15th day, he becomes entitled to 2% discount.

The credit terms shall depend on many factors, internal and external. Externally, prevalent conditions in the economy, conventions followed in an industry, ferocity of competition are some important factors. Internally, the business has to weigh the cost of effecting incremental sale with the expected profit generated therefrom.

Credit terms have a close and direct bearing on the cash flow. For instance, increased credit period will block the cash for more number of days. Impact of cash discount on the cash inflow is quite interesting. It decreases volume of cash inflows due to reduced collections but increases the speed of cash inflow through accelerated collections.

The extent to which credit standards and credit terms can be liberalised is dependent on the cost and benefit analysis arising from increased profits and expenditures due to enhancement in the sales volume. This can be illustrated in Exhibit 9.1.

Exhibit 9.1

CREDIT POLICY AND SALES

A business manufacturing toys provides following information with regard to sales in the year 1995-96.

Sales	3000 toys
Selling price	Rs. 20 per toy
Variable cost	Rs. 14 per toy
Operating margin	Rs. 2 per toy
Credit period	36 days

A study made by the business shows that in case it extends the credit period to 45 days, it is likely to have an increase of 20% in the sales. Presuming that the fixed costs remain unchanged, determine whether the business should adopt relaxed credit policy if the required rate of return is 20%.

(Rupees)

	1995-96	Proposed	Variation
Sales	6,00,000	7,20,000	1,20,000
Variable costs	4,20,000	5,04,000	84,000
Fixed costs	1,20,000	1,20,000	—
Total operating costs	5,40,000	6,24,000	84,000

Cost of investment in receivables	10,800	15,600	4,800
Total cost	5,50,800	6,39,600	88,800
Profit	49,200	80,400	31,200
	6,00,000	7,20,000	1,20,000

Working notes:	1995-96	Proposed
Turnover of Accounts Receivable	360/36=10	360/45=8
Total cost of sales	5,40,000	6,24,000
Average investment in sales	5,40,000/10 = 54,000	6,24,000/8 = 78,000
Cost of Investments	54,000× 0.20 = 10,800	78,000× 0.20 = 15,600
Cost of additional investments	15,600–10,800	= 4,800.

In the above example the business can earn Rs.31,200 by incurring an additional cost of investment of Rs.4,800. The business should therefore relax its credit policy.

9.4.3 Collection Policies

A business should have a rational policy for collection of receivables. Collection policy can be tight or liberal. A tight policy ensures better collection, fewer instances of bad debts but high collection costs. It may, however, antagonise the customers and some of them may switch to other competitors. A liberal collection policy will have opposite effect. It may delay the inflow of cash from collections. Number of slow payers and non-payers may increase but collection costs shall reduce. Of course, it acts as a magnet for enrolling new customers. A business, therefore, will have to strike a balance between cost and benefits of collection policy which it intends to follow.

Second aspect of collection policy is a follow up methodology having an orderly and sequential procedure. On the expiry of credit period a polite letter along with statement should be sent. This must be followed by a not-too-polite reminder. In the absence of any communication from the customer a stern letter, fax, telex should be despatched. Telephone call can be made. If still no response is received, personal representative should call on the customer. Finally, possibility of legal action should be considered. By and large, efforts should be made to settle the issue without any legal recourse. It is time-consuming and expensive. In any case, litigation should be avoided with permanent and established customers.

9.5 CREDIT INVESTIGATION

Extension of credit is an important and sensitive issue. Credit cannot be accorded in a blanket manner. Nor a business can afford to be too choosy in the extension of credit. It has to adopt the policy of selectivity. A proper selection can be made on the basis of an effective investigation before enlisting a customer for the extension of credit. For such an investigation it is imperative that the relevant information is collected from the various sources. Some of the sources are as follows:

9.5.1 Financial Statements

Published accounts contain plethora of information about companies. Such information is certified by the auditors and can therefore be relied upon. A business can extract the information required for the determination of credit-worthiness of a customer from such published accounts. Normally, the information pertains to profitability, liquidity and solvency of the company. Auditor's comments in the balance sheet can also provide further insight to the real position of a company.

9.5.2 Bank References

A common prevalent practice in developed countries is of getting bank reference in respect of customers to whom credit is to be extended. A bank may not supply information unless his own client, i.e., the customer makes a request. Alternatively, the information may be supplied by a customer's bank to the bank of the business requiring such information. Sometimes, the banks are evasive in replies and whatever they state is couched in not very transparent phrases. But even if it gives a good certificate it cannot be construed as a magna carta about the credit-worthiness of a company. In any case, it cannot guarantee that the customer will pay his bills at the scheduled time.

9.5.3 Other References

The customers can be requested to name the companies with which it has current dealings. Such companies can be approached by the business to get the desired information. It is necessary that such referees should be of repute.

9.5.4 Credit Bureaus

In developed countries there exist specialised agencies which can provide information with regard to various customers. The information so provided will be accurate and unbiased.

Equipped with such information a business can make its own judgement and fix credit limits for individual customers. The credit limit is invariably subject to periodical review and may be revised upward or downward depending upon the new facts brought into notice.

9.6 CREDIT ANALYSIS

Another important aspect of receivables management is credit analysis. It provides details of ageing of debts. Broadly, debts can be categorised into three categories.

9.6.1 Undue Debts

These are debts which have come into existence but have not become due contractually. If a customer is required to make payment 30 days after receipt of goods he becomes a debtor, the day, goods are received by him. But the amount will not become due till the expiry of 30 days.

9.6.2 Due Debts

These cover debts which have become due as per the terms and conditions of the mutually agreed contract. In the above referred case, debts which remain unpaid from 31st day onward shall be considered as due debts.

9.6.3 Overdue Debts

These are the debts which have remained unsettled despite the fact that a long period has elapsed after the due date.

Once such an analysis is made, thrust should be for recovery of overdue and due debts in the same order. A regular and periodical analysis will ensure recovery from all the debtors. No debtors can escape attention. It is better not to touch undue debts, because first, it is uncontractual and secondly it may give wrong signal to the customers. Of course, when there is a crisis such issues can be mutually talked and sorted out.

Both credit investigation and analysis have great impact on the inflow of cash. Credit investigation assists in the prevention of cashflow problems because credit is extended to credit worthy customers who are expected to make payment in time and also there are least chances of bad debts. Credit analysis assists in solving the cashflow problems by ensuring the inflow of cash from debt collections as and when it is due.

9.7 GENERAL FACTORS

There are some other general factors which should also be given due recognition in the mangement of receivables.

(a) The system in vogue should ensure raising of bills/invoices immediately at the completion of a transaction. When this is not possible invoices must be despatched alongwith despatch of goods or promptly thereafter. Slow or sloppy letter work breeds delays.

(b) Invoices should be prepared absolutely as per agreement. Inaccuracy if pointed out must be attended immediately lest it may provide an excuse for the non-release of payment at the due date.

(c) Special attention should be paid while dealing with government and government agencies which want documentation with meticulous precision.

(d) Accounting statements should be sent at regular intervals even if debt has not become due technically. A statement fulfils dual purpose. It confirms state of accounts so that the same can be reconciled and secondly it acts as a reminder.

(e) Credit limit so fixed should be prominently displayed in the credit file of the customer so that even an overzealous salesman does not miss the ceiling figure.

(f) Cash discount offered should invariably be linked with the interest rate prevalent in the market and must be subject to constant review.

9.8 CASH FOR AND AGAINST RECEIVABLES

The biggest drawback of sales on credit is blockade of funds for the credit period. The business uses certain techniques like offering cash discount to prod the customers to pay earlier. In addition to these, there are a number of alternatives through which cash can be brought to the business without waiting for the maturity of the receivables. Some of the alternatives which can help a business in harnessing immediate cash against receivables are as follows.

9.8.1 Factoring

The motto of factoring is "Produce, sell and forget". It is an arrangement under which a business sells its receivables to a specialised agency known as Factor. Functionally, the credit department of a business is substituted by a factor. The factor undertakes collection, accounting and management of debts. The customers at the time of sales are informed about the arrangement so that they make the payment directly to the factor.

Normally, a factor agrees to pay substantial advance against the receivables. The business thus gets the benefit of immediate availability of cash. A factor may purchase receivables without recourse or with recourse. If the arrangement is 'without recourse' then the factor becomes liable to bear the loss of bad debts. In the case of 'with recourse', such loss is borne by the business. The fees charged by a factor in the case of 'without recourse' is more than the fee charged for 'with recourse' arrangement.

From the point of cash flow, factoring is a valuable arrangement. A business has Rs 10,00,000 as receivables on a particular date and normal credit period is ninety days. If the amount is factored, the business can get 80% as advance immediately on first day. Receipt of Rs 8,00,000 eighty-nine days before the scheduled date of recovery will improve the cash flow circulation substantially. The other benefits include elimination of collection costs and costs associated with credit investigation and analysis. This also improves the cash flow in its own way.

9.8.2 Borrowings Against Receivables

Another commonly adopted method for raising money against receivables is by pledging receivables to banks as collateral for a loan. The receivables are pledged as revolving security; as soon as collections against receivables reduce its amount new receivables are assigned to bank in place of the old ones. Also, if some receivables do not materialise bank insists for their substitution with more viable receivables. It is pertinent to note that the bank acts only as a financier. The business retains the title to the receivables unlike under factoring where it is passed on to the factor. The business certifies to the bank about the solvency of the customer. If there is any bad debt, loss has to be suffered by the business. From the point of view of costs, there is no reduction in the collection, delinquency and default costs. Besides, banks are also paid interest and a certain percentage as service charges.

The biggest benefit to the business is immediate receipt of cash. The bank normally provides loan upto 60% to 90% of the value of the receivables. To that extent there is no blocking of funds.

9.8.3 Captive Factoring Unit

A business having large number of customers with high value of receivables will be incurring huge costs if it factors its receivables to some outside factoring agency. Nor, raising of loan against receivable will be in any way cheaper. The best course of action probably will be developing own credit department and running it effectively. Once the infrastructure for such a department is developed and manpower trained, the business with little costs can start undertaking factoring activities by buying the receivables of other companies. Fixed overheads of such unit shall be shared by all the companies getting its services. The collection costs for the receivables of its own business thus shall be substantially reduced.

9.8.4 Captive Financing Unit

In the present era of conglomerates it is not uncommon for big businesses to have their own captive finance companies. Such financing companies, in due course, acquire proficiency in raising finances at lower costs. This, in turn, helps the business to finance the credit sales at less than normal costs prevalent in the market. The result; a meteoric rise in the volume of sales.

9.8.5 Receivables Insurance

In advanced countries, some insurance companies provide risk coverage against unexpected large defaults by the customers. If a business has expected, as per the past trend or so, a bad debt of Rs 40,000 during next twelve months but has to face a bad debt of Rs 1,00,000, insurance companies shall reimburse part of the unanticipated loss. Presuming the risk coverage is 80% of the loss, it will reimburse the business an amount of Rs 48000 {(Rs (1,00,000 - 40,000) x 80%}. This compensates the business to a great extent in respect of default cost.

9.9 MONITORING OF RECEIVABLES

The efficiency of the receivables management can be gauged with the help of certain basic parameters. These parameters can be compared historically with the past and also with other units of the industry. The deficiencies revealed through such comparisons pinpoint areas which are required to be toned up. The prominent parameters are as follows:

9.9.1 Average Collection Period

It signifies the period during which, on an average, the receivables remain uncollected. To take an instance, a business has credit sales of Rs 43,20,000 per annum and average debtors at the year end are Rs 7,20,000. The average credit sales per day will be Rs 12,000, i.e., 43,20,000/360. It is customary to consider 360 days in an year for such calculations. The debtors of Rs 7,20,000 will signify that the average collection period is 60 days, i.e., 7,20,000/12,000.

Alternatively, the debtors veolcity can be calculated which then can be expressed in terms of number of days. Debtors velocity refers to number of times receivables get converted in terms of credit sales during a period. Higher the velocity, better the management of receivables. It is expressed as:

$$DV = \frac{CS}{D}$$

When, DV = Debtors velocity.

CS = Credit sales during the period, generally an year.

D = Average debtors (these can be average of debtors at the beginning and at the end of the year also)

$$\frac{43,20,000}{7,20,000} = 6 \text{ times}$$

$$\text{Average collection period} = \frac{360}{6} = 60 \text{ days}$$

If the average collection period was 80 days during last year the business has done well in the field of receivables management in current year. However, if it transpires that industry average collection period is 50 days the business needs to improve further its strategies for the management of receivables.

9.9.2 Detailed Ageing Schedule

While studying credit analysis we touched upon the topic of ageing schedule. At that time we categorised the debts into three groups consisting of debts which are undue, due and overdue. For the purpose of effective monitoring of receivables, we need perhaps a detailed schedule. This schedule is prepared by arranging the receivables monthwise alongwith other relevant information.

Exhibit 9.2 details the contents of such a schedule. Borrowing the data of earlier example, the annual credit sales of a business is Rs 43,20,000 and debtors at the year end are Rs 7,20,000. The average collection period turns out to be 60 days. However the average collection period masks the fact that almost 34% debtors are more than 60 days old,and out of it 7.8% are on the brink of becoming bad debts. This schedule thus prism the focus of the business wherever it is needed most.

Exhibit 9.2
RECEIVABLES AGEING SCHEDULE

Month of sales	Age of receivables (days)	Value of receivables (Rupees)	Percentage to total receivables (%)
March	1 – 30	1,30,000	18.05
February	31 – 60	3,45,000	47.91
January	61 – 90	1,10,000	15.27
December	91 – 120	79,000	10.97
Earlier	120 –	56,000	7.60
		7,20,000	100.00

It can thus be observed that ageing schedule overcomes to a great extent deficiencies associated with the method of average collection period.

We have seen that collection from debtors is the most dominant source of inflow of cash. Management of receivables, therefore, is an important issue. But at the same time it is very knotty issue too. It demands proper blending of standard and non-standard dictums for its efficient management.

Standard credit policy will ensure universal applicability regarding determination of credit limit, follow up, credit analysis *etc.* But the management of receivables, if overshadowed with fixed dogmas may lose human touch culminating in loss of good humane customers. A business deals with wide variety of customers. All of them cannot be treated equally. An old established dedicated customer if passing through a temporary liquidity crisis will not appreciate identical treatment as may be accorded to a new customer passing through similar circumstances. In such a case, it will be better if an exception is made and he be allowed more time to settle his accounts. The business may suffer in terms of short-term cash flow interests but will certainly gain in terms of over-all business interests.

QUESTIONS

1. "Selling on credit is an investment and like any other investment is guided by cost and benefit analysis". Explain the statement.
2. What are the elements of a credit policy?
3. Explain credit investigation. What are the various sources of collecting information for the credit investigation?
4. Explain the role of credit analysis in the receivables management.
5. What are the different sources for raising cash against receivables?
6. Explain the significance of the credit sales ratio.
7. What are the merits of preparing statement showing detailed ageing of receivables?
8. Write short notes on :

   a) Factoring.

   b) Value of speedy paper work in receivables management.

   c) Risks of following an inflexible credit policy.
9. Sales department of ABC & Co. has proposed its management for relaxation in the credit policy. It has proposed two options as Option I and Option II. Currently, the company has annual credit sales of Rs 60,00,000. Its accounts receivable turnover ratio is 4 times a year and loss on account of bad debts amounts to Rs 1,00,000 per annum. The company's variable costs are 70% of the selling price and fixed costs are Rs. 5,00,000. The company is required to give a return of 25% on the investments in new accounts receivable. Given the following information, which is better option if the fixed costs remain unchanged?

	Unit	Present policy	Option I	Option II
Annual credit Sales	Rs lakhs	60.00	70.00	80.00
Bad Debts	Rs lakhs	1.00	2.00	3.25
Accounts receivable turnover ratio	Times	4.0	3.0	2.40

10. Annual credit sales of ABC & Co. are Rs 30,00,000 and are spread evenly over the year. It does not offer any cash discount to its customers. They are offered a credit period of 2 months. It now proposes to offer a discount of "2/10 net 60". It is expected that 60% of the customers shall avail this facility of cash discount and the average collection period will be reduced to one month. The product of the company is sold at Rs 20 whereas its average cost is Rs 15 per unit. The required rate of return is 25%. The company intends to know whether its offer of cash discount to the customers would be beneficial for it or not?

10

MANAGEMENT OF INVENTORY

10.1 INTRODUCTION

Inventory is an important and valuable asset. It constitutes substantial portion of the total current assets of a business. Inventory covers a wide variety of items which are meant to be procured, 'used up' and sold in the ordinary course of business. It covers the whole range of items starting from input of materials and ending with output of finished products. The items forming inventory can be classified into three categories: (1) raw materials, (2) work-in-process (WIP), and (3) finished goods. Raw material inventory represents the items of basic input which are yet to be processed for transformation into final products. Work-in-process covers all items which are at various stages of production processes. These items have ceased to be raw material but have not developed into final products and are at various stages of semi-finished levels. Finished goods inventory consists of the final products which are awaiting sale.

An important feature of inventory is the *inter se* proportion of these three kinds of inventories in the overall inventory cost of a business. Much depends upon the nature of the business and product. If the raw material is ubiquitous and easily available, the business need not invest heavily into it. But if the product involves heavy input, like in steel industry, lot of stock of coal and iron ore need be available to ensure continuous production. The quantum of WIP inventory is dependent on the nature of industry/production line. Industries having large gestation have huge investments tied in work-in-process whereas a manufacturer of domestic utensils will have very little amount blocked in the work-in-process. Inventory of finished products, too, is dependent on the discipline of the industry. Manufacturing units engaged in the production and also retailing units like jewellers have large stock of finished goods. On the other hand, units engaged in tailor-made products like manufacturing of aircraft, where the product is made and sold, have almost nil inventory of finished products. These three kinds of inventory are normally available in a manufacturing unit only. A retailer or a wholesaler, for instance, may have inventory of finished proudcts only.

10.2 STOCK AND CASH

Some experts of financial management taking a broader view consider stock (inventory) as good as cash. Indeed, in the fraternity of current assets they possess strikingly identical features. Let us look at the similar features of stock and cash.

— Stock like cash, too, move in a circular fashion. The iterative process of stock is akin to circular track of cash flow. Raw material is processed into finished product for sale. The proceeds of sales are used for procurement of raw material again to start the process afresh. Like that in cash management rapid generation, efficient utilisation and effective conservation is the hallmark of efficient management of stock.

— The motive of holding stock is similar to those of holding cash. Stock is held to meet transaction, precautionary and speculative motives. Stock is held for transaction motive to cater to the demands of day-to-day production schedule. The precautionary motive persuades the business to maintain a buffer stock to meet any unforeseen requirement. And speculative motive like that of cash prods to take benefit of speculative price variation. A business will do well to procure heavy inventory if it envisions extensive price escalation of the stock items in near future.

— Management of stock like that of management of cash aims at counter balancing two conflicting objectives. On the one hand, it tries to keep the minimum balance of inventory so as to reduce the investment cost and, on the other hand, it attempts to ensure that production does not suffer due to lack of raw material. The guiding rule in both the cases is optimal utilisation since both have opportunity costs.

There are, however, elements of dissimilarity also. Cash is a legal tender. Stock is not. Cash surplus, even for a short time, can be invested to earn some revenue. Stock has no such trait. During inflation cash depreciates but stock appreciates. Stock suffers from the danger of physical deterioration or obsolescence. Cash is free from such risks.

On the liquidity ladder cash is at top, the ultimate expression of liquidity. Stock, on the other hand, is near the bottom. It is considered less liquid than receivables even.

10.3 OBJECTIVES OF INVENTORY MANAGEMENT

Like cash management, inventory management too is guided by the objective of counter balancing two conflicting aims. One, to reduce cost of holding stock so that investment in stock remains minimal and second, to reduce the risk of stock outs (running out of stock) so that production cycle operates smoothly. The first aim persuades the business to reduce the level of inventory whereas second one prompts it to increase the same. The business has to strike a balance. On a different perspective the first aim represents the cost of holding stock. The minimum the merrier. The second aim reflects the benefits accruing from holding stock. The more the merrier. The act of counter balancing is done through trade-off between the costs and benefits so that quantity of stock held is optimal and investment therein is minimum. To the extent a business is in a position to do so is the index of efficiency of its inventory management.

10.3.1 Reducing Cost of Stock Holding

The first objective of inventory management is to reduce cost of holding stock. Maintaining inventory is costly affair. Excessive stock holding will impair the profitability and affect the cash flow adversely. First, funds which have been tied in the huge inventory could have been invested elsewhere with better rate of return. Secondly, there are innumerable types of costs which keep on mounting if the business has over-stocked itself. Thirdly, huge investment in stock with less frequency of inventory turning over rate would jeopardise smooth operation of cash flow cycle leading ultimately to serious liquidity crisis. As the time passes things become more aggravated. Selling of inventory as such may become more difficult. Raw material disposal would create problems and ultimately may fetch a price below its cost price. Semi finished products are still more difficult to be sold. Even the finished products may pose problems because longer span of holding stock has given enough time and opportunities to the competitors to enter the fray or the product itself may become obsolete.

Costs associated with holding stock are of two types, (a) Costs associated with ordering stock, and (b) costs associated with carrying stock.

(a) *Ordering Costs:* Ordering costs, also known as acquisition and set up costs, refer to costs involved in the placement of order for the purchase of material. These include expenses related to preparation of purchase order, transporting, receiving, inspecting and recording of materials. Larger the number of orders, higher shall be the ordering costs. In other words, if in a period, the inventory holding is large there shall be fewer instances of order placements and lesser ordering costs. Thus ordering costs have inverse relationship with size of inventory. In order to reduce the costs of repetitive orders, the business need, to have large stock. But holding large quantity of stock entails different set of costs known as carrying costs.

(b) *Carrying Costs:* Carrying costs refer to the costs incurred for maintaining a given level of inventory. These costs can normally be grouped into four categories; (i) storage costs, (ii) servicing costs, (iii) costs of deterioration, and (iv) opportunity costs.

Storage costs cover expenses like rent of godown, depreciation of handling equipment, insurance and utilities. Servicing costs refer to costs of labour handling inventory, clerical and accounting costs for record-keeping, janitorial services *etc.* Costs related to deterioration cover pilferages, thefts, loss by fire *etc.* Stock may also become obsolete due to technological advancements or change in fashion. Finally, opportunity costs refer to the loss of revenue which a business would have earned on the amounts which have been invested in inventory. Whereas all costs other than opportunity costs are related to operative aspects of inventory management, opportunity cost is concerned with its financing aspect.

The carrying costs move in sympathy with the level of inventory. If the inventory level is increased, carrying costs too show rising trend. To minimise carrying costs it would be advisable to keep on placing orders in smaller lots. But then, placement of orders in smaller lots will increase the ordering costs. So a trade-off between ordering costs and carrying costs need be reached. This will be studied in detail later. Let us examine the benefits of holding stock as reflected in second aim of inventory management.

10.3.2 Reducing Risk of Stock Outs

A business should always ensure that it maintains enough inventory to meet any demand from production and marketing fronts. Any disruption due to non-availability of raw material will have double effect. First, disrupted production line will warrant additional cost and time to come back to normal production schedule. Secondly, the business may run the risk of losing its customers who may switch over to other competitors if they find delayed delivery schedules unsuitable. So large inventory holding ensures smooth production and marketing operations.

A study of functions of inventory in all the three segments will reveal the benefits which a business enjoys by holding large inventory. The basic function of inventory is to separate or "decouple" various activities of the business so that these need not follow the same pace rate. Raw material inventory decouple purchase and production. If no inventory is maintained purchases would have to be made at the rate of consumption in the production. It will increase the ordering costs depriving the business, economies of scales. Also, during inflation time it will lead to avoidable increase in cost. Above all, it will result in interruptions in production because it may not always be possible to procure raw material in right quantity at right time.

The origin of work-in-process (WIP) inventory is due to the fact that production is not always instantaneous. The amount of such inventory depends upon a number of factors including efficiency of production process and technology involved in the manufacture of the product. The decoupling characteristic of WIP inventory is significant when the process consists of a number of stages. It decouples the various stages enabling different pace rates for different stages.

Inventory of finished products decouple production and sale. At times, production rate is faster than the sales rate or *vice versa*. Inventory in such cases provide the requisite coordination in the production and marketing operations. This is particularly evident in a business having seasonal sales. For such a business, sales rate will be higher during season and lower in off-season period. The business under such circumstances have two alternatives. First, it gears up production during peak season and closes the plant during off season, and second, it continues production at the same level throughout the year. The former will entail expenses of discontinuity whereas latter will ensure smooth and economical production. A ready inventory of finished products gives boost to the marketing efforts as well. The business will be able to meet instantaneous demands. No waiting time for long processes. No disappointments to customers.

Thus, we see that an efficient inventory management aims at making a rational compromise between minimising cost of holding inventory on one hand and reducing risks of non-availability on the other, by ensuring that there remain, at all times, sufficient quantities in hand to meet the demands of production and marketing departments. Less quantity lessens the cost but enhances the risks of stock outs. Excessive quantities diminish the chances of disruptions but increase the costs. Situation demands trade-off between the two so that inventory is maintained at optimal level. This is done through various inventory management techniques as explained below.

10.4 INVENTORY MANAGEMENT TECHNIQUES

These techniques assist the business to determine optimal level of inventory. The determination of optimal level often poses numerous problems. It depends upon a number of factors which temperamentally are conflicting with each other. To begin with, low level of inventory is advantageous from the point of view of cost as it remains low but exposes the business to the risk of discontinuity of operations entailing extra expenditure and loss of clientage. High level of inventory will ensure smooth operation of production and sale but increases the inventory cost. Somewhere between the high and low levels will be a level where cost will be minimum and quantity enough to take care of production and sale. Through the application of various inventory management techniques such a level can be determined. We shall now study these techniques in detail.

10.4.1 ABC Analysis

A business has to deal with wide variety of items forming inventory as a whole. In some industries the number of items may not be so large but in some others it may run into thousands. But all of them cannot be on same footing in terms of their values. Quite justifiably, all the items do not deserve same attention for effective management. High value items require strict control and close monitoring whereas items with low or negligible values can afford to have somewhat liberal control measures. Such a discrimination is important for an effective inventory management otherwise the control over costly items will get diluted. Traditionally, the methodology adopted is to classify all the items of raw materials on the basis of "ABC analysis". ABC analysis is a technique which categorises the inventories into three classes. The basis of classification is cost of the items. It has been observed that items which account for about 10% of the total items, contribute to 70% of the total value of consumption. These may be put under A category. The next 20% of the items contribute to another 20% of the consumption value. These are category B items. The balance 70% of the items contribute to only 10% of the monetary value of consumption. These are category C items. Group A items as major contributor towards cost must receive maximum attention. Detailed and exhaustive inventory control measures should be employed to guard against pilferage, and should ensure effective utilisation of these items. Group B items shall require less vigorous control measures, and group C items can be subjected to liberal control measures. The benefits of this technique is that it provides simple and practical approach towards issues of inventory management. Its limitation is its allout focus on cost only. An item may be of low value but very critical for production. Assigning category C to such an item may not be justified.

10.4.2 Economic Order Quantity

Another important technique of inventory management is determination of optimum size of the order. We have seen above that the two elements of inventory cost, *i.e.*, ordering costs and carrying costs have inverse relationship. The increase in the order quantity will reduce the ordering costs but will increase the carrying costs and just opposite happens when the order quantity is decreased. Economic Order Quantity (EOQ) determines the optimal order quantity where the total cost consisting both of ordering costs and carrying costs is minimal. Material can then be procured in lot size so determined. There are two approaches for determining an EOQ, (a) Trial & Error approach, and (b) Mathematical approach.

(a) *Trial and Error Approach:* This technique is based on detailed analysis of data related to lot sizes and their costs. A table can be constructed displaying costs involved for the various lots of quantities.

The lot size having minimum cost can be identified for placement of orders. This can be illustrated by a simple example.

A business estimates its annual requirements as 600 units. The ordering cost per order is Rs 20 and carrying cost is Re 1 per unit. We are required to find out optimal size of order.

The business has a number of alternatives for buying the desired requirements. It can buy the whole of the requirement in one lot at the beginning of the year. In that case the stock in the beginning will be 600 units and zero at the end of the year. The average stock holding during the year will thus be opening balance + closing balance divided by 2, *i.e.*, (600+0)/2 = 300 units. On the other hand, if business intends to make monthly purchases, stock in the beginning of the month will be 50 and zero at the end of the month. Average stock holding in such case is (50 + 0)/2 = 25. Exhibit 10.1 displays the cost computations of various sizes.

Exhibit 10.1
ECONOMIC ORDER QUANTITY

Size of orders	No. of orders	Average stock	Cost per order (Rs)	Annual ordering cost (2 × 4) (Rs)	Carrying cost per unit (Rs)	Annual carrying cost (3 × 6) (Rs)	Total cost (5+7) (Rs)
1	2	3	4	5	6	7	8
600	1	300	20	20	1	300	320
300	2	150	20	40	1	150	190
200	3	100	20	60	1	100	160
150	4	75	20	80	1	75	155
100	6	50	20	120	1	50	170
60	10	30	20	200	1	30	230
50	12	25	20	240	1	25	265

It is evident that order size of 150 units entails minimum cost, and as such can be described as economic order quantity.

The above method though simple involves wading through a tedious work of permutations and combinations.

(b) *Mathematical Approach:* Economic order quantity can be determined by a simpler shortcut method as well. A mathematical paradigm comes to our rescue. Borrowing the data from Exhibit 10.1, we can calculate economic order quantity with the help of following formula.

$$\text{EOQ} = \sqrt{\frac{2AO}{C}}$$

where,

EOQ = Economic order quantity
A = Annual requirements of units
O = Ordering cost per order
C = Carrying cost per unit

$$EOQ = \sqrt{\frac{2 \times 600 \times 20}{1}}$$

$$= 155 \text{ units.}$$

The determination of economic order quantity as per above referred technique is based on certain assumptions. These assumptions are more theoretical than practical. To that extent the method suffers from shortcomings. The first assumption is constant consumption of the inventory as if business operates in static environment. The order placements to, and delivery from suppliers cannot be so mechanical as assumed under the method. Suppliers may not stick to delivery schedules and a business may have to have buffer stock as a cushion. Secondly, the demand of product and the consequent demand of raw materials can also not be predicted so precisely. Any variation in estimated quantity and actual quantity will change the size of economic order quantity.

10.4.3 Reorder Point

Stock like cash imprest needs constant replenishment. In other words, there is a continuous process of consumption and acquisition of inventory. There are two aspects with regard to replenishment process. The first aspect relates to quantum of replenishment, *i.e.*, how much to order. This is done by determining the economic order quantity. The second aspect relates to time of replenishment, *i.e.,* when to order. This is determined by calculating "Reorder Point". Reorder point is that level of inventory which prompts a business to initiate action for the placement of fresh order. For the calculation of reorder point three factors are taken into consideration; average consumption, lead time and economic order quantity.

Average consumption refers to the number of inventory units which on an average are consumed in a day or week or month. Lead time is the time gap involved in the placement of orders and receipt of inventory. It covers order placement time by the business, order processing time by the supplier, and transit time required for the inventory to move from supplier to business. The calculation of reorder point is explained by an example below.

Suppose the average consumption of inventory item per week is 100 units. The lead time is five weeks and the economic order quantity is 1000 units. The reorder point can be calculated by the formula:

The Reorder point = Average weekly consumption × Lead time

$$= 100 \times 5 = 500 \text{ units}$$

To put in simple words reorder point level is equal to the material consumption of lead time. It is pertinent to note that the size of the order will be equal to the economic order quantity. In the instant example, the economic order quantity has been determined as 1000 units. In terms of weekly consumption it gives requirement of 10 weeks. The business will, therefore, place an order at the expiry of fifth week so that at the end of tenth week it has 1000 units in its stock.

The critisim of this method stems from its theoretical assumptions. The method assumes existence of static business environment. The average consumption and lead time shall remain constant. It is possible that consumption of inventory may undergo change because of number of factors linked with production and marketing. Also, the lead time may change substantially due to processing delay by suppliers or excess time lost in transit.

10.4.4 Safety Stock

Precautionary motive is one of the three motives for holding inventory, other two being transaction motive and speculative motive. Precautionary motive motivates the business to hold stock in addition to its usual requirements as a cushion or buffer to meet any unforeseen needs. Such stock is known as Safety Stock.

The need for holding stock stems from the existence of uncertainty in the business operations. The assumptions of static environment considered under the methods of economic order quantity and reorder point may not be acceptable in the practical business world. The requirements of inventory may vary from time to time and so is also its supply. There may be spurt in the demand of product in the market. The business may be forced to change its chartered production schedule to make production programme compatible with the demand. Safety stock, if available, will enable the business to take benefits of such rise in demand. Similarly, lead time may get over-stretched due to economic factors like strike or non-economic factors like earthquake. Under such situations a business without safety stock will run the risk of complete stock out and it may have to halt the proudction completely. Such a possibility of stock out can be hedged by holding sufficient amount of safety stock. This leads to another question; how to determine sufficient safety stock?

We have observed earlier in this chapter that a prudent inventory management aims at determining optimal level of inventory which in turn is based on trade-off between cost of holding inventory and cost of stock outs. Calculation of safety stock, too, is dependent on the rational compromise between these two conflicting costs. Cost of maintaining inventory covers both ordering costs and carrying costs. Safety stock necessitates holding of additional units resulting in additional costs over and above the costs of holding normal inventory. Cost of stock out, on the other hand, covers costs associated with disruption of production and opportunity costs. Disruption in production is the additional cost required to be incurred for the restart of the production. Opportunity cost refers to the loss of benefits/profits which a business is deprived of due to non-availability of stock. Optimal safety stock is that level of safety stock where the total costs of these two conflicting costs is minimal. It is the fulcrum point of a *sea-saw* having costs of carrying stock, on the one hand, and costs of stock out, on the other.

10.4.5 Just-in-Time

The "Just-in-time" or the *Kanban* as the Japanese call it was invented by Mr. Taiichi Ohno, a production engineer at the Toyota Motor Corporation in 1952. It changed the basic concept of inventory from Just-in-case to Just-in-time. As discussed above, the main purpose of keeping inventory is to synchronise various activities of production process. It is also looked as a "buffer" to be utilised just-in-case the need arises. The concept of just-in-time is in contrast with the traditional concept of holding inventory. It is based on our daily experience of shopping. If one buys the goods off the shelves of a shop, he buys just what he needs in right quantities, at the right place and of right quality. Mr. Ohno thought that if the same philosophy is applied to the manufacturing companies also it would minimise inventory levels and the resultant costs, and also the risks of holding inventory. This led to the invention of the system of just-in-time or *Kanban*.

Under the *Kanban*, exact number of required units are delivered by suppliers at each successive stage of production at a rate at which these are needed by the manufacturing companies. The implementation of just-in-time requires the manufacturer to establish very close relationships with the suppliers involving efficient and effective communication of production, planning and scheduling information. The literal meaning of *Kanban* is a signboard or a label, and it acts as an important communication tool in the system. A *Kanban* (Label) is put on each box as they move to the assembly line. Since these parts are brought to the line exactly at the time these are needed the *Kanban* is returned after the parts are used. The return of *Kanban* serves two purposes; a record for actual use of the parts and a request for new parts.

The operation of just-in-time system is dependent on three fundamental principles:

- Reliability: The manufacturer must have the support of reliable suppliers who can ensure right quantity, at right time, at right place and of right quality.
- Regular communication: There should be regular flow of information from manufacturer to suppliers and *vice versa* so that suppliers are well aware of the requirements of its client all the time.

— Flexibility: The manufacturer and the suppliers must be able to respond rapidly to the changes in the demands.

Just-in-time is helpful in reducing the costs associated with holding inventory to a great extent by keeping the inventory to almost zero level. It has its own limitations as well. First, the system can function successfully only if smooth production is guaranteed. Secondly, not only the concerned business but all its suppliers must opt for adoption of just-in-time system. Thirdly, the lead time for the receipt of materials from the suppliers must be known with certainty. Due to these limitations the system cannot be applied universally. It requires a very careful appraisal of the potential advantages and a supplier's capacity to meet the demands placed on them before one opts for adoption of the just-in-time system.

10.5 CASH FOR AND AGAINST STOCK

Stock sponges cash. Cash remains tied up in stock from the date of payment for raw material till receipt of payments from the sale of finished products. The time involved in the journey may vary from industry to industry. Some industries require a few days time for the processing wherein some others like shipbuilding have long span before the final product can be manufactured and sold. Whatever be the time gap, big or small, the cash is one thing which remains blocked for the period. However, following proper financial policies stock can be made instrumental to bring cash into the business much before the expiry of input-process-output journey time. This is done by raising finance for and against stock. The various methods used for this purpose are as follows.

10.5.1 Finance Against Stock in Transit

Funds can even be raised against stock which is yet to come in the physical possession of a business. This facility is generally available when quantity to be procured is huge and delivery time is very lengthy. In such cases raw materials can be financed "en route" through a Trade Bill or Warehouse Receipt. Based on the Bill of Lading a business can draw a Bill of Exchange and can raise requisite funds even if the material is still on the high seas. Such trade bill in certain cases is negotiable as well. The warehouse receipt is an acknowledgement of the goods lying in the warehouse. As and when required, the goods can be reclaimed therefrom. The receipt can also become source of immediate cash. It can be pledged as a collateral and funds raised against it.

10.5.2 Loan Against Stock

Stock is an asset and like any other asset can be pledged to raise funds. The commercial banks offer credit facilities against the hypothecation of stock in trade. Before sanctioning credit facility bank satisfies itself regarding smooth running of production cycle and marketability of product. Items pledged should not be difficult-to-sell or obsolete. The credit is normally restricted to 80% of the value of stock. The business keeps on utilising the stock for the purpose of production and replenishing it in the normal course. The bank, however, keeps an eye on the stock level ensuring that at no stage value of stock gets reduced to less than agreed amount of collateral. If it does, the bank reduces the amount of credit. Under this scheme, the business enjoys both the possession of stock as well as cash.

10.5.3 Commodity Market

There are certain types of raw materials which are traded in a commodity market. If a business deals in such material it gets some additional benefits including that of improvement in liquidity. An item of material can be traded in commodity market if it is, (a) durable in nature (b) it is dealt in large quantities, and (c) price is normally subject to wide variation. The commodities which are dealt in London Metal Exchange, the biggest commodity market in the world, are copper, lead, zinc, aluminium, nickel and tin. At local level any other commodity satisfying above referred parameters can be chosen for trade at commodity exchange.

A business which consumes heavy quantities of traded raw materials can interface its stock requirements with trade at the commodity market in such way that cash investment in stock is reduced to minimum. If the prices are expected to rise the business can place order for material at current prices for current and future deliveries. This way prices shall be minimum and the desired quantity will be assured at the appointed time. Even if excessive quantity has been purchased, the surplus can be sold off at a profit. On the contrary, if prices are likely to fall, the business need to purchase quantities which are immediately required, may be on week to week basis. Besides, through 'Short Sales' the business can make some profit as well. Trading at commodity market thus adds element of liquidity to inventory management. Further, through an efficiently managed commodity portfolio, a business can make inventory management a profit centre.

10.6 MONITORING OF INVENTORY

The efficiency of inventory management can be judged through a number of indicators. An inter-firm or intra-firm comparison of these indicators will reveal avenues which deserve immediate attention. The monitoring of inventory, however, can be successful only if it is supported by an exhaustive and well maintained records. No other asset in a business demands maintenance of such a detailed and upto-date records as are required by stock. Material receipt notes, inspection reports, daily transfer registers, bin cards, issue slips, stock ledgers are some of the prominent records which a business must maintain. The efficacy of inventory system can be monitored through the following methods.

10.6.1 Average Age of Stock

In a business basic materials are procured to be processed for churning out the saleable finished products. Thus we see stockpile of raw materials, semi-finished products and final or finished products. We can determine the average age of stock at each stage. Average age of stock refers to the period, on an average, stock remains in its original form before being 'used up' in the business. The average age of stock can be calculated for the composite stock and also for the individual components of stock. Formula for calculating the average age of stock is akin to that for calculation of average collection period of receivables. First we determine the stock velocity which then is converted into number of days. Stock velocity indicates the number of times average stock held during the period is turned over in terms of cost of goods sold. It is expressed as:

$$SV = \frac{CGS}{S}$$

SV = Stock velocity
CGS = Cost of goods sold in a period
S = Average stock held during the year

If, in a business cost of goods sold in an year is Rs 6,00,000 and average inventory held during the year is Rs 2,00,000, the stock velocity is 3, *i.e.*, Rs (6,00,000 / 2,00,000). The average age of stock can be computed as:

$$\text{Average age of stock} = \frac{D}{SV}$$

Where, D = Number of days in a period
SV = Stock velocity

In the instant case average age of stock = 360/3 = 120 days. (It is customary to consider an year having 360 days)

The average age of composite stock calculated above refers to the total stockpile covering all three components, *i.e.*, raw material, semi-finished products and finished products. It will be better if the average collection period of each individual component is calculated separately so as to know at what stage 'turning over' needs acceleration. If it is found that average value of raw material during the year was Rs 50,000 only, then the stock velocity of raw material will be 12

{Rs (6,00,000/50,000)} and the average age of raw material stock will be 30 days (360/12). The turn around period of 30 days can be compared with the average period of trade credit accorded by the suppliers which in the present case is presumed as 45 days. This signifies an efficient utilisation of raw material as the business is in a position to utilise raw material before it is required to shell out money for its purchase. This leaves 90 days to be examined; whether something is wrong with production process which consumes more than deserving days or the business needs to improve its market strategies to speed up its sales.

10.6.2 Detailed Age Classification

Another technique adopted for monitoring inventory management is preparation of a schedule detailing age classifications of various items of raw material or the stock balance as a whole.

Exhibit 10.2 shows one such schedule as on March 31 wherein the raw material inventory has been classified based on the number of days it remains unused.

Exhibit 10.2
INVENTORY AGE CLASSIFICATION

Date of purchase	Age-Classification (Days)	Amount (Rs)	Percentage to total cost (%)
March 16	0-15	22,500	45%
March 10	16-30	12,500	25%
February 28	31-45	6,000	12%
February 08	46-60	5,000	10%
January 16	61-75	4,000	8%
		50,000	100

In the previous section we have seen that average value and age of raw material during the year was Rs 50,000 and 30 days respectively. A close inspection of the above schedule will reveal that about 30% raw material, *i.e.*, raw material procured earlier to Feb. 28 have remained unturned beyond 30 days. Total cost of such raw material is Rs 15000. Out of it some 8% (Rs 4000) remained unconsumed for more than two months. Preparation of individual items of raw material shall go a long way to identify items which are not moving in the production cycle at the desired pace.

Preparation of such a schedule for finished products can also be very useful. The products can be tabulated on the basis of production dates. Such a classification will help the business to enlist items which have become difficult to sell. With the lapse of time the market value of such items shall keep on diminishing. A quick action will be needed lest these become absolutely obsolete.

QUESTIONS

1. "Inventory management is guided by the objective of counter balancing two conflicting aims". Explain.
2. What are the similar and dissimilar features of stock and cash?
3. Define economic order quality (EOQ). Describe the various methods of its computation. What are its limitations?
4. Explain just-in-time (JIT). How does it differ from the conventional concept of inventory, being considered as just-in-case?
5. What are the various ways of raising cash for and against stock?
6. What are the methods used for judging the efficiency of inventory management.
7. Write short notes on:
   a) ABC analysis
   a) Re order point
   a) The 'decoupling" function of inventory.
8. The yearly requirement of ABC & Co. is 60,000 units. The carrying cost per unit per annum is Rs. 1.50. The ordering cost is Rs. 300 per order. The company has the option to place order in the following sizes.
   (1) 60,000 Units
   (2) 30,000 Units
   (3) 15,000 Units
   (4) 7,500 Units
   (5) 5,000 Units
   (6) 3,750 Units
   Determine the
   (a) Ordering cost
   (b) Carrying cost
   (c) Economic order quantity by trial and error method.
9. The following relations to inventory costs have been established for ABC Ltd.
   (a) Annual requirement 3,00,000 units
   (b) Purchase price per unit Rs. 3/-
   (c) Order to be placed in multiples of 100 units
   (d) Carrying cost is 25% of the purchase price of goods
   (e) Ordering cost is Rs. 25 per order
   (f) Desired safety stock is 10,000 units; this quantity is on hand initially
   (g) Three days are required for delivery.
   Determine
   (1) EOQ
   (2) How many orders should company place each year?
   (3) At what inventory level should an order be placed?
   (Adapted from CA Final, May '81)

11

INVESTMENT OF SHORT-TERM SURPLUS

11.1 INTRODUCTION

Cash surplus like cash deficit is a product of non-synchrocity of inflows and outflows. There are always recurring instances where requirements are more than the funds available and conversely where funds available are more than the immediate needs. In the former case, business examines the ideal sources for raising additional funds, and in the latter case, it looks forward for the ideal slots for investing idle funds. The various sources of raising of short-term finances are described in Chapter 12. In this chapter we examine the various avenues which are open for warehousing funds for short-term durations. As stated earlier, a prudent cash manager is capable of making cash management a profit centre. The surplus funds can be so invested as to generate additional income to the business.

There are many reasons of cash being surplus in the business. First, the cashflow movement is unpredictable. A spurt in sales can bring influx of cash. Secondly, a seasonal business may find itself flush with cash during the season. Thirdly, there can be a situation when a business is required to liquidate its long-term liability necessitating a large amount of cash; for example, redemption of debentures. It then needs accumulation of cash over a period of time. During the process of such accumulation it can be invested for a short term till the time the amount is released to the debenture holders.

It is pertinent to note that the exercise of making short-term investment is motivated to make use of fallow cash rather than encashing on investment opportunities. Return is likely to be less than what a business can earn by investing in its own operations. So the business does not intend to bind itself on a long-term basis. Its priority is to have accessibility to cash all the time so that it can invest it in its own line of business whenever required. Short-term investment is only a stop-gap arrangement.

Exhibit 11.1
CASH BUDGET

Period : January to March,1995 Date: 24/12/1994
Basis : Monthly

Particulars	Jan.	Feb.	Mar.
RECEIPTS			
Sales	33,000	55,000	50,000
Others	2,000	2,000	4,000
Sub Total	35,000	57,000	54,000
PAYMENTS			
Purchases	20,000	10,000	55,000
Salary	10,000	10,000	10,000
Others	16,000	11,000	25,000
Sub Total	46,000	31,000	90,000
DEFICIT/SURPLUS			
Balance in the beginning	25,000	10,000	10,000
Cash Receipts	35,000	57,000	54,000
Cash Payments	46,000	31,000	90,000
Forecasted Cash Balance	14,000	36,000	(26,000)
Desired Cash Balance	(10,000)	(10,000)	(10,000)
ADJUSTMENTS			
Cash Surplus	4,000	26,000	
Surplus utilised in short-term investment	4,000	26,000	
Cash Deficit			(36,000)
Cash from sale of short-term investment.			30,000
Short-Term borrowing			(6,000)

11.2 CASH MOVEMENT STATEMENT

We have seen that cash budget points out times of deficits and surpluses occurring on certain prefixed dates generally on monthly basis. The balances so revealed may not provide the desired details for implementing an effective schedule of investment. This can be done by preparing a detailed Cash Movement Statement. Such a statement helps the business to overcome limitations associated with a cash budget drawn on monthly basis. This facilitates the way for profitable short-term investment. The limitations of a cash budget are as follows:

(a) Cash budget points out the deficit/surplus as on a particular date, say, end of the month. The month may be too long a period for planning an effective strategy of profitable investment in short-term money market. A business aims at optimum utilisation of cash resources. For this, all possible avenues including efficient use of surplus cash are exploited fully to add to the business income. The money market for deployment of short-term funds is well developed. The investment can now be made for as short a period as a day or for an overnight. Hence the cash budget figures are good for broader perspective only. The cash movement statement will overcome this shortcoming by dovetailing the cash transactions on weekly or even daily basis.

(b) Cash budget may not provide insight to the monthly balances. There may be a number of transactions involving cash flow movement in a month. Monthly balances are the net outcome of series of cash transactions in a month. Exhibit 11.1 shows an extract of cash budget pertaining to a period of three months from January 1995 to March 1995. It indicates a surplus amounting to Rs 4,000 at the end of January. The cash movement statement prepared for these months is shown in Exhibit 11.2. We find that the end-of-the-month surplus is much less than during the month peak surplus of Rs 41,000. An additional surplus of Rs 37,000 is available for short-term investment for varying periods from January 7 to February 14. Thus, a decision of investment of cash surplus based on the cash budget may deprive the business the interest earnings which otherwise it could have earned had it prepared cash movement statement. Similarly, total deficit of Rs 6,000 in the month of March is in fact less than the peak deficit of Rs 15,000 during the week ending March 7. The business has to take care of peak deficits and surpluses and not merely month ending cash surpluses and deficits.

(c) The cash budget may not reveal the pattern of cash receipts and cash payments if it is prepared on monthly basis. If we look at Exhibit 11.2, we observe that receipts from sales are normally in the first week of the month whereas payments for purchases and salaries are in the third or last week. The influx of cash brought in the early part of the month can be utilised for investment in the in-between transit period. Cash budget will not throw any light on such pattern since it only indicates the closing balances.

11.3 CONSTRUCTION OF CASH MOVEMENT STATEMENT

The basic technique for the construction of detailed cash movement statement is identical to the preparation of cash budget. The data of course is reflected in more detailed fashion. For such statements normally weekly presentation is considered sufficient. However, in certain cases, daily cash movement too can be projected if heavy transactions are occurring during those particular days. During Dewali or Christmas time, for example, daily cash movement watch may yield better results for taking investment decisions.

Exhibit 11.2

CASH MOVEMENT STATEMENT - PART A

Period : January'95 to March'95 Date: 24.12.1994

Basis : Weekly

Week Ending	Expected Cash Balance	Expected Receipts			Expected Payments				Expected Surplus (Deficit)	Expected Weekly Net Increase (Decrease)
		Sales	Others	Total	Purchases	Salaries	Others	Total		
1	2	3	4	5 (3+4)	6	7	8	9 (6+7+8)	10	11
B/F	25000								15000	
JAN										
7	51000	30000	—	30000	—	—	4000	4000	41000	26000
14	49000	3000	1000	4000	—	—	6000	6000	39000	(2000)
21	47000	—	1000	1000	—	—	3000	3000	37000	(2000)
28	14000	—	—	—	20000	10000	3000	33000	4000	(33000)
FEB										
7	49000	40000	—	40000	—	—	5000	5000	39000	35000
14	55000	10000	2000	12000	—	—	6000	6000	45000	6000
21	45000	—	—	—	10000	—	—	10000	35000	(10000)
28	40000	5000	—	5000	—	10000	—	10000	30000	(5000)
MAR										
7	(5000)	—	—	—	35000	—	10000	45000	(15000)	(45000)
14	37000	50000	—	50000	—	—	8000	8000	27000	42000
21	41000	—	4000	4000	—	—	—	—	31000	4000
28	4000	—	—	—	20000	10000	7000	37000	(6000)	(37000)

Note: After accounting for Rs 10,000 as safety cash in hand.

11.3.1 Cash Movement Statement - Part *A*

Cash movement statement is prepared in two parts. Part *A* shows the weekly receipts, payments and surpluses and Part *B* displays the action plan for the investment of the surplus. Columns 1 to 9 of Cash Movement Statement Part *A* of Exhibit 11.2, detail weekly receipts, payments and cash balances. Column 10 provides information of surplus/deficit at the week-end. The surplus/deficit amount is determined after providing for a prefixed amount of cash in hand known as 'safety' or 'cushion cash'. In the instant case, this amount has been considered as Rs 10,000. Finally, last column shows increase/decrease of cash during that week. Based on the information so revealed an action plan can be chalked out for projecting investments of next three months. Such an action plan would be fairly accurate for the immediate period of 4 - 8 weeks. For an extended period, it may not be so definite.

To begin with there is brought-forward balance of Rs 25,000 as shown in column 2. After reducing Rs 10,000 as safety cash in hand, Rs 15,000 is available for short-term investment. During first week of January, the business is expecting Rs 30,000 from sales and is likely to incur Rs 4,000 for various expenses. Thus, net increase during the week will be an amount of Rs 26,000 inflating the cash in hand to Rs 51,000 by week ending January 7. The total expected surplus on Jan. 7, will be Rs 41,000 (Rs 51,000- Rs 10,000) which can be verified by adding weekly increase of Rs 26,000 with the surplus amount of Rs 15,000 pertaining to opening balance. The next two weeks project a weekly decrease of Rs 2,000 each with the result the surplus as on Jan. 21, is reduced to Rs 37,000. In the last week ending Jan. 28, the business is expected to make payment for purchases as a consequence of which the surplus at the end of the week is diminished to Rs 4,000 only. During the first week of February it is expected that cash inflow will increase by Rs 35,000, followed by an increase of Rs 6,000 in the second week. However, in the third and fourth weeks, it is expected that the weekly cash will decrease by Rs 10,000 and Rs 5,000 respectively. At the end of February, there will be cash in hand of Rs 40,000 with Rs 30,000 as surplus cash available for investment. Such a comparatively large surplus is partly due to the fact that the business is likely to defer the payment for purchases scheduled in the last week of the month to the first week of the next month.

In the first week of March, a disturbing factor is likely to emerge. The business is not expected to get receipts from sales due to some unavoidable reasons. But it has to meet its commitments to the creditors and release Rs 45,000. This will wipe out whole of the surplus of Rs 30,000 resulting in a deficit of Rs 15,000 consisting of Rs 5,000 as negative balance and Rs 10,000 as safety cash in hand. The business will have to raise overdraft of Rs 15,000 to meet its commitments. The overdraft is likely to be for one week only since during the week ending March 14, the cash inflow of Rs 50,000 on account of receipts from sales will result in weekly increase of Rs 42,000 and a surplus of Rs 27,000 after liquidation of overdraft of Rs 15,000. The surplus is likely to increase by a small amount of Rs 4,000 in the week ending March 21. In the last week of March, the business is expected to make heavy payments amounting to Rs 37,000 and to facilitate this it will again go for an overdraft of Rs 6,000. It is important to note that exactly identical position has been projected on monthly basis in cash budget of the relevant period as displayed in Exhibit 11.1. However, the cash budget fails to give requisite details for chalking out a suitable investment plan for short-term investments. This is done by preparing a Cash Movement Statement Part *B*.

Exhibit 11.3
CASH MOVEMENT STATEMENT - PART *B*

Period : January to March, 1995. Date: 24.12.1994.
Basis : Weekly

Week Ending	Weekly Increase (Decrease)	Surplus-Investment Amount	Period	No. of Days	Deficit-Requirement Amount	Period	No.of Days
1	2	3	4	5	6	7	8
B/F	15000	2000	Jan 07	07			
		2000	Jan 14	14			
		11000	Jan 21	21			
Jan 07	26000	22000	Jan 21	14			
		4000	Feb 14	38			
Jan 14	(2000)						
Jan 21	(2000)						
Jan 28	(33000)						
Feb 07	35000	6000	Feb 14	07			
		5000	Feb 21	14			
		24000	Feb 28	21			
Feb 14	6000	6000	Feb 28	14			
Feb 21	(10000)						
Feb 28	(5000)						
Mar 07	(45000)				15000	Mar 14	07
Mar 14	42000	27000*	Mar 21	07			
Mar 21	4000	4000	Mar 22	01			
Mar 28	(37000)				6000		

* After liquidating overdraft of Rs 15000.

11.3.2 Cash Movement Statement - Part *B*

Cash Movement Statement - Part *B* is in fact an extention of Part *A* statement. It projects the investment programme of the surpluses shown by Part *A* statement. Exhibit 11.3 displays one such statement. Columns 1 and 2 contain the details borrowed from Part *A* statement. Having displayed the weekly surpluses the strategy for their investment is drawn out. A study of the statement indicates that there is a brought-forward surplus of Rs 15,000. The first week ending Jan. 7 too is likely to increase cash by an amount of Rs 26,000. But the week ending Jan 14 (Jan 8 to Jan 14) will witness a decrease in weekly cash by Rs 2,000 followed by similar decrease in the next week. The investment of Rs 15,000, thus, can be sub-divided into three tranches. An amount of Rs 2,000 can be invested upto Jan 7, so that cash is available from Jan 8th onwards. Likewise, another amount of Rs 2,000 can be invested upto Jan. 14 and balance Rs 11,000 can be deployed upto Jan 21 since in the following week substantiual amount is required to make payment for purchases. The weekly increase of Rs 26,000 which is likely to be available during next week too, can be sub-divided into two separate amounts for investments. First, an amount of Rs 22,000 can be invested upto Jan 21 so that this amount coupled with Rs 11,000 also maturing on Jan 21 can take care of weekly decrease of Rs 33,000 expected in the following week ending Jan 28. The balance Rs 4,000 can be invested upto Feb 14 since the next weekly decrease is expected in the week ending Feb 21 only. Similarly, Rs 35,000 pertaining to weekly increase of week ending Feb 7 and Rs 6,000 being weekly increase of week ending Feb 14 can be suitably deployed upto week ending February 28.

The first week of March involves heavy payments resulting in weekly decrease of Rs 45,000. This decrease will not only wipe out the whole of accumulated surplus but will also necessitate an overdraft of Rs 15,000. The overdraft can be repaid out of weekly increase of Rs 42,000 emerging during week ending Mar 14 and the balance amount of Rs 27,000 can be invested till next week. Week ending March 21 is also likely to generate a cash increase of Rs 4,000. This surplus increase is very short lived. The business is expected to have a decrease of Rs 37,000 in following week ending March 28. As the cash is required in the week beginning March 22, the business can at best invest Rs 4,000 in the overnight deposit account because it is required to raise another overdraft of Rs 6,000 in the beginning of the following week which will be liquidated as and when it has surplus cash.

It is pertinent to note that the above mentioned investment programme is one such plan which can be designed in such a situation. There can be many more versions depending upon the prevalent conditions in the money market and strategies adopted by the business. It can decide to invest funds for longer duration in the initial stage itself to get higher rates of interest and bank upon overdrafts as and when required if it finds such a plan more remunerative. Alternatively, it may carve out a modicum balance for day-to-day investment and the rest for longer duration. Whatever be the strategy adopted, it must have the basic ingredients of a wholesome investment plan encompassing liquidity, safety and optimum return.

11.3.3 Advantages of Cash Movement Statement

The important advantages for preparing such a cash movement statement are:

(a) Business gets ample time to decide about the investment programme/arrangement. Whatever information is required can be obtained during this period. Interest rate movements can be studied minutely to determine best possible investment schedules. If rates are likely to rise, investment period can be shortened.

(b) Such an action plan provides the basis for investment strategy. It remains flexible and can be changed smoothly if there is any variation in the quantum of cash surplus due to unforeseen events. Also, if an investment becomes more attractive because of prevalent market sentiments than the one originally scheduled, action plan can be revised without much difficulty.

(c) Once a business becomes proficient in such investment strategies, it can chalk out the schedule in such a way that a part of the money can be carved out for investment on day-to-day basis whereas balance money can be invested in short-term deposits on weekly, monthly or quarterly basis, as per the availability of cash surplus and the period.

(d) Equipped with such detailed information a business can dare to invest for a duration beyond its scheduled surplus period. If the investment for a period of 28 days is yielding much higher interest but the surplus period is limited to 21 days, the business can invest for 28 days and for balance 7 days funds can be raised from overdraft if the economies suggest that such an arrangement is profitable. Something unthinkable if weekly cash flow statement is not prepared.

(e) Such a statement can open more avenues for the investment of surplus cash. For short-term investments, portfolio investment is normally not considered a viable proposition but with such a blueprint of investment in hand the business can afford to indulge in this activity within certain limits. It can buy fixed interest bearing bonds, debentures on discount which are nearing redemption date to get more profit than the income it can earn from the interest on short-term deposits.

11.4 SELECTION OF AN INVESTMENT OPTION

Before we consider the various options available for the investment of surplus cash let us have a look at the factors which influence the selection of a particular investment.

11.4.1 Quantum

Larger the amount, higher the interest. The size of cash surplus plays an important part in the selection of the investment. Many financial institutions engaged in financing and leasing business are ready to offer higher rates of interest if the deposit is for a substantially large amount. Otherwise also, a business with huge cash is in a much better bargaining position to attract higher rates of interest.

11.4.2 Risk and Return

Greater the risk, higher the return. Banks are bound by certain internal and external regulations and as such offer more or less uniform rates of interest for the deposits. But certain body corporates particularly in the unorganised sector offer wildely varied rates of returns for the deposits. These high yielding deposits are exposed to heavy risks and a prudent cash manager always tends to shy away from such propositions. He knows that his primary consideration is retrieval of cash when required rather earning more yield from its short-term investment. He is prepared to surrender return in order to purchase security.

11.4.3 Liquidity

The most desired feature of any short-term investment is its liquidity. All investments are undertaken for conversion speedily into cash whenever required. The emphasis on the liquidity becomes all the more greater if there is uncertainty regarding period upto which surplus cash is available for investment. In such situations a business invests in securities which are highly liquid even though the yield is comparatively lower. However, there is one compensating factor also. Such highly liquid securities normally have a very active secondary market, with the result the cost of conversion into cash is comparatively less. With the selective relaxation of controls on the money market operations and establishment of Discount and Finance House of India Ltd.(DFHI), Indian secondary market is poised for sustained growth enhancing liquidity of the investments to a great extent.

11.4.4 Volatility

Volatility prevalent in the interest rate is another feature which influences the short-term investments. This necessitates a careful watch on the money market. If the interest rates are likely to rise, it is better to invest for short periods. Conversely, if there is possibility of fall in the interest rates, investments can be made for a longer period.

11.5 TYPES OF INVESTMENTS

There is a wide variety of investments which are available for parking short-term funds. Some of the most prominent among them are explained below.

11.5.1 Term Deposits

Term Deposits are the deposits with the banks which are repayable on a fixed date or after the expiry of the pre-determined period. Unlike deposits in current accounts, these are not payable on demand but after a notice or after the expiry of a stipulated period. The terms of deposits including interest are governed by the rules and regulations framed by the bank which in turn are based on directives issued by Reserve Bank of India and ground rules/instructions issued by Indian Banks Association from time to time.

The rates of interest are dependent on the period of deposits. The bank normally offers different rates of interest for 91 days, 181 days and 366 days. Sometimes, the banks are given the leverage by Reserve Bank of India to pay interest within certain range. These rates are decided by Reserve Bank of India for various periods and are followed universally by all the banks.

Deposits in the banks ensure complete liquidity. The amount becomes eligible for repayment on the prefixed date against the surrender of the deposit receipt. Amount can even be retrieved earlier than the scheduled date, in case of emergency, if the business is prepared to sacrifice part of interest. Another advantage is getting financing facilities against the deposits. The business has the option of raising funds upto 75% of the deposit amount at a rate of interest 2% higher than the rate at which the amount has been deposited. In addition to it, a business can avail of certain other facilities rendered by a bank on the strength of these deposits. It can obtain bank guarantees against these deposits without blocking its funds for these guarantees. It is also seen that once the relationship between the business and bank takes root, the bank normally goes out of the way to provide facilities to the business. The practice of open dated deposit receipts is not very uncommon. Under this, the bank issues deposit receipts without mentioning the duration of the deposit. The due date is filled on the date of encashment. This enables the business to obtain full benefit of interest without any loss on premature encashment of the deposits. This, of course, is dependant on the mutual trust between business and bank. The bank leaves the date unfilled and the business leaves the receipts in the possession of the bank.

Term deposit is very useful instrument of short-term investment. It has least chance of default with full liquidity. However, the rate of interest offered by a bank is normally less than the other avenues available for short-term investments.

11.5.2 Certificate of Deposits

Certificate of Deposit is a term deposit with a bank to be paid after certain period with guaranteed rate of interest. This deposit is evidenced by a certificate issued by a bank and hence is popularly known as Certificate of Deposit or CD in its abbreviated form. The rate of interest agreed to be paid by the bank is dependant on the cash requirements of the bank and the prevalent rate of interest in market. During the conditions of tight money, bank may offer high rates depending upon its own needs of cash. A CD is a negotiable instrument. The holder of CD can sell the same by delivery in the market and get payment earlier than maturity. In developed countries like the U.K., there exists an active secondary market where CDs can be sold to Discount Houses. It adds to the liquidity of the investment. The risk of default in the case of CD is comparatively less as it is issued by a bank.

CD is a fairly popular instrument of investment in the developed economies. It originated in U.S. during 1960s and spread to other countries. In the U.K. the First National City Bank of New York first issued Dollar CD in 1966. By 1968 other British Banks also started issuing such certificates. In India CD is issued by banks for a period of 91 days to one year with the minimum amount of Rs 10 Lakhs. A CD is issued at a discount and the face value is payable at maturity by the issuing bank. The rates of discount keep on varying depending upon cash supply in the money market and banks' own requirement of cash. At times the rates of interest offered by the bank may be 4% to 5% more than the rate for fixed deposit of the identical period. A CD is transferable by endorsement and delivery after 45 days of issue. However, in the absence of developed secondary market of CDs in India, the holder has to reconcile for keeping the same with himself till its maturity.

11.5.3 Treasury Bills

Treasury Bills are rated as an important source of short-term government borrowings and have become an effective source of short-term investment for the commercial enterprises. These are issued for a period of 3 months to 6 months in the U.K. and for 3 months to one year in U.S.A where these are popularly known as T. Bills or Treasuries. Historically, treasury bill was first introduced by the U.K. government in 1877. They gathered momentum during the first and second world wars when the governments of the U.K. and U.S.A. wanted to raise more money from the market. In India Reserve Bank of India (RBI) introduced 182 days Treasury Bills in November 1986. Initially these were auctioned by RBI on monthly basis which was changed to fortnightly from July, 1988. These treasury bills are issued for a period ranging from 91 days to 364 days in the minimum denomination of Rs one lakh and multiples thereof*. However, in the secondary market the deals at present are transacted for a minimum amount of Rs 25 lakhs and thereafter in the multiples of Rs 10 lakhs. Treasury Bills do not carry any rate of interest, rather these are issued at a discount price to be redeemed at the full price at maturity. The return on this instrument is closely related to the prevalent call money rates.

Treasury Bills have all the virtues of a good short-term investment. Since issued by the government these have zero default risk. Also these can absorb huge funds available at the disposal of a business. Maturity periods of the bills are also short - three months to one year.

* RBI to issue Treasury Bills of various maturities—Monetary and Economic Policy 1997.

And above all Treasury Bills have an excellent marketability. These are highly liquid investment instruments since these are actively traded in a developed secondary market. The Discount and Finance House of India Limited (DFHI) is ever willing to purchase treasury bills at its ruling discount rates. A business can invest its surplus funds for a period of less than tenure of the bill also by purchasing the bills nearing maturity from their original owners or DFHI. The option of repos(buy back and sell back) transaction is also available to banks, selected financial institutions and PSU's at negotiated interest rate, if one simply wishes to warehouse the funds for a duration upto 14 days.

11.5.4 Commercial Papers

Commercial papers are large denominated promissory notes normally having maturity period of one month to twelve months. These are issued by big conglomerates or banks. A business can invest its funds by buying these papers and earning interest therefrom. Commercial papers are explained in Chapter 12. Suffice here to say that for a prudent short-term investment, commercial papers of a reputed organisation alone should be considered.

11.5.5 Short-Term Deposits with Financial Institutions

There are a number of financial institutions established by government for providing long-term finances to trade and industry. Some of the examples are SCICI, ICICI, IDBI, IFCI. In addition to these, Companies like ILFS, HDFC are also engaged in providing funds to units in their specialised sectors of operations. At times these institutions require funds for short-term, say, three to six months and offer good rates of interest. They, however, insist for large amounts of investments.

11.5.6 Inter Corporate Deposits

Inter Corporate Deposit is also an effective instrument of short-term deposits. These have become an active source of investment, in particular, when the stock market passes through depressive state. Cash liquidity of the industry as a whole is severely effected due to lower volume of transactions in the stock market. Companies facing cash drought look forward to the companies with cash surplus to meet their immediate requirements. An attractive rate of interest is bargained. Such investments are unsecured, and, therefore, exposed to heavy risks, as well. However, with the advent of credit rating agencies like CRISIL, ICRA and CARE, a business can minimise the risk considerably by depositing its funds in the companies enjoying maximum credit rating.

11.5.7 Others

In addition to these, there are many other avenues open for making short-term investments. Some of these are:

(a) *Units of Unit Trust of India:* Unit Trust of India (UTI) is the oldest mutual fund in India. It has been successfully operating since 1964. US-64 is the most popular scheme of UTI. It is an open ended scheme and as such provides a good opportunity for parking funds for a short time. Units can be purchased from UTI whenever there is a surplus cash and can be sold back to UTI or in the market whenever there is need for cash. After setting off the difference between purchase price and sale price the yield will provide return for the period the units were held by the business.

(b) *Bonds nearing maturity:* Bonds which are scheduled to be redeemed in the immediate future can also provide a slot for temporary warehousing of funds. However, the investment in such bonds should be considered only if the difference between the amount payable on redemption and the present discounted value of bond is quite attractive. The yield should be favourably comparable to the prevalent rate of interest on bank deposits.

(c) *Short Term Debentures:* Some finance and other companies issue short-term debentures having a maturity period of three months or so. It provides a good opportunity for short-term investments if such debentures have been accorded good credit rating.

Exhibit 11.4 shows comparative features of these short-term investments.

Exhibit 11.4
SHORT TERM MONEY MARKET INSTRUMENTS

Investment	Risk/Return	Period	Liquidity
Treasury Bills	Virtually risk free. Return closely related to the prevailing call money rates	30 days to 364 days.	Very high due to existence of a fairly developed secondary market.
Commercial Papers	Risk dependent on the rating of the issuing corporate. The return is higher than that of treasury bills.	1 to 12 months	A negotiable instrument. Quoted in the secondary market. However, non-availability of proper lot size may sometimes affect liquidity
Term Deposits	Low risk since bank operations are subject to strict surveillance by RBI. Return dependent on the period and deposit rate structure of the bank.	46 days to 2/3 years.	Liquid to the extent that they can be withdrawn as and when required subject to penalty applicable. Also limited loan/OD facility available.

(Contd.)

Certificate of Deposits	Low risks since banks are bound by strict statutory requirements, return dependent on the cash requirements of the bank and prevalent rates in the market. Generally, return is more than term deposits.	91 days to 1 year	Transferable by endorsement and delivery only after 45 days of issue. Besides, liquidity affected due to absence of fully developed secondary market.
Deposits with Financial Institutions	Risk not much as most of the institutions are state owned and/or have large size. Return better than term deposits.	3 months to 2 years	Liquidity medium. Some offer facility of partial loans against deposits.
Inter-Corporate Deposits	Risk dependent on the rating of the concerned corporate. Return better than term deposits with banks and financial institutions.	3 months to 3 years.	Very low liquidity.
Units of US-64 Scheme	Low risk. Return dependent on the profits made during the year. Past trend indicate a stable rate. Better than term deposits.	No specified period.	Very high. Can be sold at any time to UTI at the specified repurchase price. Can be sold in the secondary market also.

There are many more opportunities available for the short-term investment and with the development of the economy, these opportunities are growing day by day. However, one has to be careful while exploring possibilities of short-term investment. The primary motive of such investment is to ensure that cash does not remain barren and additional yield flows into the business. The cardinal principle should be to make investment in securities having moderate income with less risk as against high income with heavy risk.

QUESTIONS

1. Describe cash movement statement. What are the advantages of preparing such a statement?
2. What are the limitations of a cash budget. How does cash movement statement overcome these limitations?
3. Explain the factors which are taken into account while selecting an investment option for investing short-term surplus.
4. Describe the term deposits with bank. What are the advantages of parking short-term funds in term deposits?
5. Explain certificate of deposits' as avenue of short-term investments. What are the chief characteristics of certificate of deposit?

6. Why are treasury bills considered as one of the best sources of short-term investments?
7. Write short notes on:
   (a) Inter corporate deposits
   (b) Units of US-64 Scheme
   (c) Non-synchrocity of cash inflows and outflows.

12

SOURCES OF SHORT AND MEDIUM-TERM FINANCING

12.1 INTRODUCTION

A business regularly encounters the instances of short-term cash deficits ranging from a few days to a few months. We have already seen that cash needs of a business are dependent on transaction, precautionary and speculative requirements which have a tendency to fluctuate. There are many reasons for this fluctuation. Sales may vary in peak season and off season; cash reacts accordingly. As the inflow of cash may be less in off season, funds may be required to carry on production. Stock requirements also keep on changing. At times business buys heavy inventory to take advantage of prevalent low prices. Hence, the need for more funds. Even for moderate expansion, short-term financing becomes a handy tool to inject additional funds. Medium-term financing, on the other hand, fulfils the requirements which range from one to five years. They cater to the special type of needs like permanent addition to working capital or buying of fixed assets having commercial life of a few years.

12.2 SHORT-TERM FINANCING

Short-term financing is synchronised with short-term cash deficits and normally is provided for a few months subject to maximum for an year. It is expected that during this period cash inflow will improve enabling the business to repay the debt so raised. Funds raised through short-term financing are utilised primarily to meet requirements of working capital. Short-term financing if utilised for permanent capital like procurement of fixed assets will disturb the rhythm of short-term cash flow cycle culminating in cash drought due to jamming of operational liquidity.

Short-term financing is inherently self-liquidating. Funds are raised to bridge temporary gap between the cash required and the cash available, also known as bridging finance. Debts raised by short-term financing are liquidated through cash generated by the sale of products in the normal course of business. The repayment is out of the receipt of cash from sale of goods rather than cash generated from incremental profit.

12.3 SOURCES OF SHORT-TERM FINANCE

Funds for short-term can be arranged from many sources depending upon the nature of the business and needs of the finance. Other factors which influence the selection of the source are amount to be raised, period for which finance is required, collateral security offered and prevalent economic conditions in the market. The two important sources from where the requirements of short-term financing can be fulfilled are trade circle and money market. The former includes credit by suppliers, whereas the latter includes various types of loans and advances raised from various agencies, predominantly from commercial banks. The sources from where the short-term financing can be arranged are explained below.

12.4 TRADE CREDIT

Trade credit is a credit availed by a business when it purchases goods without making payment in cash. The credit period begins on the receipt of goods and stretches till the payment is made therefor. The business, thus, starts enjoying the goods and at the same time conserve cash till the expiry of credit period. The cash so conserved tantamounts to short-term financing provided by supplier for the duration of credit period.

There are certain features unique to trade credit as a source of short-term financing. First, the credit facility is spontaneous. The need for credit and its financing originate at the same point of time. Secondly, financing through this source is available in the conduct of ordinary course of business. There is no separate activity involved to bring cash into the business like raising of loan. Thirdly, this source of financing is comparatively free from cumbersome legal formalities and documentations. Often old relationship of buyers and suppliers makes trade credit a form of scripless financing.

12.4.1 Terms of Trade Credit

Terms of trade credit are mirror image of the terms of sale on credit. We have already studied terms of credit sale earlier in Chapters 5 and 9. The terms applicable to trade credit are just the reverse of terms of credit sale. Every credit sale for one business becomes credit purchase for another business. Terms of trade credit are, therefore, the terms which a supplier offers to a buyer.

In Chapters 5 and 9, we have noted that credit terms are expressed as "2/10, net 40". This refers to credit period of 40 days but in case the buyer intends to avail a discount of 2%, he is required to pay by 10th day. This type of credit term becomes an important source of short-term financing. The decision of the business whether to make payment by 40th day or 10th day will depend on the cost of financing through this source and cost at which finance is available in the money market. By making payment on 10th day the business is depriving itself cash enjoyment of 30 days (40-10). The benefit of discount, therefore, is to be evaluated against the cost of parting with cash. This can be done by calculating the annualised figure of 2% discount and then comparing it with costs of other sources of financing. The first step of determining the discount in annual terms can be calculated by the following formula:-

$$CC = \frac{D}{100 - D} \times \frac{360^{*}}{P - DP}$$

Where,

CC = Cost of trade credit
D = Discount percentage
P = Period of trade credit
DP = Period of discount

$$\text{Cost of trade credit} = \frac{2}{100-2} \times \frac{360}{40-10} = .245, \textit{ i.e.}, 24.5\%$$

* Traditionally number of days in a year are considered as 360

This means that cost of delaying payment or conserving cash by 30 days is 24.5%. Some writers express it as cost of foregoing discount. The business can compare this cost with cost of financing through other sources and can take decision whether to opt for discount or not. If cost of raising loan in market is say 16%, the business will do well to avail the discount. It can even raise money from the market and pay on 10th day to the supplier in case it does not have sufficient cash available with it.

Another important point to be noted in respect of trade credit is that the credit should be availed for the maximum permissible period. In the instant case the payment should be made either on 10th day or on 40th day. The business does not get any extra discount in case it makes payment by 8th day nor does it get any remission in payment if it makes payment on 25th day. On the contrary, it stands to lose cash enjoyment by 2 days and 15 days respectively.

12.5 FACTORING

Factoring has been dealt in detail in Chapter 9. We recapitulate in brief the important features of factoring. Specialist companies which are in the business of factoring undertake the management of sales ledgers of their business clients. Receivables are sold by the business to a factor who takes the responsibility of recovering money from its customers on the due dates. Factoring companies, which are normally finance houses, charge fees for providing this service. Generally, this source of financing is costlier than bank borrowings. But the business gets the benefit of immediate cash because quite often the factor provides upto 80% as advance against the factored amount. The business also saves the cost associated with administration of debt recovery.

In India RBI has permitted selected commercial banks to operate the business of factoring. At present only two government agencies are involved in this business - SBI Factors Limited and Canbank Factors Limited. In addition, many non-banking finance companies and other agencies are also factoring in book debts.

12.6 INVOICE DISCOUNTING

Invoice discounting is a method under which a business sells the invoice raised on its client to a specialist company at a discount. The discounter releases initial payment upto 75% of the invoice price. Collection of debts remains with the business which acts as an agent of the discounter. On the receipt of money from its customers the business forwards the same to the discounter, generally a finance house.

The arrangement under invoice discounting is similar to that of factoring except the two distinguishing features. First, in the case of factoring (except in the undisclosed factoring) payment of debts is received by a factor whereas in the case of invoice discounting it is received by the business itself which then repays the debts to the discounter. Secondly, the arrangement under factoring generally works as a continuous process. The business sends its invoices, say, on a weekly basis and the factor keeps on crediting the amounts in the account of the business after deducting its fees. The amounts of initial payments made against invoices are debited in the accounts of the business. As against this, invoice discounting is done at a specific time for specific invoice only.

12.7 BANK FINANCING

For the short-term financing, commercial banks are the most important source. Traditionally, the banks provide suppport to their business clients at the critical times. Being specialists in short-term lendings they have developed a number of schemes to suit the individual needs of the borrowers.

While agreeing to the short-term lending the banks look forward to three factors: safety, liquidity and profitability. Banks require some security to guard against any default by the borrower. The second factor of liquidity is important because banks should get its money back whenever due as per the terms of lendings. Banks are very much concerned with the profitability of clients business because in case clients are not likely to have incremental profit due to the loans raised from the banks, in all probability, repayment of loans gets jeopardised. Keeping these three factors in sight, the bank scrutinises the applications for loan facilities by making an in-depth study of the following:-

(a) *Purpose of Loan:* The loan raised by the borrower should be for a purpose which is likely to give profit to the business. The bank will not like to block its funds for a purpose which is unproductive and uncertain.

(b) *Quantum of Loan:* Quantum of loan is dependent on bank's own appraisal of requirements, creditworthiness of the borrower and bank's internal regulations regarding credit sanctions.

(c) *Repayment Schedule:* The bank deals in cash and is very much concerned with the retrieval of its amount with interest from the borrower. Even if it finds that the loan is for productive purposes and is likely to yield high returns to the borrower it will still be reluctant to give loan if it is not convinced regarding the cash inflow projections tendered by the borrower.

(d) *Collateral Security:* Bank normally insists for a collateral security. It is an insurance for a banker to fall back in case of an emergency. It may be in the form of mortgage of a property or hypothecation of stock.

(e) *Creditworthiness:* Another important factor to be considered by the bank is credit worthiness of the borrower. It tries to get information in this respect from internal and external sources. It may evaluate the borrower's balance sheet and ask for certain important details. It can get references from other parties also.

(f) *Minimum Balance:* Some times bank insists that certain amount of compensatory balance should be made available to it till loan is settled. The borrower is not allowed to draw against this amount.

There are various forms of credit facilities which a bank provides to its customers. The most prominent of these facilities are described below.

12.7.1 Overdraft

An overdraft is a credit facility provided by a bank to a customer to draw money over and above the amount available in his account subject to a prefixed limit and period. This is the most common credit facility which is in vogue. The overdraft facility is provided through a current account opened with the bank. The balance in the current account keeps on fluctuating from debit to credit. The bank honours the demands of the borrower provided it is within the sanctioned limit. For example, if the overdraft limit approved by the bank is Rs 20 Lakhs and there is a credit balance of Rs. 8 Lakhs in the account, the bank will honour the payment instructions of the borrower for an amount of Rs 28 lakhs. The borrower can issue cheques for payments, the way he feels like, within the limit of Rs 28 lakhs. He can also deposit any money in the account without any fear of the amount being adjusted by the bank against the overdraft facility. The basic features of an overdraft are as follows:

(a) Overdraft facility is very flexible. The borrower can keep on depositing and withdrawing money from the account. He will be charged interest only in respect of the amount outstanding on daily basis.
(b) It is a time tested method very much familiar to both bank and the borrower, with the result that the arrangement of overdraft can be negotiated and operated without much of the formalities and delays.
(c) Though overdraft is available for a short-period only, but the bank has no hesitation to keep on extending the facility at the expiry of the agreed period if it works well for the mutual benefits of the bank and the borrower. Practically, therefore, it assumes the characteristic of a permanent facility, since it keeps on rolling forward.
(d) It cements the relationship of the bank and the borrower and adds to their mutual confidence.
(e) The rate of interest charged by the bank in the case of overdraft normally covers the base rate plus some element of premium. The bank may also insist for certain security like hypothecation of stock.

12.7.2 Cash Credit

As per banking terminology cash credit is a "drawing account". Under the arrangement a business is authorised to draw cash subject to the limit pre-fixed by the bank. Cash credit is advantageous to a business. Unlike under term-loan, where full amount is made available to the borrower, in the case of cash credit, a credit limit is put at his disposal. This gives the borrower lot more flexibility. He can avail funds to the extent he desires. He will be charged interest only for the amounts so drawn against the limit. The borrower is also accorded the facility of reducing the debit balance in his account as per his convenience and save interest. He can even provide alternative securities from time to time if so agreed with the bank. Quite often a minimum interest clause is inserted by the bank which entitles it to charge interest on, say one fourth of the limit even though the borrower has not withdrawn to that extent. This way the bank gets some returns for the funds locked unnecessarily due to the borrower's inability to draw funds to the extent of the bank estimates. Operationally, cash credit and overdraft are identical. However, cash credit facility is extended by a bank to its valued customers on a regular basis for a long tenure. Overdraft facility, on the other hand, is provided occasionally and for shorter durations.

12.8 BILL FINANCING

Analogically, a 'Bill of Exchange' is like a post-dated cheque. It is an instrument containing an unconditional order signed by a drawer directing a certain person to pay a certain sum of money to or to the order of a person or to the bearer of the instrument. Thus, there are three parties in a bill of exchange—the drawer, the drawee and the payee. Any two of the three capacities can be filled by one and the same person. The method of operation is very simple. The drawer through the instrument asks the drawee to pay the specified amount. The drawee accepts the same and gets the desired credit facilities. Once accepted, it becomes a negotiable instrument. It can be bought and sold in the market. Once sold normally at a discounted value, the drawer gets immediate money. Thus, both drawer and drawee derive benefits out of the arrangement. The bill can be payable on a fixed date, generally 90 days or it can be payable when presented for payment. The former is known as Term Bill and the latter as Sight Bill.

Bill financing has become an important element of money market. Two types of bills of exchange - documentary and accommodation are in circulation alongwith the facilities of rediscounting.

12.8.1 Documentary Bills

Documentary bills can be inland or foreign bills of exchange. Such bills are very common in the international trade. The importer opens letter of credit in favour of the exporter through his banker according to which the exporter draws the bill on the importer which accepts the same with the back up acceptance of his banker. The exporter then negotiates the bill with his own banker and gets the payment against the bill. The banker of the exporter sends the bill to its correspondent in the importing country who can get it further discounted in the market or wait upto the agreed tenure to fetch full value of the bill. Almost identical procedure is adopted in the case of domestic trade. Though it is not necessary that bills should invariably have the support of L.C. but it is observed that security string of a bank enhances the property of discountability of a bill.

12.8.2 Accommodation Bill

It is a simple method of borrowing in which the borrower accepts the bill drawn on it. The bill is then discounted in the market. In U.K. there are accepting houses which are in the business of accepting such bills. These houses accept the bill directly drawn by the drawer. By accepting these bills they take the responsibility of redeeming the same on maturity. The drawer can discount the bills in the market and can get the requisite money immediately. A bill of exchange moves in the money market on the strength of the creditworthiness of a drawer and the accepter. Once the bill is accepted credit of drawer is substituted by the credit of drawee. It is an important source of short-term financing prevalent in the money market.

In India bills are discounted with the government agencies, banks or with non-banking-financing companies in accordance with the guidelines of bills discounting issued by RBI in July 1992.

12.8.3 Rediscounting Bills

Banks offer credit to their customers by discounting commercial bills. Banks too have the facilities of rediscounting these bills and getting ready money instead of blocking their funds till maturity of the bills. The eligibility criteria prescribed by the Reseve Bank of India for rediscounting a bill are as follows:

— bill should arise out of general trade or commercial transaction.
— the maturity date of the bill should be within 90 days of the date of the discounts.
— the original tenor of the bill should not be more than 120 days.

In order to facilitate multiple rediscounting and eliminate circulation of many papers, the individual bills can be substituted by usance promissory note of the equal aggregate amount and maturity issued by the bank.

12.9 COMMERCIAL PAPER

Commercial paper is a typical I.O.U. instrument. Since it is unsecured, only large business houses enjoying highest credit rating in the market can attract funds by issuing commercial paper. Normally, big finance companies associated with large conglomerates and commercial banks use these instruments as a source of raising funds.

Commercial paper can be issued in the market through an issuing and paying agent. This agent ensures that all the legal requirements necessary for the issue of commercial paper are duly taken care of. The fee charged by the agent is negotiable and ranges from 0.125 per cent to 0.25 per cent flat of the issued amount. Alternatively, these can be sold directly to the buyers thereby saving the agent's fee. This is known as direct placement. Normally, commercial papers are issued for one to twelve months. The biggest advantage of commercial papers is saving in the cost involved in their issue. The cost is cheaper than raising of funds from the commercial banks. Besides cost advantage, sometimes the very size of the funds requirement is so huge that the bank may not be in a position to meet the requirements in view of its own internal regulations or statutory constraints. The business which has a reputed name and credit in the market may opt to enter the money market through commercial paper and fetch the desired amount.

Commercial paper is a good source of short-term financing. At maturity the borrower has to redeem the paper by making payment as per terms. However, if the borrower is a large prestigeous business house, it can roll forward the maturity by substituting the issue so matured with the new issue. The disadvantage of this method of financing is that it is not available to all borrowers. Only a few reputed business can avail of the facility of raising finance through the source of commercial paper.

In India issue of commercial paper is regulated through Non-Banking Companies (Acceptance of Deposits through Commercial Paper) Directions, 1989. Reserve Bank of India has been amending these directions from time to time. The regulations as on date are as follows:

- The issuing company should have a minimum net worth of Rs 4 crores. Also, it should have a funds based working capital limits from the banks for a minimum amount of Rs 4 crores.
- The issue should be rated by a recognised credit rating agency like CRISIL/ICRA. The minimum rating should be P2/A2. Rating fee is 0.1 per cent with an annual surveillance fee of 0.03 per cent of the issue size.
- Commercial paper can be issued only by listed companies, public sector companies and closely held public companies.
- The currency of the commercial paper can be for a minimum period of one month and a maximum period of twelve months.
- The issue for the primary market shall be for a minimum of Rs 10 lakhs and multiples of Rs 10 lakhs. However, for secondary market the transactions can be in the denomination of Rs 5 lakhs.
- The maximum amount of commercial paper issue is restricted to 75 per cent of the permissible bank finance limits (funds based working capital limits).
- The current ratio of issuing company should not be less than 1.33 times.

Commercial paper is issued at a discount on face value and rate mentioned in the instrument shall be the yield to investor rate and not discounting rate. No underwriting or co-acceptance is allowed to be made in the commercial paper issue in India. The rate of commercial paper issue depends on the money supply prevalent in the short-term money market at a particular time. The secondary market for commercial paper is not yet developed in India. However, some trading activity has been initiated on the National Stock Exchange.

12.10 INDIGENOUS MONEY LENDERS

When there are pressing demands, the business small and local units in particular, are tempted to raise funds from private individuals. These money lenders operate in a highly unorganised way. The advantages of this source are simplicity and instantaneous receipt of funds. However, the biggest demerit is the exhorbitant rate of interest charged in such cases which act as deterrent for using this as a regular source of short-term financing.

12.11 MEDIUM-TERM FINANCING

Short-term sources outlined above cater to the funds requirements of less than a year. These are best suited for investment in current assets. The funds are needed for long-term as well, for procuring fixed assets like land, building and venturing for a new project. These requirements are for five to twenty-five years and are fed from sources of long-term finances discussed in Chapter 13. There are some requirements which lie in between these two extreme time horizons. Certain plant and machinery may have a commercial life of three to five years. These requirements are funded through medium-term sources of finance.

Three features of medium-term financing distinguish it from short-term financing. At the first place is the time horizon. Short-term financing is maximum for a year whereas medium term financing ranges from one to five years. Secondly, short-term financing is used as bridging finance whenever there is a cash deficit in day-to-day operations. If the debtors have increased and inflow of cash has reduced, short-term, financing will enable procurement of raw materials to keep the production cycle moving. Medium-term financing, on the other hand, is used to make permanent addition to working capital or buy fixed assets. Thirdly, the repayment of short-term financing is done by liquidating the assets being financed through them. Inventory is sold to repay short-term loans. Medium-term financing is repaid from the profits or cash flow generated from operations over a period of several years.

12.12 SOURCES OF MEDIUM-TERM FINANCES

Medium-term financing can be arranged from the following sources:

12.13 FIXED DEPOSITS

A company can raise funds by accepting fixed deposits from members, directors and the general public. The acceptance of these deposits are subject to statutory provisions of Companies Act and regulations issued by Reserve Bank of India (RBI) from time to time. A company can accept deposits for a period ranging from six months to thirty six months. The maximum rate of interest is determined by RBI which normally is in the range of 15%. The maximum amount of the deposit outstanding on the date of acceptance from public should not exceed twenty five per cent of the aggregate of the paid-up capital and free reserves of the company. The advertisement for acceptance of deposits should be signed by the majority of directors of the company and filed with Registrar of Companies before issue of the advertisement.

Fixed deposits as a source of finance is devoid of complicated formalities. Receipts of cheques and issue of fixed deposit receipts are the two major activities. The initial cost of raising funds through this method is less costly. Major costs are advertisement for soliciting deposits, commission paid to agents if employed, stationery and postage. But all put together the cost remains within moderate limits. Even the perpetual cost of interest payable to depositors is less than the interest charged by banks. Another important advantage is that the assets of the company remain unencumbered since such fixed deposits are generally unsecured.

Fixed deposits as source of medium-term finance suffer from the demerit of unreliability. The unreliability is both with regard to receipt of deposits and repayment of money. For the receipt of deposits, a company cannot bank upon this as a regular source of raising sufficient funds. Companies enjoying highest credit rating alone can exploit fixed deposits as a definite source. So far as repayment is concerned slight decline in the financial health may trigger mad rush for premature encashments of the deposits culminating in the sure downfall of the company which otherwise could have been avoided.

12.14 TERM LOANS FROM COMMERCIAL BANKS

A term loan raised from bank is for a specific amount, specific period and is subject to specific repayment terms. Such loans are provided against the security of fixed assets like land and building, current assets like shares, debentures and even fixed deposit receipts. Generally, the amount is provided in lumpsum by crediting loan amount in the account of the borrower. In certain cases like agricultural sector, loan may be provided in instalments as well. Repayment of loan by borrower can also be in lumpsum or in series of instalments.

The rate of interest is normally more than the overdraft rate. But in certain priority sectors like exports, there are provisions of providing funds on subsidised rates of interest also.

12.15 HIRE PURCHASE

Hire purchase is a system of buying an asset on credit. The buyer pays relatively small amount as initial payment and takes the possession of the equipment. The balance amount is paid in regular periodic instalments which cover both the part payment and part interest. The ownership of the equipment is transferred only after the payment of final instalment. It is an important source of medium-term financing and the period involved stretches from one year to five years.

Hire purchase is mainly useful for a business in its initial stage of fast growing period. The business at this stage is struggling hard to increase sales and the resultant cash inflow. Hire purchase helps the business to conserve well sought after cash in the business. Unlike in the case of outright purchase, the business need not part with full cash on account of the cost of the equipment. The initial down payment and periodic instalments entitle the business to use the equipment. Thus, it provides enough time to the business to get stabilised and make payments of periodic instalments from the cash generated through the use of the equipment. Hire purchase is good for such type of equipment, in particular, which is indivisible and involves heavy capital outlay. Examples are automobiles, lathe machines and the likes.

Hire purchase can be arranged directly from manufacturers or through specialised finance companies. Such companies make exhaustive enquiries about the creditworthiness of the business. The equipment is normally meant for a specific requirement and may lack general acceptability. It may not have enough residual value. The companies financing hire purchase, therefore, are very much concerned with the solvency of the business getting the equipment on hire.

Hire purchase arrangements provide an easily negotiated finance. It is a good source to supplement bank financing. In the inflationary market, it has added advantage since the real value of the instalment keeps on diminishing. Another advantage is better after sales service provided by the manufacturers in view of the fact that the equipment continues to be owned by them. However, it is not a cheap source of financing and often it becomes difficult for the business to meet its periodic commitments.

12.16 LEASING

Leasing is yet another important source of medium-term financing. It is an arrangement under which an asset is financed and owned by one party but possessed and used by the other. The owner of the asset is known as lessor and user is called lessee. The lease agreement details out the specific period and timing of the sequential payments to be made by the lessee to lessor as consideration for the use of the asset.

Lease is an imputed form of debt. It is like raising of loan not in cash but in kind. Instead of cash, lessee receives an asset. Like any other loan, the lease agreement incorporates repayment schedule for a period dependent upon the type of lease and nature of leased asset.

Earlier, lease was confined to property related assets only. During sixties, lease movement gathered momentum in the developed countries and equipment like plant and machinery, computer, automobile, aircraft, and agricultural implements were included in the net of leasing. Lease can be provided directly by the manufacturer of the asset to the user. Alternatively, lease may be provided by the financing companies, merchant bankers and subsidiaries of commercial banks. These companies though not functionally associated with the assets to be leased are in the business of leasing. They buy the assets from the manufacturers and lease them to the users.

12.16.1 Basic Features of Leasing

There are certain features unique to a lease. These are as follows:-

(a) *Period:* Probably, no other form of financing has such a large variation in terms of time. Lease can be for any period ranging from a day to hundreds of years. A car can be rented for a day under the tacit agreement of lease. On the other hand, land can be leased for 100 years by the concerned municipal authority or city development authority or by a trust to the user. The period of equipment to be leased is determined on the basis of requirements of lessee and active useful life of the leased asset. The period is normally less than its active commercial life.

(b) *Payments* : The payments for the use of the leased asset is made in a sequential pattern. Payments can be made on daily, weekly, monthly, or yearly basis depending upon the terms of the lease agreement between lessor and the lessee.

(c) *Security:* Generally, a lease transaction does not emphasise upon the security since the asset remains under the ownership of the lessor. In the event of default, asset can always be taken back. Even in the case of bankruptcy of lessee, leased asset is returned to the lessor who stands with other creditors in respect of the defaulted lease payments.

(d) *Escalation:* Lease payments are prefixed as to the amounts and the timings. But in some cases particularly in the countries experiencing high inflation, lease agreement may provide for an escalation linked with the relevant price index.

12.16.2 Types of Leases

An agreement of lease is between two parties who are at liberty to determine mutually agreed terms and conditions. However, based on the practice in vogue, leases can be categorised into following types:-

(a) *Operating Lease:* Operating lease is for a shorter duration, much less than the useful life of an asset. The amount of the asset is thus not fully amortised from a specific lease. In such cases the lessor either re-leases or sells the equipment after the expiry of lease agreement. Another important feature of operating lease is that such a lease agreement is cancellable. A common example is lease of a dwelling unit where lessee can give notice of cancellation of lease as per the terms of lease agreement and the lessor has to make arrangement for the re-leasing of the premises. Due to these features, lessor of an equipment is always exposed to the risk of technological obsolescence in operating lease.

(b) *Financial Lease:* The period of financial lease is stretched to the useful commercial life of the asset. The amount due is fully amortised during the tenure of the lease period. Lessor holding the title of the equipment, owns the residual value as well. Financial lease is not cancellable. Risk of obsolescence in such cases is borne by the lessee. In the event of equipment becoming obsolete due to technologocal advancement lessee has either to bear with it till the balance period of lease or buy the equipment from the lessor by making full payment of rental.

(c) *Net Lease :* Both operating and financial leases can be gross or net lease. A lease to be gross or net is dependent upon the fact as to who will bear the costs of maintenance, insurance and other levies associated with leased asset. In the case of net lease, lessee bears these costs whereas under gross lease such costs are borne by lessor. A finance lease is commonly a net lease. Justifiably so, because the lease agreement is non-cancellable as a result of which lessee is more careful for its maintenance. Also finance lease may be for a specific type of equipment for which lessee is better equipped to maintain instead of lessor. If a ship has been leased by a finance company to a shipping company, it is obvious that the shipping company is in a much better position to take care of its maintenance as compared to the leasing company which is operating in the field of finance. Under operating lease, the lessor is very much concerned about the risk of technological obsolescence. It, therefore, ensures that the asset continues to function normally and thus takes care of its maintenance.

12.16.3 Advantages

Both operating lease and finance lease have some advantages which are exclusive to them whereas some other advantages are common to both types of leases:-

(a) Leasing is a very simple and convenient method of financing. The individual requirements of the lessee can be taken care of.

It is quite simple for a construction company to take on lease concrete mixer for a short period at the time of concreting activity at the site and return the same after accomplishing the objective. There is no need to buy and keep the mixer idle when other activities are in progress.

(b) At the time of tight money conditions in the market it may be difficult to raise funds for buying certain equipment. Also if the amount required is small then again it may not be economical to raise a loan from money market. In such cases leasing becomes a handy tool of short-term financing.

(c) In the case of operating lease, lessee is free from the fear of technological obsolescence. On the contrary, he keeps on acquiring the latest model of the equipment.

(d) It is observed that lease payments generally are more than the admitted amounts of depreciations in the income tax. The lessee, therefore, has a benefit of lower tax burden.

(e) There is no need to sink heavy amount for buying a costly equipment.

(f) Generally, lease agreements do not contain any escalation clause. The rigid repayment instalments are spanned for large number of years. For a lessee this is economical in real terms of the values of instalments during inflationary period.

(g) Lease agreements generally are free from onerous covenents which are normally put in loan agreements.

(h) The regulated lease repayment amounts benefit the business for it can project cash flow movement in a more accurate manner. Also lease agreement insulates the lessee against increase in cost due to increase in the rate of interest as it happens in bank overdraft.

12.16.4 Disadvantages

The disadvantages of lease financing are as follows:

(a) It is costlier than the normal purchase of an asset. However, the true cost of lease needs a careful analysis. Such an analysis takes into account opportunity costs associated with buying the asset and the net present values of the sequential repayment instalments to be paid in future.

(b) Tax authorities some times provide some extra advantages for buying and owning new equipment. These are not available to the lessee, since the equipment remains under ownership of lessor. However, quite often, lessor passes to the lessee these benefits in the form of reduced rental.

(c) The rigidity of the payments particularly in the finance lease may cause some problems in the subsequent years. Finance lease is non-cancellable. The lessee, therefore, has to carry the asset with him till maturity of the contract even if very advanced technological models have entered the market.

QUESTIONS

1. Explain the trade credit as a source of short-term financing.
2. What factors are considered by a bank while scrutinising an application for loan facilities of a customer?
3. What is an overdraft? Explain its basic features. How does it differ with cash credit?
4. What are the various ways of raising short-term finances under the schemes of bill financing?
5. Explain commercial paper as a source of raising short-term finances.
6. Define leasing. What are its basic features? Describe its advantages and disadvantages.
7. Write short notes on:
   (a) Invoice discounting
   (b) Term loan by a bank
   (c) Hire purchase

13

SOURCES OF LONG-TERM FINANCING

13.1 INTRODUCTION

Long-term financing is required to cater to the needs of long-range planning. Every business tries to expand for which it requires funds which should remain at its disposal for a longer period. Thus, the thrust in the case of long-term financing is on growth and development rather than running day-to-day business. There are four basic features of a long-term financing. First, the funds are required for a longer duration. The time horizons of expansionary programmes are much longer. It, thus, warrants that funds be deployed for long period to accomplish the goals set in the plans. So much so that some of the funds may remain tied up with the business throughout its life. This, in fact, constitutes permanent financing in the form of equity capital. Secondly, the quantum of funds requirement is very large. The expansionary programmes are capital-intensive and demand pumping of large funds into the business. Thirdly, selection of an appropriate source is extremely important. The two sources of long-term financing are capital and debt. Selection of an appropriate finance-mix of the two alone will yield maximum return at the lowest cost. A wrong decision can be catastrophic for the business. Fourthly, there are plethora of statutory provisions which are to be complied with, when the funds are to be raised from the general public. It is a huge subject particularly in view of requirements of Companies Act and ever changing guidelines issued by Securities and Exchange Board of India (SEBI) from time to time. Present chapter primarily deals with the commercial aspect of long-term financing, and as such, text relating to statutory requirements have been kept out of its scope.

13.2 DISTINCTION BETWEEN SHORT-TERM FINANCING AND LONG-TERM FINANCING

The following are the distinguishing features of short-term financing and long-term financing.

13.2.1 Purpose

Short-Term Financing aims at providing solace to temporary cash droughts. The idea is to ensure that cash flow cycle keeps on moving and the business continues to operate with desired level of working capital. Long-term financing, on the other hand, is not meant for such day-to-day operations. It is concerned with ensuring sufficient finances for the achievement of long-term objectives of growth and development of the business as stipulated in the corporate plan.

13.2.2 Period

Short-term financing is confined to a maximum period of one year. The business endeavours to convert its non-cash current assets into cash as quickly as possible. As a result of which cash deficits though quite frequent are very short lived. Long-term financing has a longer time frame so as to synchronise with the long duration needs of expansionary programmes. The period of long-term financing may range from five to twenty five years.

13.2.3 Volume

The volume of funds involved in short-term financing is much small as compared to long-term financing as the former is required for day-to-day business and the latter for large-scale expansion.

13.2.4 Formalities

Raising of funds for short term is much simpler, convenient and easy. Processing of long-term financing, on the other hand, involves cumbersome procedural requirements, documentations and is more time-consuming.

13.2.5 Security

Stock and debtors are considered good securities for short-term financing. Long-term financing requires high value properties and assets as security. It is not uncommon to raise short-term finance without any security. It is, however, almost axiomatic that any lender of long-term finance will look for the best possible security.

13.3 FACTORS INFLUENCING CHOICE OF A SOURCE

Capital and debt are the two root-sources of long-term financing. These are popularly known as owners funds and borrowers funds. From these two sources flow various types of financing; each having unique characteristics of its own. A business makes an analysis of pros and cons of individual source, while making choice for the one. Each source whether belonging to equity or debt fraternity has mixed bag of advantages and disadvantages. A business weighs the relative strengths of these advantages and disadvantages in the light of following factors before opting for a particular source.

13.3.1 Initial Costs

Initial costs of raising long-term financing range from negligible to substantial. If the chosen source demands coverage of a vast market, the costs are likely to be high, *e.g.*, issue of shares or debentures to the general public shall involve heavy initial costs in the form of underwriters fee, advertisement cost, printing cost *etc.* Conversely, initial costs involved in the long-term loan negotiated with a financial institution shall not be much.

13.3.2 Perpetual Costs

This head represents recurring costs associated with a source of finance. Some sources like long-term loans or debentures and bonds bind the company to incur continuing costs as interest till the time the debt is alive. Equity finance, on the other hand, allows more discretion in the hands of management to retain the income so generated with the business or share as dividend with the shareholders to the extent it deems fit. However, considering the other side we find that whereas debenture or bond holder has to be content with the interest as per terms of issue, equity shareholders expect high returns in terms of capital appreciation and dividend. A compromise between the two is provided by preference shares.

13.3.3 Repayment Obligations

The debts are required to be liquidated in accordance with predetermined schedule. The company has to arrange cash for the repayment on the stipulated dates. There are no such compulsions for equity. Equity continues to be in the company as capital of a going concern. Preference shares however, are also redeemed as per terms of the issue. Equity becomes eligible for repayment on the liquidation of the company only. In the event of liquidation, debt holders get priority in respect of unpaid amount as against the equity holders.

13.3.4 Tax Relief

Another important factor to be weighed before the selection of a long-term source of finance is tax angle associated with it. The perpetual cost of interest inherent in a debt obligation is a charge to profit and to that extent is cheaper to the company. Dividend, on the other hand, is viewed as sharing of profit and as such is not deductible while arriving at company's tax liability.

13.3.5 Control and Management

In broad terms, control and management of a company is effected only in the case of equity financing. Such rights are not effected on debt financing. However, this may not be true in all cases. In equity financing right issue and bonus issue shall not dilute the control of existing shareholders. Likewise, there may be a clause in debt financing empowering debt holders to have access to the management of the company in case the company fails to fulfil its obligations provided for in the debt agreement.

13.3.6 Success Rate

Each source of long-term financing has its own degree of success rate. In some like bonus issue and rights issue, it may be as high as hundred per cent while in some others it is exposed to great many uncertainties. A number of factors influence the success of a source. Prevalent economic and monetary policies, booms and depressions of economy, receptivity for a particular kind of source in the market, future prospects of the concerned business, cash availability with financial institutions are some of the factors which influence the successful tapping of a particular source.

We shall study these factors in detail while examining the individual source of long-term finance.

13.4 EQUITY FINANCING

Equity financing is an important source of capital financing. It consists of shares issued by a company, subscribers of which become shareholders and collectively own the company. They exercise ownership through voting rights which are commensurate with the shares held by them. They share the profits of the company by way of dividend and also enjoy appreciation in the value of shares in case the company trades successfully. On the other hand, if the company is not making profit, they have to bear the loss. They are residual claimers in respect of profits and assets. Profits to them is distributed only after the claims of others like labourers, suppliers, lenders *etc.* are met and likewise in the event of liquidation of company their claims rank last after claims of other claimants are satisfied.

13.5 METHODS OF RAISING EQUITY FINANCE

There are three different ways of raising equity finance. These are (a) making use of retained profits and is known as Bonus Issue, (b) inviting additional capital from existing shareholders and is known as Rights Issue, and (c) inviting fresh capital from the public and is known as New Issue. These are explained below:-

13.5.1 Bonus Issue

As its name suggests these shares are issued by a company free of cost as bonus to its members. These are issued out of the retained profit. It looks paradoxical as to how a company can consider Bonus Issue as a source of equity financing when it is not likely to receive any money against it. In order to appreciate it in its proper perspective it should be well understood that the retained income which has been used for issue of bonus shares has been generated and retained in the business in consonance with the policy of the management. The company has two alternatives when it consistently makes profit. One, to distribute the income to the shareholders as dividend and ask for the additional capital from the shareholders out of the profit so distributed. Two, to retain the income in the company and issue bonus shares to shareholders at the opportune time. In the former case, the money is received after the allotment of shares whereas in latter case money has already been received in the form of income generated and retained which is now used for issue of shares. This way the undistributed profit is permanently ploughed back into the business.

From the point of view of the company, issue of bonus shares does not make any change in the total amount of shareholders' fund. The only change being that after the bonus issue, equity stands increased by an exact amount the reserves stands decreased. However, issue of bonus shares does show confidence of the management in the business which has a favourable impact on the market value of its shares. Bonus shares are issued on the pro-rata basis to existing shareholders, and, therefore, do not disturb voting rights of the shareholders.

13.5.2 Rights Issue

Right issue is an invitation to the present shareholders to subscribe to new shares to be issued by the company. The number of shares offered to a shareholder are pro-rata to the existing strength of his shareholding. A company may offer rights issue as one for two shares signifying thereby that the shareholder can subscribe to one new share for the two shares held by him. If a shareholder has 200 shares he acquires right to buy additional 100 shares. In case a shareholder is not interested in the offer, he can sell his right to subscribe to a third party who need not be a member of the company.

The fixation of appropriate share price is very vital for the success of the right issue. The right issue price of a share is kept lower than its market price. There are two basic reasons for doing so. First, it is natural for the present owners to expect some price preference. It induces them and instils a sense of belonging with the company. This way the management and control too, remain with the existing shareholders. Secondly, it increases the chances of the success of the issue. If the shares are not offered at the lower price and during subscription period market value falls below the offered price, the issue is likely to fail. Other factors which contribute towards success of a issue are future prospects of the business, the size of the issue and expected market value of the share after the rights issue.

For the rights issue, the company sends letter of offer to all their shareholders stating therein the number of shares held by them, number of shares they are entitled to subscribe as per terms of offer within the stipulated period. Sometimes, another column is provided to indicate additional shares which the shareholder may like to acquire in case some shareholders do not exercise their rights. The second part of the offer relates to renunciation of the right. As stated earlier a shareholder can sell the rights (commonly known as renunciation of rights) to someone else in the market. The person to whom the rights are sold need not be a member of the company.

The reasons for fixing the price of right shares lower than its market price has already been explained. This has an effect on the determination of new market price of the share which tends to be somewhere between the earlier market price and rights-offer price. Suppose a company has a paid-up capital of Rs 50,00,000 in the form of 5,00,000 shares of Rs 10 each. The market value of its share is Rs 200. The company proposes to make a rights issue of 1,00,000 shares @ Rs 140 per share. The market value of entire equity of the company prior to rights issue was Rs 10 Crores (5,00,000 × Rs 200) whereas the market value of the equity after the right issue is expected to be Rs 11.40 Crores (Rs 10 crores + Rs 1.4 crores). The market value of the share, thus, will be Rs 190 (Rs 11.40 crores/6,00,000). This concept indirectly adds to the success of the rights issue when we examine the options available to the shareholders, in respect of rights offer.

On the receipt of a rights offer a shareholder has three options:-

(a) to accept the offer, or

(b) to sell the offer, or

(c) to ignore the offer.

Extending the example considered above, suppose a shareholder owns 1000 shares. The market value of his shares is Rs 2,00,000 (1000 × Rs 200). He has been offered additional 200 shares on pro-rata basis of 1 for 5 at price of Rs 140. He has three choices;

(a) To accept the offer. If he accepts the offer, he will make a payment of Rs 28,000 and the market value of his shareholding will increase by exactly the equal amount. His shareholding will increase to 1200 shares which as per new market price of Rs 190 each will make the total value of his shareholding as Rs 2,28,000 (1200 × Rs 190). The pre-right issue value of his shareholding was Rs 2,00,000 (1000 × Rs 200). The net increase in his holding is Rs 28,000 which exactly is the price he paid for subscribing to the rights issue. Thus, he neither loses nor gains.

(b) To sell the rights. He can sell the rights presumably for Rs 10,000. The rights issue price is Rs 140 and the post issue market price is expected to be Rs 190. The 'advantage price' of rights issue, thus, is Rs 50 per share. He can sell the rights, for Rs 10,000 (200 × Rs 50). His net holding value then will be Rs 2,00,000 consisting of 1000 shares at the revised market value of Rs 190, *i.e.,* Rs 1,90,000 plus Rs 10,000 received as cash from the buyer of the rights Shares. Thus, he neither loses nor gains.

(c) To ignore the offer. If a shareholder allows the offer to lapse, he becomes a loser. In the instant case, the share price consequent upon the rights issue, will get reduced to Rs 190 decreasing the market value of his shareholding to Rs 1,90,000/- (1000 × Rs 190). Thus, he loses Rs 10,000 by failing to exercise his option either for accepting the rights or selling the rights.

This phenomenon greatly contributes towards the success of the rights issue making it a favourite source of raising long-term finance by a company.

13.5.3. New Issue

Both, Bonus Issue and Rights Issue are confined to the existing shareholders. New Issue, on the other hand, extends invitation to investors at large to subscribe to the shares of the company. The reasons for 'going to public', a term commonly used for New Issue can be many. Need to have large amount of funds, listing requirements of a stock exchange, dilution of shares held by foreign nationals and constructing a pattern of broad base shareholding are some of the reasons influencing a company's decision to go public. Whatever be the reason, there is no denial from the fact that New Issue involves a time- and money-consuming exercise. Despite this, in a burgeoning economy like that of India raising of capital through New Issue has become a call of the day.

New Issue is the first step towards establishing contractual relationship between the company and the new investors. These potential investors can genuinely claim lack of sufficient information about company's business and management on which rests their decision to invest or not to invest. The government, therefore, has introduced a number of statutes to protect their interests. There are plethora of provisions in the Companies Act and the Securities and

Exchange Board of India (SEBI) guidelines warranting a prospective company to display sufficient information in the document offering stakes in the company. This document is popularly known as Prospectus. The prospectus contains detailed information regarding financial strength of the company, future prospects, risk factors associated with the issue and management's perception of these risk factors, among other things.

New Issue has somewhat nebulous market. In fact, any point of contact between a prospective subscriber and the company is part of the market. To cover such a market, a company needs the services of specialised agencies. The agencies are managers, underwriters, registrars and bankers. Manager, in fact, is an adviser and supervisor to the issue. He conducts the whole operation taking into consideration financial and legal requirements. If the issue is very big and there are many managers, one of them acts as lead manager.

Another important agency is the underwriter. A new issue has many underwriters. They undertake to subscribe to shares in case the company fails to get required response from the investors. They are insurers who minimise the risk inherent in the new issue. Registrar takes care of the procedural arrangements regarding issue of shares applications, allotments and refunds *etc.* Banker collects share application money through the network of its branches.

The success of the new issue depends upon a number of factors prominent being past performance, future prospects and pricing of the shares. A company having good track record of profit and dividend can expect favourable response from new investors. Similarly, a company in a business with bright future prospects, too, becomes a favourite when it approaches public for investment to its shares. Pricing of shares has decisive role in this regard. Shares can be issued at par, premium or discount subject to fulfilling certain statutory requirements.

13.6 FACTORS INFLUENCING CHOICE OF EQUITY FINANCING

The following factors influence the choice of equity issue as a source of long-term finance.

13.6.1 Initial Costs

The initial costs of equity issue range from almost zero to 10% of the issue price depending upon the type of issue. Bonus Issue entails almost nil cost. In the case of right issue initial costs may be in the range of 3% to 5% as the company has to send notices procuring option, make arrangements with the bankers and initiate action for allotment. The new issue involves maximum initial costs normally in the range of 10% or so. Major items of expenditure are the advertisements in the media, underwriters fees, expenses related to appointment of managers, registrars and bankers to the issue, printing and stationery and the likes.

13.6.2 Perpetual Costs

Dividend represents an explicit cost. In the evaluation of this element of cost both, the aspirations and limitations of the equity shareholders are to be taken note of. The equity shareholders expect relatively higher returns since they are exposed to the risks of failure. The yield to them may be in the form of annual dividend, periodic bonus issue or capital appreciation which they can realise by selling their holdings in the market. But at the same time, they have no right to claim dividend. It is the discretion of the management to declare or defer the dividend till all the obligations to be met out of the profit are taken care of.

13.6.3 Repayment Obligations

There is no repayment obligation till the company is alive. Equity share holders being the owners are not entitled for the repayment of their money during the currency of the company. In the event of winding up of the company, however, they are entitled to the residuals after all the obligations and liabilities have been taken care of. The residuals may be more than their share holdings if the company has been a successful venture or less than that if the persistent losses have eroded the capital of the company.

13.6.4 Tax Relief

Dividend is part of profit and not cost. From the taxation point of view, it is a distribution of taxable profit and not charge against profit. It is not an admissible expense. Thus, this makes it a costly source of finances. Fifteen per cent dividend is almost hundred per cent costlier than fifteen per cent interest because the latter gets the benefit of admissibility as an item of expense for the determination of taxable profit, the rate of corporate tax being in the range of forty five per cent. Indeed, tax impact constitutes an important deterrent while making the choice of equity issue as a source of finance.

13.6.5 Control and Management

Equity shares stem management control. These carry voting rights. Every equity shareholder can exercise control over management commensurate with the strength of his holding. Bonus issue and rights issue do not disturb the voting strength of the existing shareholders as both are issued pro-rata to their existing share-holdings. However, new issue makes a big dent on the management control of existing shareholders since the new shareholders are issued equity shares which rank *pari passu* with the existing shares in all respects. This is the price existing shareholders have to pay to attract additional funds from the market.

13.6.6 Success Rate

Bonus Issue has a success rate of hundred per cent. Rights issue, too, has very good chance of success because the price offered for subscribing to the shares is normally less than the prevalent market price. The new issue is prone to all sorts of uncertainties and risks particularly during depression in the market. However, to a considerable extent the company can insulate itself against these uncertainties by taking the services of underwriters who underwrite the whole of issue.

13.7 PREFERENCE SHARES

Preference shares like equity shares are part of the ownership fraternity. But they carry preferential rights over the equity shares. These shares bestow to their owners right to the first slice in respect of payment of dividend as well as repayment of capital in the event of liquidation of the company. The right to claim dividend is confined to a pre-determined rate as and when the management decides to declare dividend. Preference shares have been branded as a hybrid security, embracing features of both equity and debt. The preference shares are akin to equity shares since they expose the company to the cost of dividend which is not an 'obligatory cost'. Dividend is declared out of the profits and is subject to discretion of the management. Management may decide not to declare it in lean periods. Preference share holders cannot claim it as a matter of right. On the other hand, like the cost of debt, the dividend cost of preference shares is prefixed. Whatever be the profit the rate of dividend is limited to the rate at which preference shares had been issued. This unique feature of preference shares has made it an extremely flexible source of finance.

Preference shares are of the following types:-

13.7.1 Cumulative or Non-Cumulative

In the case of cumulative preference shares the dividend keeps on accumulating till the time it is eventually paid. Non-cumulative shares refer to the preference shares which do not provide such rights to their holders. If no dividend is declared in a year, the right lapses.

13.7.2 Participating and Non-Participating

Participating preference shares entitle the holders to get some additional share of profit over and above its fixed rate, out of the surplus left after payment of dividend to the equity shareholders. Non- participating shares do not carry such right.

13.7.3 Redeemable and Irredeemable

Redeemable preference shares are those which have a limited life span. These are redeemed during the life time of the company. Irredeemable preference shares can be redeemed only at the winding up of the company. With the amendment of Companies Act vide Companies (Amendment Act) Act, 1988, a company cannot issue irredeemable preference shares or redeemable preference shares having maturity date of more than 10 years from the date of issue.

13.8 FACTORS INFLUENCING CHOICE OF PREFERENCE SHARES

The factors influencing the choice of preference shares as a source of raising finance are as follows.

13.8.1 Initial Costs

The initial costs involved in the issue of preference shares are similar to those of equity shares. The methodology of approaching prospective investors, statutory obligation of the company to disclose information, involvement of managers, bankers, underwriters *etc.* are same as are in the case of equity issue. So the initial costs of preference shares are quite high. It may be considerably less if other methods like private placement and auction are used in place of prospectus to attract investments from general public.

13.8.2 Perpetual Costs

Preference share as a security is of quasi-debt nature. Its perpetual costs are restricted to the pre-determined amount of dividend inbuilt in the terms of its issue irrespective of the quantum of profit being negligible or substantial. The company, thus, have the advance knowledge of its obligations towards perpetual costs. The perpetual costs, however, are likely to be somewhat lower since the preference shareholders are not exposed to as much risk as the equity shareholders. The quantum of perpetual costs which are prefixed at the time of issue of preference shares are, in fact, determined on the basis of prevalent rates of interest in the market. The financial strength and the goodwill of the company is comparatively of lesser significance. Finally, from the practical point of view it is not possible for a company to avoid this perpetual cost for a long time. We have seen that it is within the prerogative of the company to declare or not the preference share dividend, and thus avoid cost. However, non-declaration of preference share dividend for a number of years has an adverse effect on the credibility of the company which may damage its business operations as well. A company cannot afford to ignore this aspect.

13.8.3 Repayment Obligations

Companies Amendment Act, 1988 has disallowed the issue of preference share having a maturity date of more than ten years. A company issuing preference shares, therefore, must ensure that it accumulates enough cash to successfully redeem these shares at the due dates.

13.8.4 Tax Relief

From the taxation point of view preference dividend remains a dividend irrespective of the limitation of predetermined rate associated with it. It, like equity dividend, is not allowed to be deducted out of profit as an admissible expense. This makes the preference shares a costly proposition as compared to debentures or bonds.

13.8.5 Control and Management

Preference shares are part of capital and preference shareholders belong to the fraternity of owners. But they do not enjoy any right to participate in the control of management and rightly so because they are not fully exposed to vagaries of risks and uncertainties of a business. Preference shares do not carry voting rights except on the matters which directly affect the preference shareholders

13.8.6 Success Rate

The rate of dividend associated with the preference shares is dependent on the prevalent rates of interest in the market rather than the financial strength of the company. The success of the preference shares issue as source of finance is, therefore, very much dependent on the competitive rate of dividend offered by the company vis-a-vis interest yields on the other commecial instruments available in the market.

In the conclusion, it can be said that preference shares, though enjoying the merit of flexibility have some limitations which has made it less popular source of long-term finance. In fact, limitation of ten years maturity provided in the Companies (Amendment) Act, 1988 has further reduced its usefulness, if the funds are required for a longer duration. As a source of finance it is good when a company finds it difficult to sell its equity or when market sentiments are favourable towards fixed income bearing securities.

13.9 DEBT FINANCING

Debt financing is a composite term for those funds which are raised by a business as "Loan-capital". The funds are borrowed for a specific period against payment of interest at periodic interval and repayment of principal as per agreed schedule. These two legal obligations of payment of interest and repayment of principal have potential dire consequences and may result in bankruptcy if the business fails to meet its commitments. This makes the debt financing riskier than equity financing. Interest has to be paid whether there is profit or not, and the principal has to be repaid even if the business has failed to generate sufficient cash for repayment. However, on the plus side, debt financing is a cheaper source of long-term financing due to tax advantage. Interest is an allowable deduction against profit unlike dividend which is an appropriation of profit. Further, except for special circumstances arising due to default on the part of business, debt financing does not involve any dilution of control over the management of the company.

The major sources of debt financing are:

13.10 DEBENTURES

Debenture is an important segment of 'loan capital'. It is a long term-loan with specific maturity, pre-fixed interest rate and pre-determined repayment provisions. Debenture as a script is a certificate issued by a company acknowledging a debt due from it to the debenture holder. Debenture holders have no direct control on the management of the company. They are represented by trustees who have a legal duty to protect their interest. If there is any default in honouring its commitments by the company, trustees report the same to the debenture holders. The debenture holders can take legal action and can even force the bankruptcy on the company. In the event of such proceedings debenture holders have first claim over the assets of the company as against the shareholders.

The specific advantage which a company has in the case of debenture is exercise of buyback option. Unlike in the case of shares, a company can always buy its own debentures in the market. This gives the company some safeguard against changes in interest rates. If the interest rates fall significantly during the life span of debentures, the company may opt to buy its own debentures carrying higher rates of interest by borrowing funds from the market at lower interest rates and thereby reduce its interest burden.

13.11 TYPES OF DEBENTURES

Debentures are of various types as explained below.

13.11.1 Naked Debebture

These debentures do not carry any charge on the assets of the company. Normally very strong companies only, which are confident of attracting funds from the market on the strength of their reputation, issue such debentures.

13.11.2 Mortgage Debenture

These are the debentures which are secured against the company's fixed assets like land, building and machinery.

13.11.3 Floating Debenture

In this case the charge extends to all the assets of the company.

13.11.4 Irredeemable Debentures

As the name suggests these debentures are not redeemed. They remain alive till the company is wound up.

13.11.5 Convertible Debentures

Convertible debentures are the debentures which carry the right of convertion into shares at a specific price at or between pre-fixed dates. It can be viewed as a debt plus an option. The terms of conversion are decided at the time of issue of debentures. It covers two aspects. First, the date or the period during which the debentures become eligible for conversion. Secondly, the rate of conversion from debentures to shares which can either be stated as conversion price or conversion ratio. If a debenture of face falue of Rs 100 is to be converted into equity shares having a face value of Rs 10, at a price of Rs 20, the ratio of conversion will be one to five meaning thereby that one debenture will be converted into five shares. This ratio need not be static if a number of conversions are contemplated during a defined period. Each successive conversion at a future date may be at a higher conversion price. In the above example the second conversion, say after six months, can be at Rs 25 per share and third one after twelve months at Rs 50 per share, and so on.

There are certain specific advantages attached to the convertible debentures. First, these debentures can be issued at lower interest rates. This is due to the right of option made available to the investor. If the company prospers, he can convert his debentures into shares and if the company does poorly he can retain his debentures. For such a flexibility he is prepared to accept lower rates of interest. Secondly, till unconverted, these debentures are treated as loan for tax purposes, and therefore, interest is allowed as an expense. Thirdly, earning per share (EPS) remains undisturbed till the time of conversion.

13.11.6 Debenture with Warrants

A warrant is a "call option sold by the company". These are often described as "sweetners" to the debentures. They carry the right to purchase equity shares of the company at a specified price after a specified period. The basic difference between debenture with warrants and convertible debenture is that the former requires additional cash should the investor opt for equity shares whereas in the latter case his investment in debentures is converted into shares. There are many varieties of debentures with warrants. A few kinds are as follows:-

(i) Non-Convertible Debentures (NCD) with Detachable Warrants : The debentures as such are non-convertible but they carry detachable warrants which provide option to the debenture- holders to acquire equity shares of the company at a pre-fixed price after pre-determined lock-in period. Warrants being detachable can be traded separately in the market should the debenture holder intends not to exercise the option himself.

(ii) Partly Convertible Debentures (PCD) with Detachable Warrants: These debentures have two parts. Part A is convertible into equity shares at pre-fixed rate. Part B remains unconverted and is eventually redeemed as per the terms of issue. Part B also carries detachable warrants which can be traded independently in the market. The warrant-holder becomes entitled to receive equity shares as per the price determined by the company.

13.12 BONDS

Bonds are another important source of debt financing. Basic characteristics are akin to those of debentures. Bonds are issued for a specific period at a specified rate of interest. These are required to be redeemed at the end of that period. Bonds of various varieties are being issued. Some of these are explained below.

13.12.1 Tax Free Bonds

These are issued by certain public sector enterprises raising funds for a project of national interest. Interest payable on such bonds is free of income tax in the hands of investors. Rate of interest on such bonds is lower than the prevalent market rate.

13.12.2 Zero Coupon Bonds

Zero coupon bonds are the bonds which do not carry interest and are issued at a discount. The difference between maturity price and discounted price is the interest earned by the investor for holding the bond for the specified number of years.

13.12.3 Deep Discount Bonds

These bonds belong to the fraternity of zero coupon bonds. The maturity period of these bonds is comparatively much longer than the normal bonds - say for 20 to 25 years. The bonds are agreed to be redeemed at a price after 20 years which is discounted as on date. For example, a bond to be redeemed after 20 years at its face value of Rs 1,00,000 can be issued at a price of Rs 2,700. The difference between these two prices is the interest which the investor will earn for surrendering his cash to the company and bearing risk associated with this.

13.13 FACTORS INFLUENCING CHOICE OF DEBENTURES AND BONDS

The following factors influence the choice of debentures and bonds as sources of long-term financing.

13.13.1 Initial Costs

Debentures have comparatively low initial costs as compared to equity issue. There are substantial savings in the initial costs in case of convertible debentures.

13.13.2 Perpetual Costs

Debentures in general are fully secured. Being relatively low risk investment, they carry comparatively lower rate of interest. But the interest burden has to be faithfully borne till the debentures or bonds are fully redeemed. Any default in the payment of interest will have serious consequences.

13.13.3 Repayment Obligations

Except for a few types of debenture, e.g., irredeemable and convertible debentures, all other debentures and bonds need to be redeemed within a stipulated time frame. The company has to take appropriate action for accumulating cash for such redemption. The provisions of Companies Act warrant creation of special sinking funds to facilitate in time redemption.

13.13.4 Tax Relief

This is one of the most important factors weighing in favour of debentures and bonds as sources of finance. The interest payable on these instruments is treated as an admissible expense for income tax purposes. The dividend, on the other hand, is considered as a distribution of profit and does not enjoy this benefit. This makes debentures almost fifty per cent cheaper than equity as source of finance.

13.13.5 Control over Management

Debenture holders as such do not enjoy any right over the management of the company. However, in the event of failure on the part of the company to pay interest or repay principal, debenture and bond holders are entitled to take decisions directly affecting the fate of the company. During bankruptcy proceedings, debenture holders constitute a more powerful lobby than the equity shareholders.

13.13.6 Success Rate

The success rate in the case of debenture and bond issue, in general, is higher than that of the equity issue. The chances of success are further brightened if the 'sweetners' like detachable warrants are attached to the debentures.

13.14 LONG-TERM LOANS

These are negotiated loans. Specialised financial instutions are the prominent sources of these loans. The period ranges from five to twenty years and the amount involved is relatively large. Unlike debentures, these loans cannot be transferred from lender to lender nor can these be traded in the market. The special features of these loans are as follows:-

13.14.1 Security

Securities are invariably insisted upon by the providers of these loans and rightly so, in view of the large amount and length of the loan period. Such loans are usually secured on the assets which are financed through them. Another form of security commonly adopted is floating charges on the current assets.

13.14.2 Interest Rates

Fixed interest rates are negotiated at the time of raising of loans. The rate depends upon the going interest rates in the market. Since most of these financial institutions are established by government to accelerate the industrial developoment in the country borrowers may find these interest rates quite favourable.

13.14.3 Payments and Repayments

The release of the funds by the financial institutions can be in one lumpsum amount or in a series of payments depending upon terms of agreement. Repayments can be made in variety of ways. Some of the common patterns are: equated periodical payments, smaller payments initially and larger payments at later, no payment in first few years known as 'holiday' and the likes. These payments are composite amounts consisting of part principal and part interest. Early repayments (than scheduled) may involve additional interest charge to compensate the lender for interest foregone.

13.14.4 Restrictive Provisions

These loans are backed by formal agreements containing detailed provisions covering all the aspects of the deal. Some of the provisions are inserted to safeguard the interests of the lender and to ensure that the funds are used strictly as per mutually agreed programme. The provisions may also prohibit the borrower to acquire further loans, impose restrictions regarding payment of dividend and warrant strict monitoring of the progress of the project using borrowed funds. If there is any change in the scope of original plan the management is obliged to inform the lender promptly. At times financial institutions put their nominees on the Board of Directors of the company to participate in the management of the company.

13.14.5 Loan Syndication

Funds can be arranged through loan syndication as well. Two or more financial institutions can join hands to meet the funds requirements of the company. Company in such cases applies to one financial institution which in turn makes arrangements with other institutions. Alternatively, company can approach a merchant banker who does the requisite liaison with the financial institutions.

13.15 FACTORS INFLUENCING CHOICE OF LONG-TERM LOANS

The factors influencing choice of long-term loans as a source of financing are described below.

13.15.1 Initial Costs

Raising of such loans involve relatively very low costs as compared to raising of funds from general public. Costs involved are negotiation fees, legal costs consisting of preparation of various documents, stamp duty and fee of the merchant banker, if one is engaged to liaison for raising of such loans.

13.15.2 Perpetual Costs

Like any other kind of debt financing, long-term loans also require payment of interests in periodical instalments. The loans are for a longer period of five to twenty-five years and have fixed rates of interest. Thus, ever-growing inflation makes perpetual costs fairly economical in real terms.

13.15.3 Repayment Obligations

Often, loan is repaid in monthly equated instalments which cover both principal and interest. To that extent it is different than debentures and bonds which require payments of interest in periodical instalments and repayment of principal at the redemption date.

13.15.4 Tax Relief

The interest on such loans is fully exempted from the income of the company for determination of taxable liability. The real cost of interest to the company is, therefore, much less.

13.15.5 Control of Management

The lenders of these loans exercise good deal of control over the management. They need to be informed of almost every major development in the company in addition to constant monitoring of the use of the loan amount. In addition to these, certain other restrictions are provided for in the agreement to protect their interests. They also insist for their representatives to be nominated to the Board of Directors of the company.

13.15.6 Success Rate

The success rates of these loans are fairly high. These are negotiated loans and there are a number of financial institutions available to cater to the requirements of the borrower.

13.16 SPECIALISED FINANCIAL INSTITUTIONS

There are a number of specialised financial institutions available in India which cater to the long-term financing requirements of businesses. These institutions have been specifically created by Government to act as 'development catalyst' to accelerate overall development of the economy. The loan programmes are tailored to cater to the specific needs of a particular sector taking into considerations heavy amount and long periods involved in such cases. Some of the financial institutions are:

13.16.1 Industrial Finance Corporation of India (IFCI)

This is one of the oldest financial institutions which was set up in 1948 by an Act of Parliament. It has now been converted into a limited company.IFCI provides loans for setting up new industrial projects and expansion, modernisation and diversification of existing units for periods not exceeding 25 years. It also extends guarantees for loans raised by industrial houses or in respect of deferred payment by importers. The financial facilities are provided to both private and public sector companies.

13.16.2 Industrial Credit and Investment Corporation of India (ICICI)

ICICI was established in 1955 to boost up private sector in the country. It grants loans with a maturity period upto 15 years both in Indian Rupees and foreign currencies as the need be. It also subscribes to share capital of the companies in addition to underwriting public and private issue of securities. Another important activity of the corporation is rendering technical and administrative assistance to industrial units.

13.16.3 Industrial Development Bank of India (IDBI)

Since its inception in 1964 IDBI is functioning as an apex financial institution in planning, promoting and developing industrial set- up in the country. It has many direct and indirect assistance schemes to help the industrial units in their growth and development. Some of the prominent schemes are Project and Equipment Finance Schemes, Modernisation Assistance Scheme, Refinance of Industrial Loan Schemes and Bills Rediscounting Schemes.

13.6.4 Units Trust of India (UTI)

UTI is the oldest mutual fund of the country. It was established in 1964 by an Act of the Parliament with the primary objective of pooling the savings of the middle and low income groups so as to enable them to have profitable return on their investments. UTI in due course of time has acquired huge funds to invest. It provides term loans to business units. It is also actively executing bills rediscounting, equipment leasing and hire-purchase financing to the corporate sector.

13.16.5 Export Import Bank (Exim Bank)

EXIM Bank is a premier financial institution which has been established to promote exports. As an apex institution it also co-ordinates the work of other financial institutions engaged in the export-import financing. It provides assistance to the turnkey exporters by sanctioning bridging finance in foreign currencies. It grants loans in Indian Rupees to exporters for export of plant and equipment on deferred payment terms. At times, it offers credit directly to foreign buyers for import of capital goods and turnkey projects from India.

13.16.6 Small Industries Development Bank of India (SIDBI)

SIDBI was set up in 1990 by an Act of the Parliament. It is the apex financial institution for the promotion, financing and development of industries in the small scale sector.

13.16.7 State Financial Corporations

Practically every state has set up its own financial institutions to accelerate the development of its small scale industrial units. These financial institutions provide term loans to the units established in its own state.

13.16.8 Industrial Reconstruction Bank of India (IRBI)

IRBI was created to assist in the rehabilitation of sick and closed industrial units. It provides financial assistance by granting loans and advances, underwriting of shares and debentures, and by providing guarantees for loans/deferred payments. Other important facilities provided by this premier credit and reconstruction agency are consultancy, merchant banking and leasing of equipment.

13.17 PRIVATE PLACEMENTS AND AUCTIONS

In addition to methods detailed above, long-term finances can also be raised by private placements and auctions. Under the private placement a security is offered directly to the investor through negotiation. The financial institutions outlined above are the major sources of private-placement funds. This way a company is in a position to raise funds quicker than in public offering. Also, the funds can be raised on piecemeal basis as and when required. The disadvantage of the method is, imposition of restrictive provisions normally enforced by the investing financial institutions. Besides, often the price paid for the security is less than what the company can fetch in the market.

In the case of auction of shares, a company invites the general public to quote a price for shares offered. A reserve price is fixed which remain undisclosed. The offer of highest bidder is accepted. This method has the merit of low initial cost but suffers from the demerits of uncertainty regarding success. It is not a commonly adopted method of raising long-term finances by companies in India. However, recently, certain shares of public sector enterprises have been offered through auction to the public by the government.

QUESTIONS

1. What are the distinguishing features of short-term financing and long-term financing?
2. Explain the factors which influence the choice of a source of long term financing.
3. Explain the rights issue and new isue as methods of raising equity financing.
4. Define a debenture. What are the various kinds of debentures?
5. What factors influence selection of debentures and bonds as a source of long-term financing?
6. What are the special features of long-term loans?
7. Write short notes on:
   (a) Bonus issue.
   (b) Preference shares
   (c) Private placements and auctions.

14

MONEY MARKET AND INSTRUMENTS

14.1 INTRODUCTION

The importance of liquidity in cash management cannot be over emphasised; so much so that some management experts have defined cash management as management of liquidity. We have seen in the earlier chapters that liquidity depends, to a great extent, on the operational efficiency of the business which is the result of rapid generation, efficient utilisation and effective conservation of cash resources. Apart from operational aspect, liquidity in a business is enhanced by astute treasury management, particularly money market operations, as well. In a well-developed liberalised financial market deep-rooted linkages can be established between cash and money market instruments. A prudent finance manager makes optimum use of these linkages by enhancing liquidity and increasing revenue of the business. That is the reason that more and more corporates in India are now following the example of developed countries of creating a separate department for treasury operations or retaining professional agencies for this purpose. It benefits the business in the following ways:

— Business is in a position to maintain liquidity at the desired level through successful operations in money market instruments. Cash is made available as and when desired and danger of cash crunch is reduced to minimum.

— It increases the income from treasury operations. Professionally competent managers have acumen to get maximum out of the market. Treasury operations are not relegated to mere punting.

— It is often witnessed that corporates, consciously or unconsciously or combination of both, fall prey to financial adventurism. It has catastrophic effect on the liquidity. Competent managers with the techniques of risk management are in a position to take care of this eventuality.

— It helps to eliminate corporate profligacy. Penny saved is penny earned, and in the bargain cash continues to remain where it legitimately needs to be.

14.2 FEATURES OF A DEVELOPED MONEY MARKET

Money market is a place where borrower meets the lender to trade in money and other liquid assets that are close substitutes for money. The three important features of a developed money market are:

— existence of a large number of instruments, both in terms of volume and variety.

— presence of a large number of traders, engaged in buying and selling of instruments, and

— existence of requisite infrastructure to facilitate efficient settlement of transactions.

Till 1991, money market in India was in a dormant state. It lacked the above-cited three features of a developed money market. It was operating in a closely regulated environment. Interest rates were fixed. The transactions were generally restricted to overnight borrowings and lendings by banks and financial institutions. There was no instrument which was actively traded except the commercial bill. In brief, there were a few instruments with a few players and low turnover. A working group under the chairmanship of Shri N. Vaghul, chairman ICICI, was constituted by the RBI to make recommendations for the development of the Indian money market. The Working Group recommended deregulation of rates and prices of instruments, introduction of new instruments and increase in the number of participants. Based on the recommendations, the RBI initiated a series of actions which coincided with the phase of liberalisation in the economy. As a result, India now has a fairly developed money market with a number of instruments having varying degrees of costs and liquidity attached with them. These are explained below.

14.3 TREASURY BILLS

Treasury Bill is a financial instrument sold by the government of a country at a discount through its central bank. The face value of the treasury bill is payable at maturity. It is sold by auction at fixed intervals. It was first introduced in 1877 by Government of UK on the lines of a commercial bill to cater to the seasonal needs of finance. But in the 20th century it has become the usual source of borrowing by a government. It is also considered safest and is most marketable instrument in the money market. We have explained treasury bills in Section 11.5.3. A couple of its important features are reviewed below.

14.3.1 Profile of Treasury Bill

The profile of a treasury bill sold by Government of India can be discussed in three segments.

(a) *Script Profile*

(i)	Issuer	: Reserve Bank of India
(ii)	Price	: Issued at a discount price to be redeemed at full price at maturity.
(iii)	Primary Tenor	: 91 days and 364 days. (Various maturities)*
(iv)	Amounts	: — Primary market denomination Rs 1 lakh — Secondary market minimum amount Rs 25 lakhs, and thereafter denomination of Rs 10 lakhs
(vi)	Investors	: Banks, financial institutions, individuals, corporates, trusts *etc.*

(b) *Procedure Profile*

(i)	Issuance Method	: — Sold through auction by the RBI — Banks, financial institutions and primary dealers holding current account and Subsidiary General Ledger (SGL) account with the RBI permitted to participate in the auction. — Corporates, holding Constituent SGL account can bid through banks. — In the non-competitive sectors, treasury bills are issued to State governments and Provident Funds at a weighted average price of the bid allotted.
(ii)	Settlement Method	: Settlement through SGL account makes it very efficient. No loss of interest as the same day settlement is possible.

(c) *Risk Profile*

(i)	Credit Risk	: Almost nil as bills are issued by the RBI.
(ii)	Price Risk	: No risk as the tenor of bill is short.
(iii)	Liquidity Risk	: Negligible. Active secondary market exists in India.

14.4 GILT-EDGED SECURITIES

All government debt, other than treasury bills, which are traded in

---
* As per Monetary and Economic Policy 1997 issued by RBI.

money market, are known as gilt-edged securities or gilts. An important feature of these gilts is that these are 'dated' securities. The date of the maturity is specified in the instrument. The period of their currency may vary from a short period of say 2 years to long tenure of 10 years. Another important feature of the government securities is that generally these are issued at a fixed rate of interest on their nominal values. These rates are known as 'coupon' and depend upon the repayment date of security and prevalent interest rates in the market.

14.4.1 Gilts and Investors Response

Gilts are totally free from default risk. Still, it is observed that these do not have a vibrant secondary market. By and large investments in these securities is done due to statutory compulsions, e.g., by Provident Fund Trusts in view of government regulations. Retail, institutional and corporate investors of their own do not find trading in gilts very attractive. Some of the reasons for this lukewarm response, and suggestions to activate the gilts market are described below.

(a) *Returns:* There is wide difference between the coupon rate offered in government securities and yield from securities issued by other state-owned entities like financial institutions, PSUs, *etc.* The investor perceives little difference in risk between gilts and the higher yielding bonds since both have government backing albeit in the latter case, it is indirect.

(b) *Procedure:* Procedurally (both in subscribing and receiving satisfactorily service as an investor), procurement of securities like bonds is comparatively easier than procuring government security. There is need to make procedures more investor friendly.

(c) *Mutual Fund:* Mutual fund industry does not find operating in gilts very remunerative. Attractive incentives should be provided to mutual funds so that they become efficient vehicles for attracting investors into the gilts market.

(d) *Tax Incentives:* Tax incentives through specific provisions of Income Tax Act should be provided for encouraging investment in the gilts. This will widen the investor base.

(e) *Repo facilities:* Repo facilities are now being allowed to the government dated securities. However, the range of participants in the market is still rather restricted. There is urgent need to permit additional participants to make gilt market vibrant.

(f) *Index Linked Gilts:* By and large gilts carry a fixed rate of interest which is not very attractive when we look at it in conjunction with the inflation rate. Generally, it is only marginally higher but there are instances of negative return as well, when the inflation rate is very high. Thus, there is a need to issue index-linked gilts so as to protect the investor from inflation risk. The RBI had issued in 1995, bonds linked with treasury bill yield as 1.25% over 364 days treasury bills yield calculated on half yearly basis. These bonds had a maturity period of 4 years with a floor rate of 13%. However, in a liberalised economy where the market forces are allowed to play their natural roles, attempts can be made to issue gilts which are linked with Consumer Price Index. This will help to boost gilts market to a great extent.

14.5 CERTIFICATE OF DEPOSITS

A certificate of deposit (CD) is a front-ended negotiable instrument issued at a discount by a bank. The face value is payable at maturity. The discount rate is market-determined. The CD, as a source of borrowing, is useful for a bank which can attract the requisite amount of cash from the money market by offering higher discount rate than the prevalent interest rates on usual term deposits. The investor also stands to gain as he can park his funds at a higher return for a short time with safety support as good as available to term deposits. The CD has been explained in detail in Section 11.5.2. We re-capitulate the salient features of CD once again.

14.5.1 Profile of a Certificate of Deposit

The profile of a certificate of deposit can be studied in three segments.

(a) *Script Profile*

(i)	Issuer	:	Banks
(ii)	Price	:	Issued at discount price to be redeemed at full price at maturity.
(iii)	Primary Tenor	:	91 days to 1 year
(iv)	Amounts	:	Minimum amount Rs 10 lakhs
(v)	Investors	:	Individuals, corporates, trusts *etc.*

(b) *Procedure Profile*

(i)	Issuance Method	:	Negotiated deal with investor based on the discount rate quoted by bank.
(ii)	Settlement Method	:	Settled through credit to the account of investor or through pay order. Loss of interest for a day or two possible in the latter case.

(c) *Risk Profile*

(i)	Credit Risk	:	Negligible as the CD is issued by banks.
(ii)	Price Risk	:	Low risk, as the tenure of the CD is short.
(iii)	Liquidity Risk	:	Initial lock in period of 45 days. Also absence of active secondary market increases the liquidity risk.

14.6 COMMERCIAL PAPERS

Commercial Paper (CP) is a large denominated, unsecured, negotiable promissory note issued by highly rated conglomerates. It is issued at a discount. The discount is determined by the market considerations. At maturity, the CP is redeemed at face value. If the issuer is a large business house, it can roll forward the maturity by substituting the issue so matured with the new issue. CP has been discussed in detail in section 12.9. The main features are reproduced again.

14.6.1 Profile of Commercial Paper

The profile can be studied in three segments.

(a) *Script Profile*

(i) Issuer	:	Large conglomerates
(ii) Price	:	Issued at a discount price to be redeemed at full price at maturity.
(iii) Primary Tenor	:	1 month to 12 months.
(iv) Amount	:	— Minimum amount Rs 10 lakhs. — Maximum amount 75% of permissible bank finance limit. — Secondary market transactions can be in the denomination of Rs 5 lakhs.
(v) Investors	:	Individuals, corporates, banks, financial institutions.

(b) *Procedure Profile*

(i) Issuance Method	:	— It can be offered directly to the public. — Private placement is also common.
(ii) Settlement Method	:	Redemption at face value at maturity. Rolling forward also possible.

(c) *Risk Profile*

(i) Credit Risk	:	Depend on credibility of issuing corporate. Generally very reputed corporates only issue CPs.
(ii) Price Risk	:	Low risk as the tenor of the instrument is short.
(iii) Liquidity Risk	:	Negotiable instrument. But liquidity reduced due to non-existence of active secondary market.

14.7 REPOS

Though the term Repo is short for Repurchase Agreement, it is in fact an arrangement consisting of simultaneous 'sale and repurchase agreement'. Under such an arrangement one party sells a security to another and simultaneously agrees to buy it back at a later date. Although this may sound a singularly futile exercise, it is in fact useful to both sides.

A repo works as follows. Party *A* needs funds for short term. It sells to party *B* treasury bills (sale agreement) and simultaneously agrees to buy the same after a specified time and at a slightly higher price (purchase agreement). The difference between the prices represents the interest payable by party *A* to party *B*. The transaction helps the party *B* since it gets yield though a bit less than bank deposit (because it is secured by a government bond) but more than treasury bills (because he is running the risk that the price of the security may drop in the meantime). It is indeed a unique arrangement under which the 'borrower' becomes the 'seller', and the 'lender' becomes the 'buyer' as a part of the composite deal. And in the bargain repo has developed into an important money market instrument.

An open repo market has flourished in the USA since the '60s. In Europe, though the repo markets have developed only in the past few years their growth has been very dramatic. The deep linkages among the money markets of the various countries have helped repo to become an effective money market instrument. In India, repo market has a stunted growth — thanks to securities scam of 1992. However, a tight money scenario in the banking segment and lack lustre trading in government securities have helped in the development of repo market. The RBI is also supporting the repos development in the country. It makes funds available to the banks under repos through Discount and Finance House of India (DFHI) and Securities Trading Corporation of India Ltd. (STCI). The RBI has allowed repos transactions only between banks. In addition to treasury bills, all dated central government securities can be used for repos.

14.7.1 Advantages of Repos

The advantages of repos are enumerated below.

(a) Repo has an inherent quality of being self-liquidating. This is because of the two basic characteristics of repo arrangement — firm buy-back commitment and firm negotiated price.

(b) It is an arrangement under which a seller need not dilute his portfolio. This feature is of vital importance when the money market is unexorably bearish.

(c) Repos can be tailored to the specific requirements of the concerned parties. The minimum period can be as short as an overnight. The maximum period generally is 14 days.

(d) Default risk in the case of repos is comparatively much less. If the borrower is unable to buy back the securities, the lender can sell them and retrieve his money.

(e) Under repos arrangement both the lender and buyer are assured of fixed interest rate. This feature of repos enables the market operators to use it as a hedge during volatalic movements in the interest rates.

(f) Repo is considered a particularly favourable instrument when the secondary market of government securities is dull and illiquid.

(g) Repo arrangement helps a dealer to avoid capital loss which he otherwise would have incurred had he sold the securities against cash at a price less than its cost, to muster necessary liquidity in his operations.

(h) Repos are also used by central banks to conduct monetary policy. Should it feel that there is too much money slashing around, it can use repos to drain money from the market. If it thinks there is a cash crunch, it can use repos to pump money into the market. The Bank of England was the first central bank to introduce repos in 1830.

14.8. DISCOUNT AND FINANCE HOUSE OF INDIA LTD. (DFHI)

A discount house is a financial institution which acquires short term assets by borrowing short term money. It specialises in buying and selling of treasury bills and other money market instruments, at a discount. A discount house fulfills three distinct economic functions:

— It acts as a key market maker in the money market.

— Its principal liabilities form the nearest asset to cash in the bank portfolios.

— It enjoys a special relationship with the central bank of the country and becomes instrumental in implementing the monetary policies introduced by the bank from time to time.

Discount and Finance House of India Ltd (DFHI) was established in 1988 by the RBI, jointly with public sector banks and financial institutions. The DFHI was formed with the prime objective of catering to the short-term money market instruments. It actively participates in the re-discounting of treasury bills, commercial bills, certificate of deposits and commercial papers. In the inter-bank call/notice money market and term deposit market also, it participates as lender and borrower.

The DFHI performs the function of a catalyst in activising secondary money market, particularly of treasury bills. The RBI does not purchase its treasury bills before maturity, nor sells them except through auction. The DFHI provides necessary liquidity by actively buying and selling these treasury bills. It quotes its bid and offers discount rates for various instruments, on daily basis.

The RBI extends support to the banks by making funds available under repos (ready forward deal) through DFHI. The DFHI provides repos facility to banks and other financial institutions from overnight to 14 days. It also facilitates multiple rediscounting of derivative usance promissory note (DPN) by purchasing and selling the instruments at its bid and offer discount rates.

The DFHI is an important operator of call money operations. Banks are increasingly depending upon it for borrowing or lending the requisite amounts. To that extent, the DFHI has enabled the pooling of borrowers demand and lenders supplies.

Securities and Trading Corporation of India Ltd., (STCI) has also been formed (in 1994) with prime objective of catering to long term security market.

14.9 MONEY MARKET MUTUAL FUND

Money Market Mutual Fund (MMMF) is a special kind of mutual fund which operates in money market instruments. Like any other mutual fund, the underlying principle is to pool the funds of scattered investors for investment in securities and distribute the return of such investments to fund participants. However, the basic difference between mutual fund and the MMMF is that whereas the former deals in securities of capital market in general, the latter trades in instruments of money market in particular. Another important feature of MMMF is its emphasis on total liquidity. The MMMF aims at attracting the funds of investors who are comparatively more concerned with liquidity than any other factor in their investment portfolio. Money market investments have shorter maturities and as such provide right pastures to the MMMF to satisfy the fund participants. The RBI appointed a Task Force on MMMF under the chairmanship of Shri D. Basu, ex-chairman of State Bank of India . The Task Force submitted its report on June 21, 1992. Defining the primary objective of the MMMF scheme, it detailed the salient features of MMMF — "the primary objective of the MMMF scheme is to provide high rate of return on short term investments consistent with liquidity and preservation of capital through maintenance of high quality investment portfolio."

14.9.1 Features of MMMF

Salient features of the MMMF are as follows.

(a) MMMFs can be set up by banker and financial institutions. Private sector banks have also been permitted by RBI to start a MMMF.

(b) Earlier the size of a MMMF was restricted to a ceiling related to deposits and long term borrowings of the banks and financial institutions, respectively. The ceilings have now been withdrawn by RBI.

(c) MMMFs are permitted to invest in certain specified instruments only. These are — treasury bills and dated government securities having an unexpired maturity upto one year, call and notice money, commercial papers, commercial bills accepted/co-accepted by banks and certificates of deposits.

(d) MMMFs are free to determine the extent of their investments in each instrument. However, exposure to commercial paper issued by an individual company should not be more than 3 per cent of the resources mobilised by the MMMF.

(e) On the date of launch, the sale price may be at par and thereafter sale and repurchase price should be at prospective Net Asset Value.

(f) The minimum lock-in period for investment in MMMFs has been reduced from 46 days to 30 days.

(g) Participation in MMMF is open to resident individuals, HUF, trusts, societies and body corporates including companies.

(h) Nomination facility is available to fund participants.

(i) All MMMFs require prior authorisation by RBI. The private sector MMMFs need the approval of SEBI as also the RBI.

14.9.2 Advantages of MMMF to Investor

Money market is endowed with certain special features. It is very volatile. Its instruments are traded in bulk and blocks. To be successful in money market, operators should have professional skill and expertise to cope with the intricacies of its operations. Also, the operators must have a constant and regular flow of up-to-date information for taking appropriate decisions. Let us see how MMMF helps an individual investor to earn from money market operations which he otherwise would have found difficult to manage.

(a) *Accessability:* The money market instruments like certificate of deposit, commercial paper, treasury bills require huge investments. The minimum investment in certificate of deposit is Rs 10 lakhs. Similarly, for participation in the sale and purchase of treasury bills and commercial papers in secondary market minimum amounts are prescribed at Rs 25 lakhs and Rs 5 lakhs, respectively. Individual investors having moderate investible surplus funds do not have access to such instruments. The collected funds of investors aggregate to sizeable amount for MMMF to operate in the money market.

(b) *Advantages of Scales*: With the pooled funds at its disposal, MMMFs not only offer economic advantage of bulk purchases of money market instruments but also a more diversified selection of such instruments than the size of an individual investors portfolio might otherwise permit. It can buy desired instruments directly from the issue in the primary market in large blocks at a lower price. Also, it can purchase various instruments in secondary market at a more competitive price.

(c) *Special Expertise*: An average investor lacks professional acumen to trade in money market. The volatility of the money market can be skillfully exploited by a professional fund manager who possesses adequate expertise and alert mind to purchase and sell various instruments at opportune time and appropriate price so as to ensure optimum yield from such instruments.

(d) *Up-to-date Information*: Total liquidity is the hallmark of MMMF scheme. Liquidity can be ensured only through accurate and timely flow of information. A MMMF can achieve this with the help of extensive computer network backed by highly developed computer software. Such a facility may not be available to an individual investor.

(e) *Administrative Problems*: In addition to the above referred advantages, an individual by investing in a MMMF is relieved from many of his administrative problems associated with direct purchase of money market instruments. These relate to scheduling of maturities and reinvestment, safe custody of the instruments, separating principal and income *etc.*

14.10 SECURITISATION

Securitisation has been defined as "making a loan or mortgage into a tradeable security by issuing a bill of exchange or the negotiable paper in place of the loan."*

The term securitisation covers the following:

— disintermediation of bank, whereby a business raises direct finance via financial market.

— transformation of long dated, illiquid assets like receivables, mortgage loans *etc.*, into tradeable instruments by any body corporate including banks.

In recent years, major trend in the international market has been towards securitisation. Originally, it was confined to residential mortgage, whereas now all types of assets like housing loans, automobile loans, trade debtors etc. are covered. In India, ICICI was first to introduce securitisation, when it securitised its bills of exchange in 1991.

14.10.1 Process of Securitisation

The process of securitisation basically involves two functions—pooling of assets and creation of a trust.

(a) *Pooling of Assets*: Existence of assets is a prerequisite for securitisation. Assets can be of various kinds *e.g.*, trade receivables, mortgage loans, lease rentals *etc.* They are categorised to form relatively homogenous pools on the basis of type of credit, maturity pattern and interest rate risk.

*Dictionary of Accounting — P.H. Collin & Adrian Joliffe.

(b) *Creation of Trust*: A trust is created and pool of assets is transferred to the trust. Trust performs the following functions:

(i) It issues tradeable securities according to maturity and risk of the assets.

(ii) It takes responsibility for collection of interest and principal payments of loans and transfer of funds to investors.

(iii) It may obtain credit rating to infuse confidence in the investors.

(iv) The trust also obtains insurance cover.

(v) It appoints underwriter for the issue.

(vi) It may obtain some 'bridging finance' to cover up the gap between receipt of payment from loan portfolio and release of payment to security holders.

In brief, for securitisation, assets are first categorised in homogenous groups and transferred to a trust. The trust issues securities to prospective investors on the strength of these assets. Securitisation is thus sale of securities backed by packaged assets. Securities so issued represent fractional interests in such packaged pool of assets. The process is explained in Exhibit 14.1.

14.10.2 Instruments of Securitisation

The following types of securities are commonly created and issued as instruments of securitisation in the financial market.

(a) *Single Security Structure*: This involves creation of only one type of security. It is also known as 'pass through certificate' (PTC) because principal and interest on the assets are passed through to the security holder. Single security structure synchronises the period of security with cash flows from underlying asset. If the tenure of the security is two years, the asset which is backing this security will get paid off in two years. Under a phased programme, monthly payments consisting of principal and interest are paid to investors and the final payment is released when the last asset in the pool is retired.

(b) *Multi Security Structure*: Under this structure two or more types of securities are issued. They have different maturities pattern and as such are serviced by different cash flows. These are called 'pay through securities' (PTS). Unlike under single security structure, the different maturities pattern necessitate distribution of pooled cash from various assets in different fashion to the security holders. The guiding principle is maturity dates of the securities. Securities maturing earlier are paid first (senior debt). Junior debt follows thereafter and the third category known as equity is paid in the last. This process continues till the claim of the last security holder is satisfied.

(c) *STRIPS Structure*: These are separate tranche of interest only/principal only securities and are popularly known as STRIPS. Securities issued under this category are classified into two groups.

Exhibit 14.1
SECURITISATION

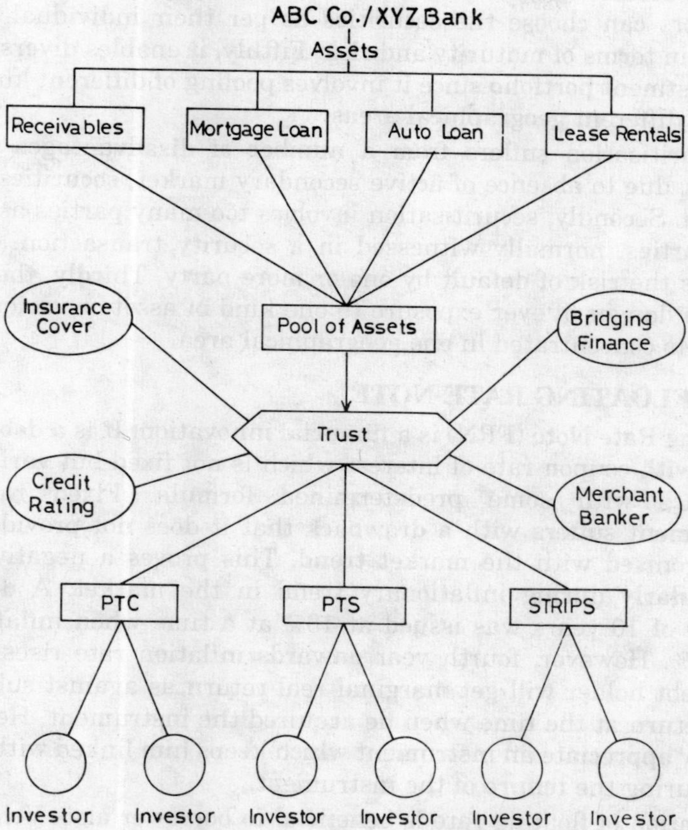

These are called 'interest only' (I.O.) and 'principal only' (P.O.) securities representing two different segments of a payment. The security holder of 'interest only' are paid back out of interest only and likewise security holder of 'payment only' are paid out of principal repayments only. The value of an 'interest only' security is increased if the interest rates go up because more interest is collected on underlying mortgage. And conversely, the value of 'principal only' security tends to increase if the interest rates go down because efforts are made to prepay existing mortgages and undertake fresh loans at lower rates of interest. These two types of securities are speculative in nature and therefore have no government backing.

14.10.3 Advantages and Disadvantages

Securitisation offers many advantages. Firstly, the liquidity of the business is increased through sale of receivables in the form of securities. Secondly, banks can raise additional finances without disturbing the liabilities side of their balance sheets. Thirdly, assets backed securities are considered safe by risk-shy investor. Fourthly, investors can choose the securities as per their individual requirements in terms of maturity and risk. Fifthly, it enables diversification of investment portfolio since it involves pooling of different kind of assets in different geographical areas.

Securitisation suffers from a number of disadvantages as well. Firstly, due to absence of active secondary market, securities become illiquid. Secondly, securitisation involves too many parties as against two parties, normally witnessed in a security transaction. This increases the risk of default by one or more party. Thirdly, there is always a danger of over exposure to one kind of asset or various kinds of assets concentrated in one geographical area.

14.11 FLOATING RATE NOTE

Floating Rate Note (FRN) is a financial innovation. It is a debt instrument with coupon rate of interest which is not fixed but varies in accordance with some predetermined formula. Fixed rate debt instrument suffers with a drawback that it does not provide return synchronised with the market trend. This proves a negative factor particularly during inflationary trend in the market. A debt of a tenure of 10 years was issued at 13% at a time when inflation rate was 6%. However, fourth year onwards inflation rate rises to 11%. The debt holder will get marginal real return as against substantial real return at the time when he acquired the instrument. He will obviously appreciate an instrument which keeps him linked with market rate during the tenure of the instrument.

Fixation of floating rate is beneficial to borrower also. Volatility in the interest rate may reduce the prevalent interest rate in market much below the committed rate of interest on a fixed coupon instrument. In the above example, suppose the interest rate falls to 8%, the borrower may have to borrow additional money to service his debt raised at 13%. Thus a borrower too, may like to have an instrument with interest rate moving in sympathy with market rate.

14.11.1 Linking Variables of FRN

The instrument can be issued linked with many types of variables. Some of these are explained below.

(a) A FRN can be issued with interest rate linked with treasury bills yield calculated on half yearly basis.

(b) An instrument can be issued linked as plus percentage on prime lending rate (PLR) of a specified bank.

(c) Another variation is FRN with coupon rising in steps until it reaches at market level after several years.

(d) FRN can be issued with 'drop-lock' arrangement also. Under this, the instrument is issued with interest linked with inter bank rate. The interest keeps on varying in accordance with the money market conditions. However, if short term interest rates are declining, then at a predetermined level FRN 'locks' into a fixed rate instrument. For example, if the interest rates are continuously declining from 20% and the pre-determined level is 12%, then the FRN get converted into a fixed rate instrument of say 11% for the remaining period to maturity once the market rate declines to 12% or less.

14.12 DERIVATIVES

The literal meaning of derivative is an item which is not a product of new ideas, but has been developed from something else. In economic parlance derivative refers to a financial instrument, such as option contracts, which is derived from ordinary bonds and shares. The transaction of a sale and purchase of a security involves two parties, each of them having a different perception of price variation of the security at a future date. One who wishes to avoid the risk of price variation is known as hedger and the other who seeks to profit from price variation is known as speculator.

Their perceptions makes the market competitive and derivative as an instrument provides impetus to such competition. In the process it produces an important hedging mechanism, as well. We shall now study two important instruments of derivaties — futures and options.

14.12.1 Futures

A future contract is an arrangement where a buyer/seller agrees to take/give delivery of the securities on a pre-specified date at a predetermined price. A future contract has following three important ingredients.

(a) *Parties*: There should be two parties to the arrangement; the buyer who is called 'long' and the seller who is referred to as 'short'. Both have opposite perceptions regarding price variation in the value of a security at a future date.

(b) *Clearing House*: The clearing house functions as a counter party in such agreements. The market is large and both the buyer and the seller interact with each other with the help of clearing house. A margin is deposited at the clearing house for the deal.

(c) *Infrastructure*: An efficient futures operations warrant the existence of a high level computerised trading. It not only quickens the pace of transaction but also provides much needed transparency.

Moralists criticise futures as an instrument of untamed speculation which results in gambling, as the parties in this transaction can settle for the price difference on the date of settlement. But market players of the futures in the developed countries consider it a fine instrument of risk transfer. It enables the transfer of risk from those who feel shy of it (hedgers) to those who are willing to accept it (speculators).

Three distinct advantages emerge from futures. They provide, (i) hedging against price risk, (ii) they are instrumental in discovery of the price of a security, (iii) they enable accumulation of a large pool of risk capital.

14.12.2. Options

An option is a contract between two parties where an option maker agrees to buy or sell a specified security to the option holder for a specific price on or upto a particular date. In capital market parlance option maker is known as 'option writer', option holder is known as 'option buyer', specified price is called 'strike price' and the particular date is termed as 'answer date'. It is important to note that the option buyer/holder has the option but not the obligation. He has to notify the option maker on the answer date if he intends to exercise his right or not. Because the right is valuable, the option buyer is required to pay upfront price, the call premium, to the option writer. The premium is determined on the basis of prevalent interest rate, tenure of the option, market volatility, spot price of the security *etc.* Option contracts can be of two kinds — call option, i.e., to buy an option, Put Option, i.e., to sell an option. Like futures, option also stimulate competition in the market. They provide hedging against price risk. In fact, an option acts as a hedge within hedge. They help in the price discovery of a security, too.

14.12.3 Derivatives in Indian Market

In India options have been thriving in the un-official market where call options are known as "teji" and put option as "mandi", and call and put option is called "duranga". SEBI has now lifted ban on the trading of derivatives and National Stock Exchange (NSE) has been permitted to trade in futures and options.

As per the proposal of National Stock Exchange, the trading in futures will be done on the basis of National Stock Exchange-50 index (NIFTY) and dealers shall be taking positions on the basis of accepted value of the NIFTY index, on a future date. The operation of futures at NSE is explained in the following example.

Suppose the current value of NSE-50 index is Rs 1,000. *X* offers to buy 300 units of NIFTY for a 30 days futures at Rs 1,050 per unit. *Y* agrees to sell these units at that particular price. After the expiry of 30 days if the value of NIFTY is Rs 1,100, *X* will get Rs 15000 (300×50) and party *Y* will incurr a loss of the same amount. However, if the value of NIFTY is Rs 1020 on that day *Y* becomes entitled to receive Rs 9000 (300×30) from *X*. During the currency of the 30 days period both *X* and *Y* can trade in this index on daily basis. Any one of them can clear the position any day by executing a reverse trade, i.e., he buys now if he has sold earlier, and he sells now if he has bought earlier and book profits or restrict his losses.

On the same basis option trading at NSE is also explained. Suppose *X* who is a member of NSE agrees to sell (put option) 300 units of NIFTY to *Y*, who is an investor, at a premium of Rs 10 per unit, for a price of Rs 1100 after 30 days. If the value of NIFTY is Rs 1200 after 30 days, *Y* has a right of not exercising his option by losing Rs 3000 (300 × 10) paid as premium. On the contrary, if value of NIFTY is Rs 1050, *Y* becomes entitled to profit of Rs 15000 (300 × 50). *X* however can restrict his risk by selling both put and call options on day to day basis.

14.12.4 Derivatives — A Controversial Instrument

Derivative is one of the most controversial financial instruments. A lot has been written about the complexities and dangers associated with derivative trade. Its opponents compare the derivative operation in stock market with gambling in casino. They quote the infamous case of Barings, the oldest bank of England becoming bankrupt due to rash deals in future derivatives by one person named Nick Leesons. On the other hand, the derivative players world over consider derivative as an important instrument for hedging. In their support, they quote the findings of two Noble laureates, Arrow and Debreu who have demonstrated in their model that derivatives are absolutely integral to the social optimal results. It is a hedge against future risk, so instead of representing a market aberration, derivative is necessary condition for removing aberration. As stated above, SEBI has permitted NSE to trade in derivatives. The main motivation for the introduction of derivatives is to make an effective mechanism of hedging operative in the market. But one thing is certain; taking into consideration the magnitude and operative skills of our traders, it is necessary that the derivative trade should always be kept under constant watch, lest it drains out the savings of general investors.

QUESTIONS

1. Define money market. How does successful treasury operations help a business in enhancing liquidity and increasing return?
2. Describe gilt-edged securities. What steps should be taken to make them more attractive to investors?
3. What do you understand by repos? Describe the advantages of repos.
4. Define a treasury bill and describe its main features.
5. Define DFHI and its role in money market.
6. Explain Money Market Mutual Fund. What are its main features?

7. Describe the securitisation. What are its advantages and disadvantages?
8. Describe derivatives with special reference to options and futures.
9. Write short notes on:
(a) Commercial paper
(b) Certificate of deposit
(c) Floating rate note.

15

INTERNAL CONTROL — CASH AND TREASURY

15.1 INTRODUCTION

The broad sweep of the term 'treasury' covers cash and other liquid assets like money market securities. The basic parameters of internal control mechanism are same for cash and treasury instruments. Both warrant effective internal control system to ward off against frauds and misappropriations. The transactions of cash and treasury must invariably be subject to internal audit. Also, their inflow and outflow movements are kept under constant watch by the management. In fact, the transactions between the two are often intervowen to such an extent that their separation becomes difficult. A simple example is sale and purchase of treasury bills on regular basis through bank, acting as an agent, for the business. However, in certain aspects variations in respect of internal control measures for cash and treasury instruments, do exist. This is primarily due to the fact that cash in addition to being a liquid asset is also a legal tender — a feature which exposes it to additional risks of thefts and defalcations. We shall describe internal control for cash and treasury separately, but before that let us study the fundamentals of an efficient internal control system.

The internal control as a mechanism is structured on three pillars:

— Internal Control Measures

— Internal Audit

— Management Reporting

These are explained in detail as follows.

15.2 INTERNAL CONTROL MEASURES

Statement on Standard Auditing Practices (SAP) issued by the Institute of Chartered Accountants of India defines internal control as

"The system of internal control is the plan of organization and all the methods and procedures adopted by the management of an entity to assist in achieving management's objective of ensuring, as far as practicable, the orderly and efficient conduct of its business, including adherence to management policies, the safeguarding of assets, prevention and detection of fraud and error, the accuracy and completeness of the accounting records, and the timely preparation of reliable financial information."

The important objectives of internal control as per above statement are to ensure the following.

— Transactions are executed in accordance with the authorisation of the management.
— All transactions are recorded in the correct amount and appropriate account.
— Assets are safeguarded from unauthorised use or disposition.
— Physical assets are compared with reorded assets periodically and appropriate action is taken with regard to any differences.

There are two important segments of a system incorporating internal control measures — designing the system and its effective implementation.

15.2.1 Designing the System

Prevention is better than cure. An efficiently designed system will go a long way in preventing the occurances of errors, omissions and malpractices. The following are the features of a well designed system.

(a) *Internal Check System*: Internal check is an important constituent of internal control system. Spicer and Peglar have defined it as "Internal check is an arrangement of staff duties whereby no one person is allowed to carry through and record every aspect of a transaction so that, without collusion between two or more persons, fraud is prevented and at the same time the possibilities of errors are reduced to a minimum". Two important elements of an internal check are:

(i) No single person handles alone a transaction from beginning to end.

(ii) Work of one person is checked by the other as a matter of routine.

(b) *Comprehensive*: The system should be comprehensive covering all the functional wings of a business. The responsibilities and duties of individual persons should be clearly demarcated based on their functions.

(c) *Practical*: The system need to be ideal but not unpractical. It may insist for proper documentation and procedural requirements but not to the extent that these become burden on the system.

(d) *Cost-benefit.* The system should satisfy the criteria of cost-benefit analysis. Cost considered should be both in terms of money as well as time spent by the employees in following the system. These should be weighed against the benefits derived from the system. Though, the evaluation of benefit is subjective and cannot be quantified in terms of money saved on account of non-occurance of frauds and embezzlements but the underlying idea is that overzealous attempt should not be made to introduce a complex and too detailed system. It should never breed delays.

15.2.8 Implementing the System

The system can yield dividend only if it is followed in letter and spirit. Nonchallant attitude towards adherance to procedures framed under the system will prove more harmful than the absence of the system itself. In this context existence of a strong control environment plays a vital role. Statement on Standard Auditing Practices (SAP) 7 issued by the Institute of Chartered Accountants of India states "The environment in which internal control operates has an impact on the effectiveness of the specific control procedures. A strong control environment, for example, one with tight budgetary controls and an effective internal audit function, can significantly complement specific control procedures. However, a strong environment does not, by itself, ensure the effectiveness of the overall system of internal control. The system of internal control must be under continuing supervision by management to determine that it is functioning as prescribed and is modified as appropriate for changes in conditions." Unless these control measures are reviewed constantly they become redundant and the attitude of the employees towards them become lax.

15.3 INTERNAL AUDIT

The Institute of Internal Audit, USA has defined Internal Audit as "An independent appraisal activity within an organization for the review of accountancy, financial and other operations as a basis for service to the management. It is a managerial control which functions by measuring and evaluating the effectiveness of other controls."

Internal audit is an important deterrant against the possibilities of frauds and defalcations.

15.3.1 Objectives of Internal Audit

The area of operation or objectives of internal audit are as follows.

(a) Internal audit reviews the accounting system and the associated internal controls. It monitors their operations and recommend improvements thereto.

(b) It verifies the financial and operating information put up to the management.

(c) Internal audit examines the economy, efficiency and effectiveness of operations including non-financial controls of the business.

(d) It verifies the physical existance and controls of the tangible assets of the business.

15.4. MANAGEMENT REPORTING

A report is a vehicle for communicating information to the management. It describes the state of affairs, prompting the management to take corrective measures, if there is need to do so. There are many kinds of reports generated as per the requirements, *e.g.*, information, performance, control, *etc.* They cater to different hierarchical levels helping the concerned person to take decisions relevant to their levels of operations — top level for strategic decisions, middle level for managerial decisions and bottom level for operational decisions.

15.4.1 Contents of a Report

The information contained in a report can be classified into three sections, (a) Factual, (b) Standard, and (c) Variations.

(a) *Factual*: This refers to the description of the actual facts of the performance. The facts detailed in this section should be relevant, clear and accurate. Irrelevant and ambiguous facts distort the underlying message of a report. Inaccurate facts can defeat the very purpose for which the report is being presented.

(b) *Standards*: Incorporation of actual facts in a report shall not be of any significance. By comparison alone the efficiency of actuals can be judged. Standards can be fixed based on internal factors — past actuals or external factors— those of other units in the same industry. If the budgets have been prepared carefully, they shall serve as very good standards because targets fixed therein take into account not only internal and external factors but also the aspirations of the management.

(c) *Variations*: Comparison of actuals are made with the standards and variations are calculated under this section. Variances so revealed throw light on the efficiencies or inefficiencies of the actual performances. Wherever possible, variances should be quantified so as to avoid the element of subjectivity in comparison. However, the conclusions cannot be drawn merely by comparisons. Variances should be analysed further. It is likely that during the period of actual performance the circumstances have undergone seachange than those assumed in the preparation of budgets. Due considerations should be given to these factors before initiating corrective measures.

15.4.2 Features of a Report

A report should have following features.

(a) *Standard Format*: So far as practicable, a standard format should be designed for each report which is presented at periodical intervals. It obviates the possibility of omission of any information required to be put in the report. It permits easy and comprehensible comparison with the reports of the other periods. Also, once accustomed with the format, it becomes very convenient for the report-maker to prepare it and for report-user to comprehend it.

(b) *Clarity*: A report should be unambiguous so as to get its message registered in clear terms. To the extent possible, it should be devoid of complicated jargons. Use of percentages, ratios *etc.*, can make the presentation much clear. A report should be brief and crisp. But the clarity should not be sacrificed at the cost of brevity. At the same time, deluging the decision maker with unnecessary details will obscure the underlying message of the report.

(c) *Timings*: Report should provide information when it is needed most. If the report is submitted much in advance, it is possible that the decision maker may lose track of its contents at the opportune time and obviously presentation of report after the due time will be of archival value only, devoid of any practical significance.

(d) *Period of coverage*: The duration of the period covered in the report will depend upon the nature of items to be reported and the level of authority to whom report is presented. The ideal period, however, should neither be too short nor too long. Too short a period will be influenced by the random factors that would have been averaged out in due course of time. So the contents of the report may not be representative of the true facts. Too long a period, on the other hand, may allow the problem to deteriorate to an unreprievable extent by the time report reaches the management.

(e) *Cost of Reporting*: The cost of reporting should be evaluated in terms of benefits derived therefrom. It is difficult to quantify monetary benefits accruing from reports. It is also not easy to measure the costs involved in reporting since in addition to hardware, software and overheads costs, it also involves cost of manhours that the decision makers spent reading the reports when they might be doing something else. But still, efforts should be made to ensure that the cost of reporting remain within reasonable limits. Useless reports are not very uncommon. It is necessary that the set of reports in use should be reviewed periodically, to weed out redundant reports, so as to save time and cost involved in this activity.

15.5 INTERNAL CONTROL — CASH

Cash as a liquid asset becomes an easy prey to misappropriation and embezzlement. Only a strong internal control system can insulate it against fraud by the unscrupulous employees. There are many ways for misappropriating cash. Receipts on account of cash sale can be suppressed. Miscellaneous receipts like sale of scrap can be omitted. A malpractice known as 'teeming and lading' can be indulged into. 'Teeming and lading' is a process under which money received from one party is deliberately not recorded in the books and siphoned off for personal use. Money received from the second party is credited in the name of first party and that of third party is credited to the second party. This way payment of one party is all the time available for the personal use. This practice is more common where identical payments are to be received from various parties. For example in a finance company, re-payment instalment of Rs 10,000 on account of vehicle advance from *X* can be utilised for the personal purpose and the payment of *Y* received next day can be credited to *X*'s account; payment of *Z* received subsequently can be credited to the account of *Y*. Ultimately, one payment of Rs 10,000 is always in the hands of the person indulging in this practice. Such practices are common and unless vigorous internal control measures are enforced, there is always a danger of the cash being defalcated.

Howsoever, effective internal control measures may be designed for cash, there are always possibilities of development of loopholes in the system after the lapse of some time. Cash payments offer many opportunities for misappropriation of cash. One common method involved is known as 'kiting'. Under this method, a cheque is drawn and encashed from a bank. The transaction is not recorded in the books of accounts. Subsequently, one more cheque is drawn on another bank and deposited in the first bank as a cover against the cash withdrawl. Similarly, a cheque is drawn on third bank and deposited with the second bank. This way, the process goes on. The statements issued by all the banks shall show contra entries except the statement of the last bank which can easily be projected as cheque issued but not yet presented by the payee. Internal audit helps to detect such a malpractice.

In the realm of management reporting, cash flow reporting figures quite prominently. A typical cash flow reporting framework covers cash planning in the form of cash budget, cash receipts, cash payments and reports on optimum utilisation of surplus cash. The management has to keep itself abreast with upto date information of cash flow movements, lest it wakes up after the total evaporation of this sensitive liquid asset. Bankruptcies of giants like Rolls Royce in early 70s and Polly Peck in early 90s were due to faulty cash adjustments.

The internal control mechanism regarding cash can be studied in the following segments:

— Cash Receipts
— Cash Payments
— Cash-in-Custody
— Cash Surplus Investment

15.5.1 Cash Receipts

The internal control system of cash receipts is detailed below.

(a) *Internal Control Measures:* The internal control measures should include the following.

(i) All the incoming cheques should be recorded in the check list prepared by an independent person.

(ii) Cheques must be deposited immediately with the bank. Pay-in-slips should be filled by a person other than the one who is responsible for preparing the list of incoming cheques.

(iii) Attempts should be made to deposit the cheques in the bank on the same day or maximum the next day. Under no circumstances the internal deposit float should be more than one day.

(iv) If the banking system in operation permits, cheques of large amounts should be sent to high value clearing under special arrangement.

(v) Acknowledgement for the receipt of cheques and cash should be issued by a person responsible for recording the same in the account books. The acknowledgement book should be serially numbered with auto carbons.

(vi) With the help of cash management techniques of concentration banking and lock box system, cash should be pooled at one place and payments made from the centralised account.

(vii) The cashier should not have any access to book writing, as well as invoices, credit notes *etc.*

(b) *Internal Audit*: The internal audit should cover the following.

(i) Cash receipts particularly from cash sales, should be reconciled with the sales records independently.

(ii) Pay-in-slips should be verified with the check list prepared on receipt of cheques.

(iii) It should be verified that the credits on account of receipts are accorded to appropriate accounts.

(iv) The casting of cash book column of the total receipts should be checked to ensure that the receipts accounted for in the books are not less than the actual receipts.

(c) *Management Reporting*: The following reports should be submitted to the management.

(i) The monthly cash report detailing the receipt of total cash during the month be prepared and compared with the cash receipt projections in the cash budget. Variances pertaining to cash sales and receivables should be gone into detail so as to ascertain the reasons thereof.

(ii) Periodical calculations of ratio of cash in sales and debtors velocity should be reported to management alongwith the ratio of previous years for the same period.

15.5.2 Cash Payments

Internal control system for payment should take into account the following factors.

(a) *Internal Control Measures*: Internal control measures should cover the following.

(i) Cheque book should be kept in safe custody.

(ii) Cheque signing authority should be specific and delegation structured on the basis of hierarchical level.

(iii) Signing of cheque by a single person should be avoided. At least two persons must sign a cheque.

(iv) Voucher authorising payment be prepared by one person and verified by the other, before any cheque payment is authorised.

(v) The payment should be supported by unambiguous documentary evidence.

(vi) All the vouchers and the relevant documentary evidences should be stamped as 'PAID' so as to obviate the possibility of duplicate payment. The stamp should be prominently endorsed on the supporting documents.

(vii) Petty cash system should be introduced for the payments of small amounts pertaining to routine type of expenses like conveyance, medical, travelling allowances *etc*.

(viii) Cash imprest of pre-determined amount should be given to the cashier which should be subject to replenishment on utilisation.

(ix) If the cheque issued to the party has been misplaced, the new cheque should be issued after receiving necessary undertaking from the payee in respect of indemnification of any loss accruing due to the misplaced cheque. The bank must be immediately instructed to stop payment of the concerned cheque.

(x) All cheques should be issued with an endorsement of 'Account Payee'. As per the Income Tax Act, payment on account of expenditure can be released in cash only if the amount involved is less than Rs 10,000. All other payments are required to be released by cheques. It is better if this limit is lowered down further by the business so as to have an effective internal control system for the payments.

(b) *Internal Audit*: Internal audit programme should be chalked out to cover the following items.

(i) Vouchers and supports for release of payments should be checked to ensure whether these are authorised by the competent authorities.

(ii) It should be verified whether the discount has been availed of by the business and also the payments are released "not sooner than due".

(iii) Cheques have not been issued without crossing except for cash withdrawals.

(iv) It should be verified that cheques are signed strictly as per the delegated authority.

(v) Cheques which have long remained uncleared should be investigated and stale cheques should be adjusted in the books of accounts.

(vi) It should be verified that no personal expenses have been booked to the business.

(vii) It should be ensured that the payment is released for the authorised amount only. Wage payment should invite extra attention to ensure that no dummy workers are being paid.

(viii) Verify that all the credit notes from suppliers have been check listed and accounted for.

(ix) Make in-depth check of a few payments to detect possibilities of 'kiting'.

(c) *Management Reporting*: The following reports should be put up to the management.

(i) Monthly report for the total payments released during the month alongwith details of the major recipients should be prepared for reporting to the management.

(ii) Total receipts should be compared with cash budget projections envisaged for the period and reasons of major variances reported to the management.

(iii) A report, listing major suppliers from whom discounts have been availed of during the period should be put up to management.

15.5.3 Cash-in-custody

The internal control system in respect of cash-in-custody should be designed as below.

(a) *Internal Control Measures*: Measures should include the following.

(i) Access to cash should be restricted. Cash box key should preferably be with two persons.

(ii) The person handling cash should be provided with necessary insurance cover including the transit cash cover.
(iii) The physical cash in hand and cash balance as per cash book should be reconciled daily.
(iv) The post of cashier should be subject to constant rotation.
(v) Surprise check of cash in hand should be conducted periodically.
(vi) It should be ensured that cash in hand of the business is not inter-mingled with other cash balances like those of provident fund trust, cooperative society *etc.*
(vii) Bank reconciliation statement should invariably be prepared by the appointed day *i.e.,* at the end of the day, week or month as the case may be.

(b) *Internal Audit*: Internal audit programme be designed on the following lines.

(i) Surprise checks of the physical cash should be made periodically. If cash is lying at more than one place, cash verification for all the places should be attempted at one time.
(ii) It should be verified that the cash book is kept upto date, invariably.
(iii) It should be ensured that cash box does not contain IOUs in place of cash amount.
(iv) Carry forward of balance in the cash book should be verified from one page to another, *e.g.,* Rs 7321 can be carry forward as Rs 3721 on the next page and the balance amount can be defalcated.

(a) *Management Reporting:* The management should be reported about the following matters.

(i) A daily cash report should be prepared which should contain the overall view of receipts, payments and cash/bank balance.
(ii) Ratio of cash turnover to sale should be reported at definite intervals.
(iii) A periodical review of cash in current assets ratio say quarterly or half-yearly basis be reported to management.

15.5.4 Cash Surplus Investment

The system of internal control should be designed to cover the following.

(a) *Internal Control Measures* : Internal control measures should include items mentioned below.

(i) Level of cash balance desired by the business to be retained for day to day operation should be determined.
(ii) Cash in hand in excess of this balance should be invested with minimum cost and maximum return.

(iii) Investment must be authorised by the competent authority.

(iv) If the amount involved is large, recommendation for investment should be approved by a higher authority.

(v) If the investments are done through brokers, more than one broker should be empanelled for a specific period of time. This will generate competition among them. A ceiling of amount should be fixed for dealing with a particular broker.

(vi) Proper record should be maintained for accounting all the receipts of dividend, interest *etc.*, in the surplus investment register.

(b) *Internal Audit:* The internal audit programme should take into account the following issues.

(i) Internal audit should ensure that the investment has been effected as per the delegated authority.

(ii) Periodical review should be conducted in respect of return pattern from the short term investments to ascertain the efficiency of the investment programme.

(iii) Investment details should be compared with the projections made in Cash Movement Statement, explained in Chapter 11.

(c) *Management Reporting:* The following reports should be sent to the management.

(i) Daily cash report should be put up, displaying cash in hand and the desired cash balance alongwith surplus if any, for investment.

(ii) Report should indicate the bank balance as per bank book also, so that 'float' is exploited to the maximum extent.

(iii) Periodical review of investment programme envisaged in the Cash Movement Statement and actual investment done during the period should be submitted to the management.

15.6 INTERNAL CONTROL—TREASURY

We have seen in the earlier section of the chapter that cash as a liquid asset is more susceptible to theft and misappropriation due to its inherent feature of being a legal tender. Treasury instruments may not be exposed to such type of pilferage. But there is a danger of different kind in the case of such instruments. If not checked in time, defalcations in these instruments may acquire enormous proportion wiping off the entity of the business itself. Three cases can be quoted as evidences. All of them pertain to banks which are considered leaders in the money market operations and are supposed to have most effective internal control mechanism.

The first case is that of security scam which rocked India in 1992. The scam exposed the weaknesses of internal control mechanism prevalent in the banking sector. Unscruplous brokers colluding with some bank officials managed to siphon off bank funds to brokers for speculative trasactions in shares. In this case, not only the weak system but also the nonchallant attitude of the bank officials towards established rules and guidelines was responsible for the collapse of the internal control mechanism.

The second case pertains to Daiwa Bank of Japan. This was a typical case of violation of basic principle of internal control that no single person should be allowed to deal with a transaction from beginning to end. Mr. Toshihide Iguchi, the head of securities trading of the bank was allowed complete authority with regard to trading, recording and reporting of securities. The result was an embezzlement of $ 1.1 billion. This case not only exposed the weakness of internal control system but also ineffectiveness of the internal audit which could not detect the fraud for eleven years.

Third instance is related to one of the oldest bank in the world—Baring Bank of England. In this case also one official Mr. Nick Leesons based in Singapore had unrestrained power to trade in derivatives. Reckless speculative dealings in derivatives resulted in the collapse of the bank. It is also stated that the management of the bank at head office was not fully kept informed by Leesons. This is another case of week system of internal control and loose system of management control.

The layout of an internal control system for treasury instruments in a business will depend upon the magnitude of its treasury operations. Banks are the major players in treasury trade. RBI has issued guidelines for an effective internal control system for treasury operations of banks. Such an elaborate system may not be necessary for a business entity. However, the basic tenets of the bank's system can be borrowed to tailor an internal control system befitting to the requirements of the business.

An important fact to be considered in this regard is that the investments should match with the available fund profile of the business. Short term funds should be used for short term securities, medium term for medium term securities and long term funds for long term securities. Mismatching may result in negative return because the business may have to borrow or settle for premature liquidation of securities. Cash Movement Statement explained in Chapter 11 can assist in the establishment of appropriate fund–investment match.

In the treasury operations 'transparency' in the deals is very important. Money market is a very sensitive and volatile market. Traders cannot afford to trade with conventional methods of calling quotations, constituting committees *etc.* Decisions have to be taken on the spot. As a matter of fact it is called a 'telephone market' where deals of crores of rupees are done on telephone. In the back drop of it, only an effective internal control system can ensure transparency.

If the deals are proposed to be conducted through brokers, the business should prepare a panel of approved brokers. Empanelment of a broker should be done after taking into account his credit worthiness and market reputation. So far as possible, an aggregate contract limit should be fixed with each broker. Brokerage payable should be stipulated in the agreement.

The business should have an investment policy which should clearly lay down the broad investment objectives to be followed regarding undertaking transactions in securities. Such a policy should cover areas relating to authority to put through deals, procedural aspects, prudential exposure limits and the reporting system. As stated above banks' structure of internal control system regarding investment in treasury operations can provide basic framework for designing an internal control system for a business. The system so designed can be classified into three sections:

— *Trading section* : This section is authorised to negotiate deals. The section should be equipped with the latest in equipment for communication and data dissemination.

— *Settlement section* : This section is responsible for recording and processing, including seeking confirmation from the counter party of the transaction negotiated by the trading section. The activities include settlement, monitoring and control including safe custody of the instruments.

— *Accounting section* : The function of this section is to accord accounting treatment to all the transactions independently, on the basis of advices received from settlement section.

Like that of cash transaction, internal control mechanism of treasury operations is also founded on three pillars viz., internal control measures, internal audit and management reporting. We shall study these separately for trading, settlement and accounting sections.

15.6.1 Trading Section

The internal control system of the trading section should be on the following lines.

(a) *Internal Control Measures:* Internal control measures should cover the issues mentioned below.

(i) Preferably two persons should be delegated authority to negotiate deals on behalf of the business.

(ii) Specific limit should be fixed upto which one can negotiate the deal. The transactions beyond the specified limit should be negotiated after getting the approval of the competent authority.

(iii) A deal slip should be prepared for every transaction. The deal slip should be serially numbered.

(iv) The deal slip should contain the requisite details like name of the counter party, nature of the deal, whether it is a direct deal or through a broker *etc*.

(v) The deal slip should be immediately passed on to settlement section for recording and processing.

(b) *Internal Audit*: Internal audit should pay attention to the following.

(i) It should be ensured that the negotiated deal is within the specified limit.

(ii) The deal is supported by immediate issuance of deal slip.

(iii) Once the deal is concluded there is no substitution of counter party and/or security.

(iv) If the deal is through a broker, ensure that the broker is on the panel of the business and the brokerage charged is as per agreed terms.

(c) *Management Reporting:* Daily/weekly/monthly Deal Report should be put up to the management. The report should detail the name of the counter party, amount and nature of the transaction conducted during the period.

15.6.2 Settlement Section

The system of internal control should be designed to cover the following.

(a) *Internal Control Measures:* Internal control measures should include matters mentioned below.

(i) It should be ensured that all the deal slips are recorded in register as soon as these are received from dealing section.

(ii) Written communication should be issued to counter party. Also, it should be ensured that timely written communication is received from the counter parties also.

(iii) On the receipt of confirmation, advice should be prepared and sent to accounting section for passing the necessary accounting entries in the books.

(iv) There should be suitable arrangement for the safe custody of the securities.

(v) Necesary insurance cover should be taken.

(vi) Entries should be made in the movement/location register alongwith necessary details so as to keep track of the securities.

(vii) If the deal is struck through brokers, same procedure to be followed except that deal slip shall be substituted by brokers contract note.

(viii) All the procedures relevant for payments through cheques to the counter parties and brokers as explained in the earlier section of the chapter should be followed.

(b) *Internal Audit:* The internal audit programme should take into account the following issues.

(i) Scripts should be verified physically and compared with the security register.

(ii) If the scripts are in a form of acknowledgement of money received or allotment letter required to be exchanged against the designated security, verify that it has been exchanged on the due date.

(iii) It should be ensured that settlement has been done as per the terms of the negotiated deal and the total consideration has been received.

(iv) It should be ensured that the interest on the securities has been received on the due date.

(v) The location/movement register should be examined in detail to ensure that security is lying with the third party for valid reasons, *e.g.,* for putting required endorsement on the script. In any case, if it is lying with the third party for a long period, necessary follow-up action should be taken.

(c) *Management Reporting:* The following reports should be sent to management.

(i) Details of all the transactions settled during a period should be reported.

(ii) A statement of interest collections made alongwith amounts pending for collection should be prepared and reported to management at fixed intervals.

(iii) Reports detailing allotment letters pending for exchange with the securities should be put up.

(iv) Statement indicating transactions against which written confirmation from counter parties have not been received should be submitted to the management.

15.6.3. Accounting Section

The internal control system is detailed below.

(a) *Internal Control Measures:* The measures should include the following.

(i) The accounting entries should be passed based on the advices received from the settlement section.

(ii) Vouchers should be prepared by one person and verified by the other.

(b) *Internal Audit:* Intenal audit should verify the following.

(i) Entries as appearing in the books should be examined independently with the back-up records maintained at settlement section.

(ii) It should be checked that amounts are debited and credited in the appropriate accounts.

(c) *Management Reporting:* Management should be sent a reconciled statement of all transactions detailing nature, amount, settlement *etc.*, of the securities at a particular date.

The internal control mechanism should be reviewed annually. The review should be a broad-base one. It should scrutinise the whole system, right from zero level, to detect infirmities and loopholes creeping in the system before these acquire unmanageable dimensions. Above all, the investment policy of the business too, should be thoroughly reviewed to find out whether it has rewarded the business with the return and liquidity as was envisaged at the time of its introduction.

QUESTIONS

1. What do you understand by internal control system? Describe its objectives and features.
2. What is the role of management reporting in an effective system of internal control? Describe the chief features of a report.
3. Describe the internal control mechanism relating to cash receipts and payments.
4. Enumerate the points which on internal audit should examine while checking cash-in-custody and investment of surplus cash.
5. Write short notes on:
   (a) Teeming and lading
   (b) Kiting
   (c) Internal check system
6. What important facts should be taken into account while designing a system of internal control relating to treasury?
7. Describe the internal control system for 'settlement section.'
8. Write brief note on internal control failure in the case of:
   (a) Securities Scam of 1992
   (b) Daiwa Bank of Japan
   (c) Baring Bank of England

SELECTED BIBLIOGRAPHY

Anthony N. Robert and Glenn A. Welsch, *Fundamentals of Management Accounting* D.B. Taraporewala Sons & Co. (P) Ltd., Bombay in collaboration with Richard D. Irwin Inc., Illinois USA, 1981

Batty J., *Management Accountancy* Macdonald & Evans Ltd., London, U.K., 1970

Beehler Paul J., *Contemporary Cash Management*. John Wiley and Sons, New York, USA, 1978

Bolten Steven E., *Managerial Finance - Principles and Practices.* Houghton Mifflin Company, Boston, USA, 1976

Brayshaw R.E., *The Concise Guide to Company Finance and its Management* International Thomson Business Press, UK, 1992

Business Week, International edition/June 12, 1995, A Publication of the McGraw Hill Companies.

Chartered Secretary/July 1993, Journal of the Institute of Company Secretary of India, N. Delhi.

Clarkson G.P.E. & B.J. Elliot, Managing Money & Finance. Wildhood House, UK, 1986

Collin P.H. & Advian Joliffee, *Dictonary of Accounting* UBS Publishers, Distributors, N. Delhi in arrangement with Peter Collin Publishing Ltd., Middlesex UK, 1994

Dobbins Richard & Stephen F. Witt, *Practical Financial Management* Basel Blackwell Ltd., Oxford UK.

Emery Toncre, *Maximising Cash Flow* John Wiley and Sons, New York, USA, 1986

Financing Strategies and Investment Consultancy (Background Material for Seminar) - The Institute of Chartered Accountants of India, New Delhi, 1993.

Franks J.R. & H.H. Scholefield, *Corporate Financial Management*. Prentice Hall, USA. 1992

Garbutt Douglas, *How to Budget and Control Cash* Gower Publishing Company Ltd., UK - 1985

Gillian Clegg, *How to Maintain A Positive Cash Flow* Business Book, London, UK, 1991

Glynn John J., John Perrin & Michael J. Murphy, *Accounting for Managers* International Thomson Business Press. UK, 1994

Hanson J.L., *A Dictionary of Economics and Commerce* Macdonald and Evans, London UK, 1977

Hartley W.C.F., *Cash: Planning, Forecasting and Control* Business Books Ltd., London UK - 1976

Harlon D. Platt, *Why Companies Fail - Strategies for Detecting, Avoiding & Profiting from Bankruptcy* Lexington Books, Massachusetts, USA

Hargreaves P.L. & R.H. Smith, *Managing Your Company Finances.* Heinemann, UK, 1981

Howard Leslie R., *Working Capital - Its Management & Control* Macdonald & Evans Ltd., London, UK 1971

Jaidicke Robert K. & Robert K. Sprouse, *Accounting Flow : Income Funds and Cash.* Prentice Hall Inc., New Jersey, USA, 1965

Jones Ernest, *Understand Business Finances : A Guide for Managers* Pitman Publishing, UK, 1991

Knott Geoffrey, *Financial Management* Pan Books, London, 1981

Leon Hopkins, *Cash Flow and How to Improve it* Kogan Page, UK, 1993

Mac Cormac M.J. & J.J. Teeling, *Financial Management* Gill and Macmillan, Dublin, UK, 1980

McLancy E.J., *Business Finance* Pitman, UK, 1986

Pearce David W., *Macmillan Dictionary of Modern Economics* Macmillan Press Ltd., London, UK, 1992

Puxty Anthony G. & J. Collins Dodds, *Financial Management - method and meaning* Chapman and Hall, UK, 1988

Samuels J.M. & F.M. Wilkes, *Management of Company Finance* International Thomson Business Press, UK, 1995

Simeon Ibitoye, *How to Manage Your Business Cash Problem* G. Burn, UK, 1986

Sundharam K.P.M., *Money Banking and International Trade* Sultan Chand & Sons, N. Delhi, 1963

The Chartered Accountant/March 1995, Journal of the Institute of Chartered Accountants of India, N. Delhi.

Valrie Hawkes & Ken Slater, *Cash Flow and Credit Management* Kogan Page, UK, 1988

Wilson Peter, *Financial Management for the Small Business* Kogan Page, UK, 1988

GLOSSARY

ABC ANALYSIS: A technique which classifies the inventories into three categories on the basis of their investment values (i) Category A includes items with largest values (ii) Category B consists of items with moderate values and (iii) Category C covers items having smallest values. The technique helps to focus more vigorous controls on the items having highest values.

ACCRUALS: Expenses or liabilities which have been incurred but not yet paid.

ACCRUED BUT NOT DUE: Amounts which though accrued become eligible for receipt or payment after the lapse of some time. For example, interest on bank deposit is considered as accrued upto the end of the financial year but becomes due after the expiry of pre-determined period of deposit.

AGEING SCHEDULE: A schedule which displays all the debts of a business usually in descending order of age so as to determine how long they have been outstanding.

AMORTISATION: A process which involves setting aside of money to liquidate a loan amount or writing off the value of an asset in the accounts over a defined period of time.

BAD DEBTS: Receivables which have become impossible to be retrieved from customers.

BALANCE SHEET: A statement displaying the values of assets and liabilities of a business as on a specific date.

BARTER: A system where goods are exchanged directly with other goods without involving any "medium of exchange."

BILL OF EXCHANGE: An instrument containing an unconditional order signed by a drawer directing a certain person to pay a certain sum of money to or to the order of a person or to the bearer of the instrument.

BOND: A bond is an instrument acknowledging debt of a long period.

BONUS ISSUE: Shares issued by a company to its existing shareholders free of cost, pro-rata to their share holdings.

BRIDGING FINANCE: Loans raised to cater to the short-term requirements.

BUDGETARY CONTROL: A system involving a continuous process of fixing the targets in the budgets, comparing the actuals with the targets and taking appropriate action to remedy the variances.

CAPITAL EMPLOYED: The sum total of owners capital, reserves and long-term liabilities indicating the total funds invested in a business.

CASH: Refers to money in coins, currency notes and deposits repayable on demand with a bank.

CASH BUDGET: A summary statement presented in an orderly format, containing forecasted figures of receipts and disbursements of cash over a given period of time.

CASH COW: A product/unit/subsidiary/company that consistently makes good profit and generates rich cash.

CASH CREDIT: Also known as "drawing account" is an arrangement under which a business is authorised to draw cash subject to the limit pre-fixed by the bank.

CASH DISCOUNT: A reduction in price if the payment is made before a stipulated date.

CASH EQUIVALENTS: Short term highly liquid investments that are readily convertible into cash with minimum cost and discount and are exposed to insignificant risks of changes in values.

CASH FLOW CYCLE: Circulatory movement of cash starting with the purchase of raw materials and ending with the collection of cash from the sale of resultant finished products.

CASH IN CURRENT ASSETS RATIO: The ratio of cash balance to total current assets.

CASH INFLOW: Actual receipts of cash during a given period. The receipts of cash are from various sources normally being sales of finished products, collection of receivables, sale of assets, raising of loan or equity and various miscellaneous receipts.

CASH OUTFLOW: Actual payment of cash during a given period. The payments of cash are on various accounts normally being purchase of raw materials, payment to creditors, purchase of assets, repayment of loan, payment of dividend and various expenses.

CASH TURNOVER IN SALES: The ratio represents the number of times the initial cash balance is turned over in terms of sales effected during a period.

CASH TURNOVER IN TOTAL FUNDS: The ratio measures the turnover of cash in the total fund flow movements occurring during a period.

CASH TURNOVER RATIO: The ratio indicates the velocity of "cash flow cycle" in an year.

CERTIFICATE OF DEPOSIT (CD): A term deposit with a bank to be paid after certain period with guaranteed rate of interest. The certificate issued by a bank evidencing deposit is a negotiable instrument.

COLLECTION POLICIES: Procedures followed to collect receivables from the customers which have not been paid within the credit period.

COMMERCIAL PAPER (CP): An unsecured, short-term, discounted debt instrument issued by large business houses to meet their short-term cash requirements. It is a negotiable instrument. It is also popular as an instrument of short-term investment.

CONCENTRATION BANKING: A system under which cash is concentrated in a bank account by pooling the receipts from various decentralised collection centres for making centralised disbursements therefrom.

CONVERSION PRICE: It is the price at which convertible instruments like debentures can be converted into equity shares.

CONVERTIBLE RATIO: The ratio which determines the number of equity shares to be issued against the conversion of convertible securities.

CONVERTIBLE SECURITIES: Securities like debentures or bonds which at a pre- determined price and during a pre-stated period may be exchanged by the holders with the equity shares of the company.

CORPORATE PLAN: A document detailing long-term strategies developed by a business to achieve defined corporate objectives.

COST BENEFIT ANALYSIS: An analysis involving trade-off of economic costs and benefits, so as to determine optimum point of an variable. For example, optimum level of inventory is determined by counter balancing economic costs and benefits of holding inventory at a specified level.

COVENANTS: Stipulations inbuilt in a loan agreement so as to protect the interests of the lender.

CREDIT ANALYSIS: Classification of debts into three categories (i) Undue debts - which are yet to become due contractually (ii) Due debts - which have become due as per mutually agreed terms and conditions and (iii) Overdue debts - which have remained unrecovered for long period of time.

CREDIT POLICY: Policy of a business to extend credit to the customers based on its own formulated credit standards, credit terms and collection systems.

CREDIT STANDARDS: The laid down criterion permitting sales on credit.

CREDIT TERMS: The terms and conditions in respect of payments which are agreed with the customers as a part of credit sales.

CURRENT ASSETS: The assets which are 'used up' in the ordinary course of business by getting converted into cash within next twelve months.

CURRENT LIABILITIES: Payables and other liabilities which are due for payment within next twelve months.

CURRENT RATIO: It is the ratio of total current assets to current liabilities of a business and is calculated by dividing the former by the latter.

DEBENTURE: It is a long term debt having a specific maturity, prefixed interest rate and predetermined repayment provisions. Debenture as a script is a certificate issued by a company acknowledging the debt.

DEBT-EQUITY RATIO: The ratio which indicates the relative proportion of lenders debts and owners funds including reserves and surpluses.

DEBTORS-TURNOVER RATIO: Also described as debtors velocity, refers to the number of times debtors get turned over in terms of credit sales during a period.

DEBT AFFORDABILITY RATIO: The ratio determines the number of times the fixed interests on borrowings are covered by operating cash flow.

DEFENSIVE-INTERVAL RATIO: The ratio establishes the relationship between quick assets and the projected daily cash requirements of a business by measuring the number of days the quick assets can enable the business to operate without resorting to future revenues.

DIVIDEND: Part of the current or previous years' profits which is distributed to the shareholders.

DEPRECIATION: Depreciation is an accounting convention of allocating the cost of a fixed asset over its useful commercial life in recognition of efflux of time and wear and tear of the asset.

ECONOMIC ORDER QUANTITY: The optimal size of the inventory order which bears minimal cost determined on the basis of trade off between its carrying and ordering costs.

ELECTRONIC CASH: Digital cash being developed for circulation in future through computer software.

EQUITY FINANCING: It consists of shares issued by a company, subscribers of which become shareholders and collectively own the company.

FACTORING: An arrangement under which receivables are sold by a business to a specialised collecting agency known as factor who takes the responsibility of recovering money from the customers on due dates.

FINANCE MIX: It indicates the *inter se* proportion of debt and equity in the total funds deployed by a company in the business.

FINANCIAL LEASE: Lease that is stretched to the useful commercial life of the asset, during which period it is fully amortised and is not cancellable. The cost of maintenance is generally borne by the lessee.

FINANCING ACTIVITIES: The activities which are instrumental in changing the size and composition of the owners capital and borrowings of a business.

FIXED EXPENSES: Expenses which remain constant irrespective of the level of business activity.

FIXED ASSETS: The long lived properties of a business which it owns and uses as an aid to generate profits.

FLOAT: The sum total of the amounts of (a) cheques deposited in the bank but not yet credited and (b) cheques issued but not yet presented in the bank. The (a) is known as Collection Float and (b) as Disbursement Float.

FLOATING RATE NOTE: A debt instrument having a rate of interest which varies in accordance with some predetermined formula.

FUTURES : A contract where a buyer/seller agrees to take/give delivery of the securities on a pre-specified future date at a pre-determined price.

GILT-EDGED SECURITIES : All government debt instruments other than treasury bills which are traded in money market.

HIRE PURCHASE: Buying an item on credit by paying series of relatively small amounts which include part debt repayment and part interest, regularly at defined intervals.

INVESTING ACTIVITIES: The activities which result in the acquisition and disposal of long term assets and other long term investments.

INVENTORY: The stock consisting of raw materials, semi-finished goods and finished goods held by a business at a particular point of time.

INVENTORY-TURNOVER RATIO: The ratio indicates the number of times average stock held during the year turned over in terms of cost of goods sold. It is also known as Stock Velocity Ratio.

INVOICE-DISCOUNTING: A method under which a business sells the invoice raised on its client to a specialist company, at a discount.

JUST-IN-TIME: Under this system exact number of required units are delivered by suppliers at each successive stage of production at a rate at which these are needed by the manufacturing companies.

LEASE: A contractual agreement under which an asset is owned and financed by one party but possessed and used by the other, against the payment of a fee.

LETTER OF CREDIT: A document issued by a bank on behalf of a customer guaranteeing payment to a supplier on the fulfilment of the conditions mentioned therein.

LIQUIDITY: The ability of a business to convert its assets into cash incurring minimum cost and time.

LOCK BOX SYSTEM: A cash management technique for speedy collection of receivables and reduction of float. Under this, cheques are remitted by customers directly into special post office boxes which are owned by a business but operated by its banker.

LONDON METAL EXCHANGE: The biggest commodity market in the world trading in copper, lead, zinc, aluminium, nickel and tin.

MATCHING CONCEPT: An accounting convention of identifying revenues with their associated costs and *vice versa* for a given accounting period so as to determine profits for that period.

MONEY MARKET: A financial market in which highly liquid short-term debt instruments like treasury bills, certificates of deposit, bills of exchange and commercial papers are traded.

NET WORTH: The difference between what a business owns and what it owes. As an accounting term, it is the sum total of owners capital plus reserves and surpluses less cost of intangible assets.

NET LEASE: A lease agreement under which the costs of maintenance, insurance and other levies associated with the leased asset are borne by the lessee. A finance lease is commonly a net lease whereas an operating lease is generally a gross lease.

OPERATING CASH FLOW TO SALES RATIO: The ratio measures the relationship of operating cash flow to sales.

OPERATING CASH FLOW TO CAPITAL EMPLOYED: The ratio establishes the relationship of operating cash flow with the amount of capital deployed in the business during a period.

OPERATING CASH FLOW TO NUMBER OF SHARES: The ratio measures the operating cash flow per share.

OPERATING CASH FLOW TO EMPLOYEES: The ratio measures the level of operating cash flow generated by a set of employees.

OPERATING ACTIVITIES: The principal revenue earning activities of a business.

OPERATING CASH FLOW: The cash flow generated from the operating activities.

OPERATING LEASE: The lease having a duration of much less period than the useful life of the asset and is cancellable. The cost of maintenance and insurance is generally borne by the lessor.

OPPORTUNITY COST OF CASH: The rate of interest lost by holding cash as such, instead of putting it into interest bearing assets.

OPTIONS : Option is an arrangement between two parties where an option maker agrees to buy or sell a specified security to the option holder for a specific price on a particular date.

OVERDRAFT: A credit facility provided by a bank to a customer to draw money over and above the amount available in his account subject to a pre-fixed limit and period.

PRE-AUTHORISED CHEQUES: An arrangement authorising a business to raise a demand on the bank of a customer for the payment of a pre-determined amount on a pre-determined date.

PRE-AUTHORISED DEBITS: An automatic system involving paperless operation under which the bank account of the customer stands debited with the pre-determined amount on the due date.

PROFIT CENTRE: A responsibility centre, generally a decentralised unit, which is independent enough to calculate its own centre-specific return on investment.

PROFIT: An accounting term for difference between revenue and cost, calculated on the basis of matching concept, for a given period of time.

PROMISSORY NOTE: An instrument containing an undertaking signed by a maker to pay a certain sum of money to or to the order of a certain person.

QUICK RATIO: Also known as "Acid Test Ratio" is the ratio of those current assets which are readily convertible into cash to current liabilities. Thus, it is calculated by dividing current assets excluding inventory and prepaid expenses by current liabilities.

RECEIVABLES: Amounts to be collected from customers on account of goods sold on credit.

REDISCOUNTING BILLS: Discounting of the bills generally by banks, which have already been discounted by the sellers.

REORDER POINT: The minimum level of inventory that prompts a business to initiate action for the placement of fresh order equal to the economic order quantity so as to ensure availability of adequate inventory at all times.

REPO: An agreement under which one party sells a security to another and simultaneously agrees to buy it back at a later date on slightly higher price.

REQUIRED RATE OF RETURN: The minimum rate which a business expects to earn on making an investment. It is a judgemental rate.

RETAINED EARNINGS: Portion of profits retained in the business for financing its activities instead of distributing it to the owners.

RIGHT ISSUE: An invitation by a company to the existing shareholders to buy specified number of new shares pro rata to their holdings, usually at an advantageous price.

SAFETY STOCK: Additional inventory retained as a cushion to hedge against the risk of running out of stock.

SALVAGE VALUE: The expected value of a capital asset at the end of its amortised period.

SECURITISATION: A process of raising finance from the market by transformation of long dated assets into tradeable securities.

SEMI-VARIABLE EXPENSES: The expenses which have both fixed and variable parts and move in the same direction in which the business activity moves but not in the same proportion.

SHORT-TERM DEBTS: Debt obligations which have maturity dates of less than one year.

SOLVENCY: Ability of a business to meet its obligations on due dates.

SWOT ANALYSIS: A systematic process of evaluating strengths, weaknesses, opportunities and threats of a business to develop long-term strategies for the achievement of defined corporate objectives.

TERM DEPOSIT: Deposit with the bank bearing a fixed rate of interest repayable on or after a pre-determined period. It is also known as Fixed Deposit with the bank.

TERM LOAN: A loan raised for a specific amount, specific period ranging usually from one year to five years and is subject to specific repayment terms.

TRADE CREDIT: Credit enjoyed by a business when it purchases goods for sale without making immediate payment in cash.

TRADE DISCOUNT: A rebate offered in the scheduled price.

TREASURY BILLS: Treasury Bills are issued in the form of discounted promissory notes by the government through Reserve Bank of India for a period ranging from 91 days to 364 days.

TRUE COMMERCIAL LIFE: Number of years a revenue-producing-asset is reasonably expected to generate income.

UNDERWRITING: An arrangement under which a person agrees to buy the agreed number of securities of a new issue if the same remains unsubscribed by the public.

UNSECURED LOAN: Loan against which no asset is pledged as collateral.

VARIABLE EXPENSES: Expenses which move in total sympathy with the business activity.

WORKING CAPITAL: Generally connoting net working capital, refers to the difference between current assets and current liabilities. Total current assets are termed as gross working capital.

YIELD: Return on investment calculated as a percentage of money invested.

INDEX